A BRIEF GUIDE TO WRITING FROM READINGS

Why Do You Need This New Edition?

If you're wondering why you should buy this new edition of *A Brief Guide to Writing from Readings,* here are a few great reasons!

1. Ten new readings on a range of topics that are directly relevant to students' lives or address topics students typically find interesting

   - Whether schools should impose student dress codes
   - Possible links between television viewing and childhood violence
   - Campus privacy issues
   - The nature of "Generation Y" students
   - Animal welfare and abuse issues

2. More readings drawn from academic sources across the curriculum

3. Six new sample student essays

4. Redesigned exploration of and instruction in writing from visual texts

5. Clear, step-by-step instruction on writing the most common types of source-based essays in college, including abstracts (new to this edition)

6. Revision checklists for every type of essay included in the textbook

7. Fully updated coverage of MLA and APA documentation conventions

PEARSON

Sixth Edition

A BRIEF GUIDE TO WRITING FROM READINGS

Stephen Wilhoit

The University of Dayton

Boston Columbus Indianapolis New York San Francisco Upper Saddle River
Amsterdam Cape Town Dubai London Madrid Milan Munich Paris Montreal Toronto
Delhi Mexico City São Paulo Sydney Hong Kong Seoul Singapore Taipei Tokyo

Senior Acquisition Editor: Brad Potthoff
Senior Marketing Manager: Sandra McGuire
Senior Supplements Editor: Donna Campion
Production Manager: Denise Phillip
Project Coordination, Editorial Services,
  and Text Design: Electronic Publishing
  Services Inc., NYC
Art Rendering and Electronic Page Makeup:
  TexTech

Cover Design Manager: Wendy Ann Fredericks
Cover Designer: Nancy Sacks
Cover Photo: © iStockphoto
Senior Manufacturing Manager:
  Dennis J. Para
Printer and Binder: R.R. Donnelley/
  Harrisonburg
Cover Printer: R.R. Donnelley/
  Harrisonburg

Credits and acknowledgments borrowed from other sources and reproduced, with permission, in this textbook appear on the appropriate page within the text and on pp. 311–312.

Library of Congress Cataloging-in-Publication Data

Wilhoit, Stephen.
  A brief guide to writing from readings/Stephen Wilhoit.—6th ed.
    p. cm.
  ISBN 978-0-205-24574-1
  1. English language—Rhetoric—Handbooks, manuals, etc. 2. Academic
writing—Handbooks, manuals, etc. 3. Interdisciplinary approach in education.
4. College readers. I. Title.
  PE1408.W586 2011
  808'.0427—dc23

                                                              2011038640

10 9 8 7 6 5 4 3 2 1—DOH—14 13 12 11

ISBN 10:   0-205-24574-9
ISBN 13: 978-0-205-24574-1

CONTENTS

Preface   **xv**

Chapter 1 CRITICAL READING   *1*

Definition and Purpose   1

Asking Questions about What You Read   3
 Questions to Ask before You Begin a Close Reading of a Text   4
 Questions to Ask while You Read and Reread Material   7

Marking Texts   11
 Highlighting Texts   11
 Annotating Texts   12

Sample Annotated Reading: "Hard Choices," by Patrick Moore   15

Note Taking   18

Additional Reading: "Getting Serious about Eradicating Binge Drinking,"
 by Henry Wechsler   20

Summary Chart—Critical Reading: Asking Questions   24

Summary Chart—Critical Reading: Marking Texts   26

Summary Chart—Critical Reading: Note Taking   27

Chapter 2 QUOTATION   *29*

Definition and Purpose   29

Guidelines on When to Quote Material   30
 Quote Passages When the Author Has Written Something in a
  Distinctive or Especially Insightful or Interesting Way   30
 Quote Material That Lends Support to a Position You Are Trying to
  Make in Your Paper   30
 Quote Authorities Who Disagree with a Position You Are Advocating
  or Who Offer Alternative Explanations or Contradictory
  Data   31

Guidelines on When Not to Quote Material   32
 Do Not Quote Passages Merely to Fill Space   32
 Do Not Quote Passages as a Substitute for Thinking   32
 Do Not Quote Passages Because You Do Not Understand the
  Author's Ideas Well Enough to Paraphrase Them   33

Integrating Quotations into Your Writing   33
   Two Basic Types of Quotations   33

Reading: "Generation Text," by Mark Bauerlein   34
   The Block Quotation   36
   The Integrated Quotation   38

Altering Quoted Material and Avoiding Misquotations   41

Summary Chart: Guidelines on Quotations   43

Summary Chart: Integrating Quotations into Your
   Writing   44

Quotation Revision Checklist   45

Chapter 3   PARAPHRASE   47

Definition and Purpose   47

Qualities of a Good Paraphrase   48
   Thorough   48
   Accurate   48
   Fair   49
   Objective   49

How to Paraphrase Material   50
   Changing Words   50
   Changing Sentence Structure   52
   Combining Sentences   53
   "Unpacking" Sentences   54
   Combining Strategies: Paraphrasing Longer Passages in Source
     Texts   55
   Blending Your Writing with Paraphrased Material   57

Documentation   57

Summary Chart: How to Paraphrase Material   58

Paraphrase Revision Checklist   59

Chapter 4   SUMMARY   61

Definition and Purpose   61

Types of Summaries   62

Qualities of a Good Summary   63
   Comprehensive   63
   Brief   64
   Accurate   64
   Neutral   65
   Independent   65

How to Summarize a Text   66
    Read, Reread, and Annotate the Source Text   66
    Summarize Each Section of the Source Text   66
    Check the Section Summaries against the Source
      Text   66

How to Write an Abstract   66

How to Write an Informative Summary Essay   67

How to Write an Explanatory Summary Essay   68

Documentation   69

Reading: "From *Animal House* to *Big Brother:* Student Privacy
    and Campus Safety in an Age of Accountability," by Ron
    Chesbrough   69
    Sample Abstract   75
    Sample Informative Summary Essay   75
    Sample Explanatory Summary Essay   76

Summary Chart: How to Summarize Texts   78

Summary Revision Checklist   80

Chapter 5   RESPONSE ESSAYS   *81*

Definition and Purpose   81

Qualities of a Good Response Essay   82
    Honest   82
    Informed   82
    Clear   83
    Well Supported   83

Writing the Response Essay   84
    Carefully Read the Material   84
    Compose Your Rough Draft   85
    Write Your Conclusion   87
    Revise Your Rough Draft   87

Sample Response Essay   89

Summary Chart: How to Write a Response Essay   91

Response Essay Revision Checklist   93

Chapter 6   CRITIQUE   *95*

Definition and Purpose   95

The Film Review as Critique   96

Writing a Critique   99

Step 1—Carefully Read and Annotate the Source Text   99
Step 2—Analyze and Evaluate the Reading   100
Step 3—Write Your Thesis and Decide Which Aspects of the Reading
Will Be the Focus of Your Essay   107
Step 4—Write Your Rough Draft   108
Step 5—Rewrite Your Critique   110

Reading: "Zero Tolerance and Student Dress Codes," by Nathan L.
Essex   112

Reading: "A Uniform Look," by Yasmine L. Konheim-
Kalkstein   115

Sample Critique   119

Summary Chart: How to Write a Critique   123

Critique Revision Checklist   125

Chapter 7   RHETORICAL ANALYSIS OF WRITTEN TEXTS   *127*

Definition and Purpose   127

The Rhetorical Situation   128
Elements of the Rhetorical Situation   129

Rhetorical Strategies   130
Content   131
Structure   134
Style   134

Analyzing a Text's Rhetorical Strategies—An Example   135
Lincoln's Second Inaugural Address   135
A Rhetorical Analysis of Lincoln's Speech   136

Writing a Rhetorical Analysis Essay   137
Step 1—Carefully Read the Assignment   137
Step 2—Establish the Source Text's Rhetorical Situation   138
Step 3—Determine the Author's Goal   138
Step 4—Identify and Evaluate the Source Text's Rhetorical
Strategies   138
Step 5—Determine Your Thesis   139
Step 6—Write Your Rough Draft   139
Step 7—Revise Your Essay   141

Sample Rhetorical Analysis Essay   142
Rhetorical Analysis of Lincoln's Second Inaugural Address   143

Summary Chart: How to Write a Rhetorical Analysis Essay   145

Rhetorical Analysis of Written Texts Revision Checklist   147

Chapter 8   RHETORICAL ANALYSIS OF VISUAL TEXTS   *149*

Definition and Purpose   149

Reading Visual Texts Critically   150
   Questions concerning the Visual Text Itself   150
   Questions concerning the Visual Text's Creator or
      Source   151
   Questions concerning the Visual Text's Purpose   152
   Questions concerning the Visual Text's Audience   153
   Questions concerning Your Response to the Visual Text   154

Reading a Visual Text—An Example   155
   Questions concerning the Visual Text   155
   Questions concerning the Visual Text's Creator or Source   157
   Questions concerning the Visual Text's Purpose   157
   Questions concerning the Visual Text's Audience   157
   Questions concerning Your Response to the Visual Text   158

Writing a Rhetorical Analysis of a Visual Text   158
   Step 1—Carefully Read the Assignment   158
   Step 2—Analyze and Describe the Text   159
   Step 3—Establish the Text's Rhetorical Situation   159
   Step 4—Determine How the Text Attempts to Achieve Its Rhetorical
      Goals   159
   Step 5—Determine Your Thesis   160
   Step 6—Write a Rough Draft   160
   Step 7—Revise Your Essay   162

Sample Rhetorical Analysis of a Visual Text   163

Summary Chart: How to Write a Rhetorical Analysis of a Visual
   Text   167

Rhetorical Analysis of a Visual Text Revision Checklist   169

Chapter 9   INFORMATIVE SYNTHESIS   *171*

Definition and Purpose   171

Types of Synthesis Essays   172

Reading: "Media Violence and Children's Emotions: Beyond the 'Smoking
   Gun'," by Joanne Cantor   173

Reading: "Television Violence and Its Effects on Young Children," by Betty
   Jo Simmons, Kelly Stalsworth, and Heather Wentzell   181

Reading: "Does Cartoon Violence Beget Aggressive Behavior in Real Life?
   An Opposing View," by Fran C. Blumberg, Kristen P. Bierwirth, and
   Allison J. Schwartz   189

Informative Synthesis   195
  Definition   195
  Writing an Informative Synthesis   197

Sample Informative Synthesis   204

Summary Chart: How to Write an Informative Synthesis   208

Informative Synthesis Revision Checklist   210

Chapter 10   ARGUMENTATIVE SYNTHESIS   *213*

Definition and Purpose   213

The Elements of Argument   214
  Claims   214
  Grounds   215
  Warrants   218

Argument and Persuasion   219
  Appeals Based on Reason   220
  Appeals Based on Emotion   220
  Appeals Based on Character and Credibility   222

Writing an Argumentative Synthesis   223
  Step 1—Analyze the Assignment   223
  Step 2—Annotate and Critique the Readings   224
  Step 3—Formulate a Thesis   224
  Step 4—Choose an Organizational Plan   226
  Step 5—Write Your Rough Draft   229
  Step 6—Revise Your Draft   229
  Step 7—Check Quotations and Documentation   230

Sample Argumentative Synthesis   230

Additional Reading: "Four Legs Good, Two Legs Bad: The Anti-human
  Values of 'Animal Rights'," by Wesley J. Smith   235

Additional Reading: "Building a Culture of Animal Welfare: Past, Present
  and Future," by Leticia V. Medina   243

Additional Reading: "Animal Suffering: Learning Not to Care and Not to
  Know," by William Crain   253

Summary Chart: How to Write an Argumentative Synthesis   260

Argumentative Synthesis Revision Checklist   262

Chapter 11   PLAGIARISM   *265*

Definition   265

Forms of Plagiarism   265
  Purchasing a Paper   266

Turning in a Paper Someone Else Has Written for You   266
Turning in Another Student's Work without That Student's
        Knowledge   266
Improper Collaboration   266
Copying a Paper from a Source Text without Proper
        Acknowledgment   267
Cutting and Pasting Material from Sources   267
Lifting Images from the Web or Other Sources   267
Copying Statistics   268
Copying Material from a Source Text, Supplying Proper
        Documentation, but Leaving Out Quotation Marks   268
Paraphrasing Material from a Reading without Proper
        Documentation   268
Self-Plagiarism   268

How to Avoid Plagiarism   269
Do Your Own Work   269
Take Good Notes   269
Paraphrase Properly   270
Supply Proper Documentation   270
Online Plagiarism Check   271
Clarify Collaboration Guidelines   271

Summary Chart: Plagiarism   272

Plagiarism Checklist   273

Chapter 12   DOCUMENTATION   *275*

Definition and Purpose   275

Types of Documentation   275

Primary Academic Style Manuals   276

APA Guidelines   277
In-Text Documentation   277
Footnotes and Endnotes   281

MLA Guidelines   281
In-Text Documentation   281
Footnotes and Endnotes   285

Chapter 13   REFERENCE LISTS AND WORKS CITED
    ENTRIES   *287*

Definition and Purpose   287

APA Format   288
Sample Reference List Entries   288
Sample APA-Style Reference List   295

MLA Format   297
    Sample Works Cited Entries   297
    Sample MLA-Style Works Cited List   303

Appendix PEER REVIEW GUIDELINES   *307*

Credits   311
Index   313

PREFACE

In the sixth edition of *A Brief Guide to Writing from Readings*, my goal remains unchanged from the earlier editions: to help students master one of the most common academic genres—writing from readings. Toward this end, and based on responses from students and faculty using the book, I have made several significant changes to the sixth edition. The changes include the following:

- twelve new readings: three readings on school dress codes, three readings on the link between television viewing and childhood violence, three readings on animal welfare, and single readings on campus privacy and security and Generation Y
- greater emphasis on readings drawn from academic sources
- six new sample student essays
- new instruction on writing abstracts
- refashioned coverage of working with visual texts, emphasizing their rhetorical analysis to better match the instruction on writing rhetorical analyses of written texts
- documentation samples that incorporate guidelines established by the 2008 *MLA Style Manual and Guide to Scholarly Publishing* and the 2010 *Publication Manual of the American Psychological Association*

To accommodate these changes, I have reduced the number of appendices in this edition, integrating the material into the body of the text, and I have dropped both instruction on CSE documentation and writing timed essays, which reviewers indicated were little used.

Though much has changed in this edition of *A Brief Guide*, much also remains the same. Faculty and students have long noted the collegial tone of the book and the utility of the summary charts located at the end of each chapter in addition to the revision checklists. These features have all been retained. From the first edition, I have tried to maintain a clear, process-oriented approach to writing instruction, laying out for writers a series of steps they can follow or modify as needed when composing source-based essays.

As in previous editions of the textbook, the sample readings are drawn from a range of disciplines; however, this edition places greater emphasis on academic sources. Readings vary in length and in difficulty, but all are intended to pique student interest and serve as prompts for class discussion. Each sample student essay I include in the text can serve as a model for students to follow in terms of its thesis, organization, and use of sources, but none of them is perfect. Students should be encouraged to read the sample essays in this textbook as critically as they read any other material in college. They may identify several ways each essay can be improved. In fact, instructors might consider asking their students to do just that: to use the instruction offered in *A Brief Guide* to critique and revise these sample essays.

In the end, my hope, as always, is that the instruction offered in this textbook will help students develop the skills they need to successfully complete source-based college writing assignments, to read texts honestly and critically, and to explore connections they find between the material they read and their own knowledge, experience, and beliefs.

SUPPLEMENTS

Instructor's Manual

An Instructor's Manual is available for *A Brief Guide to Writing from Readings*. The Instructor's Manual includes a brief introduction to each chapter, an examination of problems students commonly face when writing each type of source-based essay, and a series of exercises and assignments designed to help students improve their writing.

The New MyCompLab Web Site   mycomplab

The new MyCompLab integrates the market-leading instruction, multimedia tutorials, and exercises for writing, grammar, and research that users have come to identify with the program with a new online composing space and new assessment tools. The result is a revolutionary application that offers a seamless and flexible teaching and learning environment built specifically for writers. Created after years of extensive research and in partnership with composition faculty and students across the country, the new MyCompLab provides help for writers in the context of their writing, with instructor and peer commenting functionality; proven tutorials and exercises for writing, grammar, and research; an e-portfolio; an assignment builder; a bibliography tool; tutoring services; and a gradebook and course management organization created specifically for writing classes. Visit www.mycomplab.com or ask your sales representative for more information.

ACKNOWLEDGMENTS

I would like to thank the following reviewers for their helpful suggestions as I prepared each new edition of *A Brief Guide to Writing from Readings*: Curtis R. Burdette, Central Michigan University; Jennifer Campbell, University of Denver; Jacqueline E. Cason, University of Alaska, Anchorage; Tim Catalano, Marietta College; Jane Creighton, University of Houston–Downtown; Sally Ebest, University of Missouri, St. Louis; Daniel P. Galvin,

Clemson University; Karen Gardiner, University of Alabama; Monica E. Hogan, Johnson County Community College; Wesley Jones, University of Mary; Greg Luthi, Johnson County Community College; David D. Knapp, Front Range Community College; Raj Mohan, Cleveland State University; Anne Pici, University of Dayton; Kathy Overhulse Smith, Indiana University–Bloomington; and Mary Trachsel, University of Iowa.

Stephen Wilhoit

A BRIEF GUIDE
TO WRITING
FROM READINGS

Chapter 1

CRITICAL READING

DEFINITION AND PURPOSE

Most successful college writers are also sophisticated, critical readers. They assume a skeptical attitude toward texts: instead of believing whatever they read, they critically examine the author's ideas and their own responses to the reading. They are active, reflective readers who ask questions about the words on the page, mark passages, take notes, and draw connections between the author's ideas and their own experiences and knowledge. They are open to new ideas, but do not accept them without serious, reflective consideration. Unreflective readers, however, tend to accept unquestioningly what they see in print. In their view, if something has been published, it must be accurate. Instead of asking questions about what they read, they tend to accept the author's words at face value.

A major difference, then, between reflective and unreflective readers is the way they try to learn from what they read. Unreflective readers usually believe that the meaning of a text can be found in the words on the page: to understand a text, all a reader has to do is understand the meaning of the author's words. For them, reading is a rather simple, straightforward process: they read through a text, look up any words they do not know, isolate the author's main ideas, perhaps take some notes, then move on to the next reading. They also tend to believe that because the meaning of a text resides in the author's words, students reading the same material ought to come away with the same information; the text should mean roughly the same thing to any competent reader who studies it.

Reflective, critical readers, however, tend to adopt a different view of reading. They believe that the meaning of a text resides in the *interaction* between the reader and the words on the page: to understand a text, readers must be aware of how their own knowledge, feelings, and experience influence their *interpretation* of the words on the page. For them, reading is a rather dynamic, fluid process: they read through a text skeptically, assess the author's words and ideas in light of their own knowledge and experience, jot down some notes that capture their questions and responses, reread the text after they have had some time to consider what the author had to say, and then move on.

Viewing reading as an interactive process can help you better understand the complex nature of writing from sources and the need to be an active, critical reader. For example, it helps you understand why a story you read your first year in high school means something different to you when you read it again your first year in college. The words on the page have not changed, you have, and because you have changed, the "meaning" of the story has changed for you as well. This interactive view of reading also helps explain how twenty students in an introductory philosophy class can read the same meditation by Descartes and come away with twenty slightly different interpretations of the piece. Active, critical readers understand that for any given person the meaning of a text results from the interaction between the words on the page and that reader's knowledge, feelings, and expertise; reading involves more than a simple transfer of information from the words on the page to the mind of the reader.

Does this mean that all interpretations of a reading are equally valid? No. While every person forms his or her own understanding of a reading, people can and often do misread texts: they may not read carefully, they may not understand certain terms or ideas, or they may lack the knowledge and experience they need to form an adequate interpretation of the text. As a safeguard against misinterpretation, critical readers discuss the material with others who have read it. Comparing their own reading of a text with a teacher's or a peer's reading can help clarify the material and prevent misunderstanding.

In addition, the author of the piece plays an important role in reading. Good writers try to influence their readers' understanding of and response to a text. When writing, authors manipulate the language, structure, and content of their prose to achieve a certain effect on their audience. Success is never guaranteed, but good writers know that they can at least influence how readers might respond to their work through the choices they make while composing. Critical readers take this into account when approaching a text—they try to be aware not only of what they bring to the reading, but also of the choices the writer has made to achieve a certain goal.

Learning to read material actively and critically can be difficult. However, critical readers tend to understand course material more fully, prepare for class more efficiently, and write from readings more effectively. Following are a number of suggestions aimed at helping you become a more active, critical reader.

Central to this process is the ability and willingness to ask good questions about your reading of a text and to keep a written record of your responses. Critical readers refuse to sit back passively while they read; they actively question and respond to texts in light of their own knowledge, feelings, and experience.

ASKING QUESTIONS ABOUT WHAT YOU READ

Instead of passively accepting the ideas an author presents, a critical reader attempts to engage in a dialogue with the text, posing and working out answers to tough questions concerning the material's purpose, audience, language, and content.

The most productive critical questions center on the connections that exist between a text's author and his or her audience, subject, and language. Everything you read has been written by someone for someone about something using certain words on a page. Learning how to identify and question the relationship between these various aspects of a reading can help you understand the material more fully and determine its meaning and importance.

Typical questions you should ask of a reading include:

- Who is the author of the piece?
- What is her stand on the issue she's addressing?
- What are her interests, qualifications, or possible biases?
- What was her intent when writing this piece?
- Who is the intended audience?
- How does the author support her contentions?
- What language has she used to convey her ideas on this topic to this audience for this purpose?
- Based on my own knowledge and experience, what do I think about her ideas, intent, language, and support?
- How well does the author achieve her goal?

When you are confronted with conflicting sources of information on a topic (as is frequently the case in college), asking questions such as these is a particularly important way to sort out the authors' different positions, evaluate the worth of each source, and decide who presents the clearer, more convincing case.

Forming a full, critical understanding of a reading requires asking the right kinds of questions about the author, subject, audience, and language of the piece. In the next section you will find a series of questions to ask before, during, and after your reading. However, these questions are merely suggestive, not exhaustive; they indicate only starting points for your critical assessment of a text. Your teacher and peers may suggest other questions to ask as well. Finally, it is a good idea to write out your answers to these questions. Do not rely on your memory alone to keep track of your responses.

QUESTIONS TO ASK BEFORE YOU BEGIN A CLOSE READING OF A TEXT

Whether you are assigned to read material in history or art, biology or sociology, before you begin you need to ask yourself a series of questions concerning the author and publication in which the piece appeared as well as your own knowledge of and attitude toward the topic. Answering these questions may help you determine any biases present in the reading and help ensure that you remain open to any new perspectives or information the author has to offer.

Questions concerning the Author

- Who is the author?
- What are his credentials?
- What else has he written on the topic?
- What possible biases might have influenced his work?

Before you begin to read a text, try to assess the credibility and expertise of the person who wrote the piece. Who is the author, and what are his or her qualifications for writing on this topic? If, for instance, you are writing a paper about global warming for your English class and find an article you want to use in your essay, note whether you are reading a research report produced by a scientist who conducted her own studies on the topic, an informative article composed by a reporter who interviewed that scientist, or an opinion piece written by a television star who has no particular expertise in climatology. The first author is probably well qualified to offer expert opinion; the second author, while less qualified than the first, may still be a legitimate source of information. However, approach the third author skeptically: good actors are rarely good scientists. If you plan to use any of these readings to support a position of your own in an essay, understand that academic readers will tend to believe authors with solid, professional credentials and demonstrated expertise in the topic.

Also determine, as best you can, any biases operating in the authors' work. Note who the writers work for, who supported their research, who publishes their results. No writers are completely objective; all writers bring to their work certain biases or preferences, whether political, religious, or methodological. These biases may influence the type of study authors conduct, the type of evidence they use to support their contentions, the language they employ, and the conclusions they draw. When researching a paper on abortion, for instance, it would be important to note whether the author of a piece is a member of the National Abortion Rights Action League or Operation Life, even if the writer claims to be presenting the results of an objective study. In college you will often read expert testimony that presents conflicting views and interpretations of the same topic, data, or event. Often your job as a *writer* is to examine these different perspectives, compare their quality or worth, and use them to form and defend a position of your own. However, recognizing potential authorial bias in a reading does not disqualify it as a legitimate source of information: it simply puts you in a better position to read the work skeptically and to ask better, more critical questions.

Most academic journals include brief biographical entries on the authors at the beginning or end of each article or in a separate section of the journal typically labeled "Contributor Notes" or "Contributors." Many popular magazines also include some information on the author of each article they publish. (If you cannot find this information, see a reference librarian for help locating biographical dictionaries. Later, including in your essay the credentials of the authors whose work you are quoting or paraphrasing can help increase the credibility of your assertions.)

Questions about the Publication

- In what regard is the publication held by professionals in the field?
- Toward what type of readership is the publication aimed?
- How long ago was the piece published?
- What, generally, is the editorial stance of the publication?

When assessing the quality of a publication, your first questions ought to address its credibility and audience. Do members of the profession or the academy consider this a reputable journal? Does it publish scholarly work or general interest features? What type of reader is this publication trying to reach: scholars or the general public? Answering these questions can help you determine whether work published in this journal or magazine is appropriate for inclusion in an essay of your own.

To answer these questions about the publication, first consult your teacher. He or she can probably tell you in what regard a particular journal is held by professionals in the field. Also, if you want to consult only scholarly sources of information, you may want to limit your research to scholarly indexes and databases—drawing information from *The Applied Science and Technology Index* or ABI/Inform rather than from *The Readers' Guide to Periodical Literature* and InfoTrac. Again, your teacher or a reference librarian can help you identify scholarly reference works.

Just as individual authors have certain biases or preferences that may influence their writing, publications have certain editorial slants that may influence what they print. Some publications will have definite political or ideological agendas. For example, *The New Republic* and *The National Review* are not likely to publish the same article on gun control. Other publications may exhibit certain methodological biases: they prefer to publish only historical studies or empirical studies or Marxist studies of a topic. Determining the editorial or methodological slant of a publication can be difficult: if you have not read widely in a field, you may not know a great deal about its principal publications. Often, your best recourse in gathering this type of information is to scan the titles and abstracts of other articles in the journal to determine its political or methodological preferences or, if you are reading newspaper or magazine articles, to read the editorials.

However, a particular periodical's political or methodological slant does not necessarily make it any more or less valid a source of information. Recognizing these preferences, though, should help you read material more skeptically. A publication's biases may affect the content of the articles it publishes, its authors' interpretations of statistics, even the nature of the graphics and illustrations accompanying the text. When you are thoroughly researching a topic, gathering information from several different sources is one way to guard against one-sided, unbalanced treatments of a topic.

Questions concerning Your Own Views of the Topic

- What are my beliefs about the issue addressed in the reading?
- How open am I to new ideas on this topic?

Just as every author and publication presents material from a particular perspective, readers, too, bring their own prejudices and preferences to a text. Though absolute objectivity may be impossible for readers and writers to attain, knowing your own predispositions toward the topic an author addresses can help you guard against unfairly judging someone else's arguments or shutting yourself off from potentially helpful ideas.

Author Peter Elbow suggests two frames of mind students ought to assume when reading material. First, he advises students to play the "believing game"—that is, to assume that what the writer has to say is correct. If the author of the piece is right in what he says, how do his ideas influence your current views on the topic? What are the implications of the author's ideas? Can you draw any connections between what the author has to say and what you already know? Next, Elbow suggests that students play the "doubting game"—that is, assume a more critical stance toward the author's ideas. What are the weaknesses in the writer's arguments? What are the limitations of his ideas? In what ways are the author's ideas incompatible with what you already know about the topic?

Being aware of your own stance on an issue *before* you begin to read something for the first time can help you play the believing and doubting games more effectively. First, reading with your own beliefs firmly in mind can help you recognize which ideas are hard for you to accept or even to consider fairly. We all resist ideas that run counter to our beliefs: giving them legitimacy forces us to question our own positions. However, being a critical reader means you are willing to do just that, to consider ideas that you might otherwise ignore or reject. When you dismiss an idea in a source text, consider why: if it is only because that idea runs counter to your views, try playing the believing game before moving on.

Second, reading with your beliefs firmly in mind can help you recognize which ideas are hard for you to question and criticize. We all like to read material that confirms our present positions, because such reinforcement is comforting and reassuring. However, as a critical reader you must be willing to question authors who voice opinions you endorse, to criticize fairly and thoroughly ideas you are predisposed to accept unquestioningly. If you accept information without question, consider why: if it is only because you agree with the author, try playing the doubting game before moving on.

QUESTIONS TO ASK WHILE YOU READ AND REREAD MATERIAL

After you have read material with these questions in mind, reread it. If necessary, read it a third or fourth time—very few of us truly understand a text the first time we read it. When rereading material, though, you should consider another set of questions that focus your attention on the audience, purpose, content, and organization of the piece, along with your response to the author's ideas.

Questions concerning the Audience of the Piece

- What audience does the author seem to be trying to reach?
- What type of reader would be attracted to the author's writing, and what type would be alienated by it?
- How does your sense of the text's audience influence your reading of the piece?

Audience is one of the most important concepts in writing: an author's sense of audience will greatly affect, among other things, the language she uses, the material she includes, and the organizational strategy she employs. However, *audience* can be a difficult term to define. In one sense, it refers to actual people a writer may know. When composing a letter to a friend, for instance, a writer can make fairly accurate predictions about the way her reader will react to what she says or the language she uses.

In another sense, though, *audience* can have very little to do with specific people the author has in mind as he writes a text. Much of what you read in college, for example, was written by people who possessed a much more nebulous sense of audience as they wrote. They knew the *type* of reader they were trying to address (for example, a first-year student taking an introductory geology course) or perhaps the *type* of reader they wanted to interest (for example, people curious about feminist interpretations of literature). When writing, they did not have in mind as their audience a specific, individual reader. Instead, they were trying to produce prose that would attract or interest a particular type of reader.

Therefore, as you read and reread material, try to determine the audience the author is trying to address: how is she attempting to interest or appeal to that type of reader? How successful is she in achieving that goal? Pay attention to the language, content, and organization of the piece as you try to answer questions such as these:

- Was the author trying to reach a general reader, an educated reader, or a specialist?
- What language does the author use to try to reach this audience? What examples? What graphics?
- What type of reader would actually find the work helpful, informative, valuable, or difficult?
- Would any readers be alienated by the material in the piece? Why?

Answering these questions will help you better understand how the text you are reading came to assume its present form. When writing, authors choose language, examples, and a structure they believe will help them achieve their desired effect on an audience. Part of reading a text critically is determining in your mind how successful each writer has been in making these choices.

Realize, too, that when you read something, you become a member of that writer's audience. *Your* response to what you read is extremely important to note as you try to understand what the author has to say. Is the writer communicating his ideas effectively to you? Do you find the material in the piece interesting or boring, helpful or irrelevant, engaging or alienating? What choices has the writer made that led to these responses? What knowledge or experience do you bring to the text that contributes to your reaction? Understanding the complex relationship between the audience and the writer of a piece can help you become a more sensitive, critical reader.

Questions about Purpose

- What was the author's purpose in writing the piece?
- What is the author's thesis?
- Does the author successfully achieve his or her goals?

Generally, when writing a text, an author will have one of three aims: to entertain, to inform, or to persuade his readers. Many times a work will serve multiple purposes—it will both entertain and inform, or inform and persuade. However, as a critical reader, you ought to identify the primary purpose of the piece you are reading. To criticize an article for failing to present an effective argument on a topic would be unproductive and unfair if all the author intended was to write an informative essay.

However, determining an author's purpose or goal can be difficult. In social science and natural science journals, look for the author's stated purpose in his abstract or thesis ("The purpose of this article is . . ." and "The authors seek to prove that . . ."). The conventions of most humanities journals, however, require authors to be less straightforward or declaratory in stating their purpose, but again thesis statements and abstracts are good places to start your search. Even if the author states his or her goal somewhere in the paper or abstract, be wary. When you finish rereading the piece, ask yourself, "Given the content, language, and structure of this piece, what do *I* believe to be the writer's primary goal or purpose?"

Questions about Content

- What are the author's major assertions or findings?
- How does the author support these assertions or findings?

When examining the content of any reading, try first to locate the author's thesis and paraphrase it. A thesis statement will be either stated or implied. If it is stated, you will be able to point to a sentence or two in the reading that serves as the thesis. If it is implied, a general idea or argument unites and guides the writing, but the author never explicitly puts it into words. When you paraphrase this general idea or argument, you have identified the thesis. In either case, as a first step in analyzing a reading's content, restate the author's thesis in your own words to form a clear idea of what the author is trying to accomplish in the piece.

Next, note how the author supports her thesis—identify her primary ideas, arguments, or findings and the evidence, reasons, or examples she offers to support them. As you reread the piece, ask yourself what empirical, philosophical, theoretical, or other type of evidence or reasoning the author has provided to support her thesis and achieve her goal.

Finally, be sure to examine what you already know about the topic—what you have learned in the past and what you are learning now by reading *this* piece. Has the author left out any important information or arguments? Has she neglected certain interpretations of evidence others have offered? If so, why do you think that is? How can the reading's content be explained by its author, audience, or purpose?

Questions about Organization

- How is the material organized?
- What headings and subheadings does the author provide?
- What does the organization of the essay tell you about the author's view of the material?
- What gets stressed as a result of the organization?

As a writer composes his piece, he has to make a series of decisions about organization: he needs to determine the order in which he will present his findings, ideas, or arguments. Good writers organize their material purposefully—to make their article clear, to make their book more persuasive, or to make their findings more accessible. Through the order in which they present their material and through their use of paragraph breaks, headings, and subheadings, they try to help the reader understand or accept their views.

As you read a source text, think critically about its organization. First, form at least a rough idea of how the writer has organized his ideas. What are the major sections of the text? In what order are the ideas, arguments, or findings presented? You might want to produce a scratch outline or list that captures the reading's organization. Also, use the headings and subheadings the author provides to get a better understanding of how he views his material and how he sets priorities among his findings. For example, what ideas, arguments, or findings get emphasized through the author's selection of headings? How do the headings and subheadings guide you through the piece? Are there any instances in which you think a heading or subheading is misleading or poorly stated? Why?

Questions about the Author's Sources

- How does the author use other people's ideas or findings?
- How credible are the sources the author uses to support his ideas or findings?

As you analyze the content of a reading, examine the sources the author relied on when writing. What is documented? Flip back to the works cited list or bibliography at the end of the piece. Where does the author's information come from? Is the paper based on library research, primary research, or interviews? If much of the text's material comes from previously published work, how credible are the sources the author used to support her claims? For example, is the author relying on scholarly sources of information? Is there any apparent bias in the author's use of source material: is most of her material taken from journals that share similar editorial stances, or has the writer tried to draw information from sources representing a variety of political, theoretical, or methodological perspectives? Answering questions such as these can help you determine the credibility and utility of the author's ideas, arguments, or findings.

Questions about Graphics

- How clear are the charts, graphs, tables, or illustrations the author provides?
- How well does the author explain the graphics?
- How well do the graphics support or explain what the author has to say?

Graphics include charts, tables, graphs, drawings, and pictures. While authors may add graphics to entertain readers, most include them to support arguments, summarize findings, or illustrate ideas. As you read a text, try to determine how the author is using graphics in her work and how clear, helpful, or informative you find them.

Questions about Your Reactions and Responses

- How do I feel about the topic, issues, or findings addressed in the reading?
- What is convincing? What is unclear?
- What ideas in the piece contradict my understanding of the topic?
- What ideas in the piece are new to me? Which ones do I accept and which ones do I reject?

People's beliefs and knowledge influence how they read material—what they take note of, what they understand the author to be saying, what they remember after they read the piece. Understanding your response to the material you read can help you become a more critical reader and a more effective writer in several ways. First, honestly assessing your response can help you be balanced and fair. As a skeptical reader you need to be both critical of ideas you at first enthusiastically support and open to ideas you at first strongly reject.

Second, examining your response to what you read can help you decide on and develop effective paper topics—your responses may help you identify an interest or question you can later pursue more thoroughly in an essay. Especially consider what you learn from a reading. What information is new? How do the author's ideas or findings confirm or contradict what you have come to think? Examining your answers to questions such as these can result in some interesting essays.

MARKING TEXTS

Look at the books of active, critical readers and you will see pages filled with underlined passages, marginal comments, questions, and reactions. Because they have recognized the close link between reading and writing, they rarely read without a pencil in hand. They underline the reading's thesis statement and any important passages they find. As they question the material they are reading, they annotate the text and write down the answers to the questions they ask so that when they return to the material later they can recall the author's purpose and findings, remember how they responded to the author's ideas, and locate the information they want to use in their papers.

The two most common ways of marking texts are highlighting and annotating. Highlighting typically involves underlining, circling, bracketing, or color coding passages, while annotating involves writing comments or questions in the margin or at the end of the text.

HIGHLIGHTING TEXTS

Highlighting involves underlining, color coding, or in some other way marking important passages in a reading. Most students tend to highlight too little or too much. Some never make a mark in their books. Perhaps they were trained in high school not to mark up readings, or maybe they are concerned about the resale value of their books. Whatever their reason, these students rarely, if ever, highlight material they read. Other students highlight too many passages in a reading—practically every sentence is underlined, and almost every paragraph is shaded yellow or pink. You have to be selective in what you highlight: you mark up a reading in order to understand it more clearly and to identify important passages you may return to later when you write your paper.

In order to highlight a reading effectively, you need to develop your own marking system, a kind of code that helps you locate certain types of information in a text. Good writers usually develop unique ways of highlighting readings: they underline certain kinds of passages, place brackets around specific types of information, and circle other parts of the text. Later, when they return to the reading to write their paper, they can easily find the information they need. Following are some suggestions about what to mark in a text:

1. Mark an author's thesis, primary assertions, and supporting evidence.
2. Mark the names of authors, dates of studies, locations of research projects, and other important facts mentioned in the reading.
3. Mark key passages you might want to reread, quote, or paraphrase later as you write your paper.
4. Mark words or terms you do not know so you can look up their definitions.

Establish your own way of highlighting a text: circle authors' names, bracket dates, use a yellow highlighting pen to mark any passages you may want to quote and blue ink to indicate questionable statements, or whatever variations make sense to you. Once you establish your own highlighting system, writing from readings will become much easier for you.

ANNOTATING TEXTS

While you are highlighting a reading, you should also annotate it—that is, *write out* your responses, questions, observations, or conclusions. Generally, there are two types of annotations you will use: marginal and end comments. Marginal annotations are notes that you make to yourself in the top, bottom, or side margins of the page; end annotations are notes that you make at the end of the text.

Marginal Annotations

Marginal annotations are typically short and in many cases may make sense only to the person who wrote them. Generally, they can be divided into content notes, organization notes, connection notes, questions, and responses.

Content notes typically identify the meaning or purpose of the marked passage. For example, after bracketing an author's first argument—that eliminating a particular government program may have negative consequences on the poor, for instance—you may write in the margin, "Argument 1—consequences for poor." When you review a reading to find material you want to use in your paper, content notes help you easily locate what you need, which is particularly important if you are completing a research project involving multiple readings.

Organization notes identify the major sections of a source text. After underlining an article's thesis, you may write *thesis* in the margin in order to find it more easily later, then bracket the first few paragraphs and write *introduction* in the margin. You might draw a line down the margin beside the next few paragraphs and write *first argument* in the margin, then highlight the next section and write *refutation of first argument*. Organization notes help you understand how the author has structured the piece and may help you locate particular sections of the text you would like to review.

Connection notes identify the links you see between an author's ideas and those offered by other writers or between ideas an author develops in different sections of a reading: "this idea echoes Weber's argument," "illustrates first point," or "contradicts teacher's position." As you read an article, you should note how the author's ideas confirm or refute ideas developed by other writers. Note the connections in the margin of the essay you are reading in case you want to examine the link more closely later: do not rely on your memory. If you are reading multiple sources on the same topic, distinctions between the texts can quickly blur; you may have a difficult time remembering who wrote what if you do not write good connection notes. Also, use connection notes to trace the development of each writer's thesis. Note in the margin of the reading the link between the various ideas, arguments, or findings the writer offers and his or her thesis.

Questions can serve several purposes. First, they can identify passages you find confusing: in a question, try to capture *precisely* what you find confusing in a passage, especially if you will have a chance to discuss the reading in class. Second, questions can help you identify in a reading the material you want to dispute. Try to capture in a critical question or two why you disagree with what the author has written. Finally, questions can identify where the author has failed to consider important information or arguments. These are typically "what about" questions: "What about the theory proposed by Smith?" "What about people who can't afford day care?" Your goal is to indicate with a question possible limitations to an author's ideas or arguments.

Response notes record your reactions to what you read. These notes may indicate which ideas you accept, which ones you reject, and which ones you doubt. They can range from a simple "yes!" or "huh?" to more elaborate and detailed reactions that allow you to explore your response in some detail.

Remember to keep your marginal notes brief. Their purpose is to help you read the text more critically and recall your responses and questions when you reread the material.

End Annotations

End annotations typically make some type of comment on the source as a whole and can assume different forms, including summaries, responses, and questions.

Summaries offer brief, objective overviews of a reading. You may want to write a one- or two-sentence summary at the end of a reading, especially if you are reading several source texts for your paper. The purpose of these summaries is to jog your memory about the reading's content or thesis so you don't have to reread the entire text. These summaries are especially helpful if you have to read several texts with similar titles: it is easy to confuse these readings, and the summaries can often help you find the particular text you need.

Responses capture your reaction to the work as a whole. Try to capture in your note your response to the author's ideas, argument, writing style, or any other aspect of the reading that strikes you as important. These responses can help you form comments to offer in class when you discuss the piece, and often they serve as a good starting point for developing a topic for a paper: you may want to investigate and develop your response more thoroughly and formally in an essay.

Questions written at the end of a reading typically address the source's clarity, purpose, or effectiveness. Your questions might address the reading's claims, evidence, or reasoning; its syntax, tone, or structure. Other questions might address the reading's relationship to what you already know about the topic or what you have already read. These questions help you draw connections between the readings and your own knowledge and experience. Still other questions might indicate specific aspects of a topic you still need to investigate ("I wonder how his ideas might have an impact on part two of my paper—need to reconsider?") or links between two or more authors' claims that need further consideration ("Do her arguments refute the textbook's claims?").

You will usually jot down several different types of endnotes when you finish reading a text. You may write out a brief one- or two-sentence summary, a few questions, and a response. These endnotes can prove very helpful when you return to the material later: they indicate your assessment of the source text's content, strengths, weaknesses, and worth.

Together, highlighting and annotating can help you fully understand a reading and determine the best way to use it in your own writing. A word of warning, though: do not be blinded by your own annotations and highlights. When you review a source text you have already marked and annotated and are now planning to use in your paper, be critical of your *own* highlighting and annotations. Be sure to question whether your highlighting and annotations *really* capture the source's key points. As you review your comments and marked passages, ask yourself whether you feel the same way now about the reading. If you have been engaged in researching a topic, are you now in a better position to assess the value and meaning of the reading before you? Have your views changed? Also, try to answer the questions you asked in the margins or at the end of the article. Reassess your original reactions.

SAMPLE ANNOTATED READING

Review the following sample annotated reading. Your system for marking a reading will likely be different from the system used here. Note, though, how the reader used highlighting and annotations to gain a better understanding of the author's content, structure, language, and purpose.

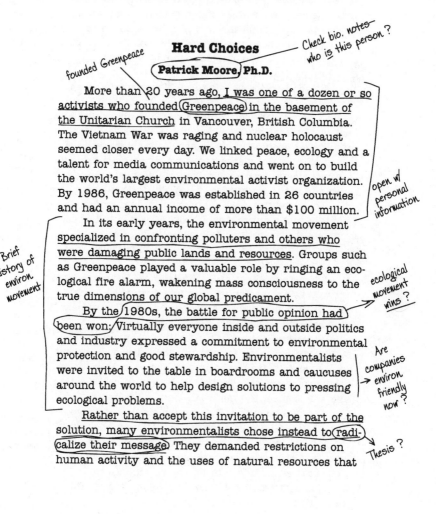

founded Greenpeace

Hard Choices

Check bio. notes — who is this person?

Patrick Moore, Ph.D.

More than 20 years ago, I was one of a dozen or so activists who founded Greenpeace in the basement of the Unitarian Church in Vancouver, British Columbia. The Vietnam War was raging and nuclear holocaust seemed closer every day. We linked peace, ecology and a talent for media communications and went on to build the world's largest environmental activist organization. By 1986, Greenpeace was established in 26 countries and had an annual income of more than $100 million.

open w/ personal information

In its early years, the environmental movement specialized in confronting polluters and others who were damaging public lands and resources. Groups such as Greenpeace played a valuable role by ringing an ecological fire alarm, wakening mass consciousness to the true dimensions of our global predicament.

Brief history of environ movement

ecological movement wins?

By the 1980s, the battle for public opinion had been won. Virtually everyone inside and outside politics and industry expressed a commitment to environmental protection and good stewardship. Environmentalists were invited to the table in boardrooms and caucuses around the world to help design solutions to pressing ecological problems.

Are companies environ friendly now?

Rather than accept this invitation to be part of the solution, many environmentalists chose instead to radicalize their message. They demanded restrictions on human activity and the uses of natural resources that

Thesis?

too "radical"

anti-science ?

not build on earlier successes

far exceed any scientific justification. That tactical decision created an atmosphere in which many environmentalists today must rely on sensational rhetoric and misinformation rather than good science. Programs have gone forward without input from more knowledgeable environmentalists and other experts; the public debate has been needlessly polarized as a result of the movement's unwillingness to collaborate with others less radical.

environ. not work w/others ?

In addition to choosing a dubious tactic, the environmental movement also changed its philosophy along the way. It once prided itself on subscribing to a philosophy that was "transpolitical, transideological, and transnational" in character. Non-violent direct action and peaceful disobedience were the hallmarks of the movement. Truth mattered and science was respected for the knowledge it brought to the debate.

says current movement rejects truth & science

Thesis →

That tradition was abandoned by many environmental groups during the 1990s. A new brand of environmental extremism has emerged that rejects science, diversity of opinion, and even democracy. These eco-extremists tend to be:

note headings

*Anti-technology and anti-science. Eco-extremists entirely reject machinery and industry; they invoke science as a means of justifying the adoption of beliefs that have no basis in science to begin with.

anti-science

*Anti-free enterprise. Although communism and state socialism have failed to protect the environment, eco-extremists are basically anti-business. They have not put forward an alternative system of organization that would meet the material needs of society.

anti-business

point not developed well

*Anti-democratic. Eco-extremists do not tolerate dissent and do not respect the opinions and beliefs of the general public. In the name of "speaking for the trees and other species," we are faced with a movement that would usher in an era of eco-fascism.

anti-democratic

The international debate over clearcutting offers a case study of eco-extremism in action. Groups such as Greenpeace and the Sierra Club have mounted major

example of clearcutting

need clearcutting

campaigns against clearcutting, claiming that it is responsible for "deforestation" on a massive scale in Canada and elsewhere. In fact, no such deforestation is taking place in Canada or the United States, and a ban on clearcutting could do more harm than good.

It is an (ecological fact) that many types of forest ecosystems thrive most successfully when they are periodically cleared and allowed to regenerate. Fire, volcanic eruptions, windstorms, insect attacks, disease and climate change (ice ages) destroy massive areas of forests, part of a natural cycle of forest destruction and renewal that has existed since long before modern humans arrived on the scene.

ignores diversity— usually replanted w/only one type of tree

The use of (hype and myths) by Greenpeace and the Sierra Club is symptomatic of the larger problems facing the modern environmental movement. Confrontation too often is preferred over collaboration, and (eco-extremism) has shoved aside the earlier spirit of tolerance and concern for the fate of humanity. The results have been harmful to the movement as well as to the environment we seek to protect.

hype and myths of Green & Sierra

As an environmentalist in the political center, I now find myself branded a traitor and a sellout by this new breed of saviors. My name appears in Greenpeace's "Guide to Anti-Environmental Organizations." But surely the shoe belongs on the other foot: The eco-extremists who have taken control of the nation's leading environmental organizations must shoulder the blame for the anti-environmental backlash now taking place in the United States and elsewhere. Unless they change their philosophy and tactics, the prospects for a protected environment will remain dim.

he is in political center— how defined?

founder now an enemy?

why a backlash?

Patrick Moore earned a Ph.D. in ecology from the University of British Columbia in 1972. He was a founding member of Greenpeace and for seven years served as director of Greenpeace International.

credentials but who does he work for?

Summary— "Eco-extremists" reject science, truth, alternative views → why lose pop. support?

NOTE TAKING

Especially when working on an extended writing project, you may want to take notes on a source text after carefully reading and annotating it. If you are working on a research paper for a class, check with your instructor about any requirements he or she might have concerning your notes. Some teachers, for example, require their students to take notes on index cards following rather specific guidelines. Other teachers set no guidelines concerning notes. It is always a good idea to check with your instructor concerning his or her requirements.

If you take notes on index cards, be sure you indicate somewhere on each card the title and/or author of the work you are reading. If your cards get out of order, you need some way of identifying the source of the information on each card. If you are more comfortable taking notes on paper, try to use only one side of each sheet. Using your notes to write your essay is easier if you are not constantly flipping over sheets of paper to find the information you need.

Some writers like their notes to consist only of quotes; others mix quoted, paraphrased, and summarized material. Some write notes in complete sentences; some use a combination of sentences, sentence fragments, and even single words or diagrams. As with annotations, you will need to work out your own system for taking notes, one that helps you sort out and organize the useful material you find in the sources you read.

The next sections provide some guidelines to keep in mind as you take your notes. Following them can help you avoid problems later as you use your notes to write your paper.

Before Jotting Down Any Notes, Always Write Down the Source Text's Full Bibliographic Information

Whenever you take notes on a reading, be sure to write down the author's full name, the exact title of the piece, the full title of the publication, all the publication information, and the inclusive page numbers. Often students will be completing a paper the night before it is due and realize they used material that needs to be documented. Without having the full bibliographic information with their notes, they have to make a frantic last-minute dash back to the library. If you are careful to write down this information before you take your notes, you can avoid some problems later.

In Your Notes, Carefully Distinguish between Material You Quote and Material You Paraphrase

One of the major sources of unintentional plagiarism is faulty note taking. This problem occurs when, in taking your notes, you copy down a passage word-for-word from a source text but fail to enclose that passage in quotation marks. If you then copy that material directly from your notes into your paper—thinking you originally paraphrased the passage—and fail to quote it in your essay, you will be guilty of plagiarism. You can avoid this problem if you carefully indicate with quotation marks which passages in your notes are exact quotations and which are paraphrases of an author's ideas.

Carefully List Page Numbers

In your notes, be sure to indicate the exact page number of the source text that contains the material you are quoting, paraphrasing, or summarizing. You will need this information later for proper documentation.

Pay Attention to the Punctuation in the Source Text

If you are quoting material in your notes, reproduce the original punctuation exactly as it appears on the page. Many times students misquote material because they incorrectly copied the original punctuation into their notes.

In Your Notes, Clearly Differentiate between the Author's Ideas and Your Own

Again, failing to differentiate between what an author says about a topic and what you have to say is a major source of unintentional plagiarism. As you take your notes, you may want to jot down some observations or ideas of your own—reading other people's ideas will often lead you to new insights of your own. However, if you do not make the distinction clear in your notes—if, when reviewing your notes, you cannot tell which ideas were yours and which were the other writer's—you might attribute ideas to authors who never suggested them or take credit for ideas that were originally developed by someone else. To make this distinction clear in your notes, perhaps you could place your ideas and reflections in brackets.

Be Consistent with Your Note-Taking System

Whether you use a notebook, looseleaf paper, index cards, or a personal computer for taking notes, be consistent in how and where you note bibliographic information, page numbers, and your responses to the material. Adhering to a system will make it easier for you to find material in your notes and will help you avoid making mistakes.

Additional Reading

Getting Serious about Eradicating Binge Drinking

Henry Wechsler

Henry Wechsler directs the College Alcohol Studies program at Harvard's School of Public Health.

Most of us are aware that binge drinking is a major problem on many college campuses. Since the Harvard School of Public Health's first College Alcohol Study used that term, in 1994, to describe the drinking pattern of significant numbers of American college students, the problem has drawn media attention across the nation. Despite this, the problem has not declined over the past four years. In fact, our latest research findings, released in September, showed little change in the proportion of college students who binge. Among more than 14,500 students surveyed at 116 institutions, 43 percent reported that they had binged at least once in the preceding two weeks, compared with 44 percent in the earlier study.

Although the number of students who abstain from alcohol grew to 19 percent this year from 15.6 percent in the first study, among students who drink we found an increase in drunkenness, in drinking deliberately to get drunk, and in alcohol-related problems—including injuries, drunk driving, violence, and academic difficulties. For example, among students who drink, 52 percent said a major motivation was "to get drunk," compared with 39 percent in the first study. Thus, despite a spate of widely publicized student deaths in alcohol-related incidents, the binge goes on.

Why isn't this behavior decreasing? For one thing, binge drinking has been so deeply entrenched for so long at colleges that it can't be expected to disappear overnight. However, the more important reason that change eludes us is that some colleges have relied too much on one approach to solve the problem—trying to get the binge drinkers themselves to stop, rather than focusing equal attention on factors that make it easy for students to drink too much.

Of course, some campuses use multiple approaches to attack the problem, but many focus most of their energies on educational efforts directed at drinkers, particularly during events such as the recent Alcohol Awareness Week. Such educational efforts are an important way to teach some students the facts about alcohol abuse. But those efforts overlook the environment around binge drinkers that condones and supports and often even encourages their behavior.

So what are the factors that promote binge drinking at colleges? One is that students who binge tend to think they represent the norm; they argue that they're just doing what most of their peers do. Most binge drinkers don't think they have a problem. They think they are only having fun, and most consider themselves to be moderate drinkers. Doing research into actual behavior and then informing students about how many students actually binge—generally fewer than binge drinkers believe—can help to reduce the behavior.

Another approach to changing student norms is to focus on the disruptive behavior of binge drinkers. Colleges are civic communities, and all too frequently they are disrupted by the behavior of students who drink excessively. Rather than search for contraband alcohol, a college would be wise to engage student leaders in helping administrators work out a clearly worded code of conduct that penalizes drunken behavior—and then to enforce it consistently.

Students who become drunk and disorderly should be made to take responsibility for the messes that they have created: They should have to clean up vomit in the bathrooms made unusable on weekends, help care for drunken students at the college health center, repair damage from vandalism, and pick up litter. The punishment should fit the crime.

But with repeat offenders, colleges need to consider enforcing a "three strikes and you're out" policy for alcohol-related violations of the student conduct code.

At the center of binge drinking on many campuses are fraternities and sororities. While they attract only a small percentage of students nationally, they continue to play a prominent role in campus life at many institutions. Our data shows that in fraternity houses, four of five residents binge, and more than half are frequent binge drinkers. And fraternity parties are attended by many more students than just members. They attract even some high-school seniors—future college students who are introduced to binge drinking as a social norm. Not surprisingly, most of the alcohol-related deaths of college students recently reported in the media involved fraternity parties.

While some colleges have begun to address the drinking culture created by fraternities, many administrators are still hesitant to move strongly against fraternities, for fear of angering alumni donors who fondly remember their own college years of partying. But administrators have a responsibility to protect all of their students against alcohol-related disruptions and injuries, and should not wait for tragedy to strike before they revoke official recognition of fraternities that consistently cause problems. Colleges also can require all first-year students who live on campus to reside in dormitories, and not in fraternity or sorority houses. Of course, then those colleges must work to create interesting alcohol-free activities centered in the residence halls, to show students that out-of-control drinking need not be the focus of social life.

A third impetus for binge drinking on college campuses—one rarely mentioned publicly—involves alumni at tailgate parties during homecoming activities and sporting events. Any alcohol-control measures adopted for students must also apply to visiting alumni. Banning alcohol at home sporting events for everyone except alumni who contribute more than $50, as one college did recently, is not a good way to win students' support for new alcohol-control policies. I would hope that most alumni, if informed that an institution is trying to cope with a serious problem, would cooperate. Colleges that base their decision making on fund-raising concerns must ask themselves: What will cost the college more money—alumni who might decrease their contributions if they're cut off from alcohol at sporting events, or a few large jury awards of damages to families of injured or deceased students?

Another center of college binge drinking is found in athletics programs. Athletes binge more than other students, according to our data. In fact, involvement in athletics—compared with time spent in other activities— increases rather than decreases a student's propensity for binge drinking. Students involved in athletics are one and a half times as likely to be binge drinkers as are other students. This tradition is kept alive through the beer-advertising blitz that surrounds sports. After all, Mark McGwire's 70th home run was hit at Busch Stadium.

As a first step, college athletics officials should stay clear of alcohol-industry promotions and advertising. Further, although coaches at some colleges require team members to abstain from alcohol during the competitive season, relatively few coaches are involved in campus-wide programs to reduce alcohol abuse. Colleges should make it a priority to enlist their coaches and athletics directors in programs designed to reach all students with the message that binge drinking interferes with performance in every area of their lives. The National Collegiate Athletic Association should encourage this. Colleges also should press coaches to stress the institution's commitment to preventing alcohol abuse when they recruit high-school athletes.

Another important point of intervention is at the high-school level. Half of college binge drinkers start in high school. Colleges should begin to address this problem at high schools that send a large number of freshmen to their campuses, by sending college students from those high schools back to talk to the younger students about alcohol and other substance abuse. The volunteers should stress that one in five college students nationally abstains from alcohol, and that another two in five drink, but not to excess.

High-school students are more likely to believe the messages of college students than those of teachers and other adults. Let future freshmen get their first view of college life from these volunteers, rather than from attending fraternity parties or tailgate events. Once freshmen have unpacked and settled in, it may be too late to tell them about college rules on alcohol use. That message should be sent before they even apply.

Colleges also need to focus more attention a block or two away from the campus—on the ring of bars and liquor stores that encircles many institutions. Colleges need to map the density of those establishments; many institutions have more than 50 such alcohol outlets surrounding them. These are formidable competitors for students' attention, and cannot be coped with by the college alone; community leaders must be enlisted to help, particularly in barring the low-price specials that the outlets use to compete with each other: two-for-one offers, cut-rate drinks and free food during happy hours, and free drinks for women on certain nights. Some states and communities already have laws that ban those types of sales. Remember, the problem is not alcohol itself; it is the availability of a large volume of alcohol at a low price, usually to be consumed in a short period of time.

All of the problem areas that I've cited cannot be attacked by every college at once. Some issues may be more pressing than others on particular campuses, and the solutions must be fashioned to fit local circumstances.

Some important actions are being taken by colleges and universities across the country. Many are trying to sever the connection between alcohol and sports by banning advertising in the programs for sporting events and prohibiting alcohol at college stadiums. Some colleges are discontinuing the practice of not holding classes or exams on Fridays, and are no longer allowing local bars to advertise drink specials in campus publications. And some colleges are experimenting with new student-housing arrangements, such as living–learning centers that take faculty members and classes into the dorms, to try to completely change the environments there.

Institutions also are trying to give students more alcohol-free entertainment options. Some are working with neighborhood groups, as well as community and state officials, to find legal and other means of controlling students' behavior off campus. Other colleges are imposing stricter sanctions on students who break the rules—notifying parents after a certain number of infractions, and suspending or expelling repeat offenders.

What institutions need to avoid are one-dimensional programs that focus on particular students but ignore the ways in which colleges help enable some students to continue binging for four years. Not holding classes or exams on Fridays, for example, enables students to binge from Thursday to Sunday without interruption. Making new rules, but not enforcing even the old ones—for example, banning alcohol in the dormitories, but allowing it to be carried in unmarked cups—tells students that the college is not serious about eradicating the problem.

To anyone who thinks that binge drinking is behavior that cannot be changed, I offer the following challenge. At the next meeting you attend, look around and count how many people are smoking. Not many years ago, the room would have been filled with smoke. Today, because of the wide recognition that smoking hurts both the smoker and people nearby, through secondhand effects, the air is clear. Binge drinking can become equally unacceptable on college campuses.

Summary Chart

CRITICAL READING: ASKING QUESTIONS

1. **Questions to Ask before You Begin a Close Reading of a Text**

   Questions concerning the author
   - *Who is the author?*
   - *What are her credentials?*
   - *What else has she written on the topic?*
   - *What possible biases might have influenced her work?*

   Questions concerning the publication
   - *In what regard is the publication held by professionals in the field?*
   - *Toward what type of readership is the publication aimed?*
   - *How long ago was the piece published?*
   - *What, generally, is the editorial stance of the publication?*

   Questions concerning your own views of the topic
   - *What are my beliefs about the issue addressed in the reading?*
   - *How open am I to new ideas on this topic?*

2. **Questions to Ask while You Read and Reread Material**

   Questions concerning the audience of the piece
   - *What audience does the author seem to be trying to reach?*
   - *What type of reader would be attracted to the author's writing, and what type would be alienated by it?*
   - *How does your sense of the text's audience influence your reading of the piece?*

   Questions concerning the purpose of the piece
   - *What was the author's purpose in writing the piece?*
   - *What is the author's thesis?*
   - *Does the author successfully achieve his or her goals?*

   Questions concerning the content of the piece
   - *What are the author's major assertions or findings?*
   - *How does the author support these assertions or findings?*

   Questions concerning the organization of the piece
   - *How is the material organized?*
   - *What headings and subheadings does the author provide?*

- *What does the organization of the essay tell you about the author's view of the material?*
- *What gets stressed as a result of the organization?*

Questions concerning the author's sources
- *How does the author use other people's ideas or findings?*
- *How credible are the sources the author uses to support his ideas or findings?*

Questions concerning graphics in the piece
- *How clear are the charts, graphs, tables, or illustrations the author provides?*
- *How well does the author explain the graphics?*
- *How well do the graphics support or explain what the author has to say?*

Questions concerning your reactions and responses to the piece
- *How do I feel about the topic, issues, or findings addressed in the reading?*
- *What is convincing? What is unclear?*
- *What ideas in the piece contradict my understanding of the topic?*
- *What ideas in the piece are new to me? Which ones do I accept and which ones do I reject?*

Summary Chart

CRITICAL READING: MARKING TEXTS

1. **Highlighting Texts**

   Highlight the text's thesis, primary assertions, and supporting evidence.

   Highlight the names of authors, specific dates mentioned, and principal sources cited.

   Highlight key passages you may want to reread, quote, or paraphrase later.

   Highlight terms you do not understand or want to discuss in class.

2. **Annotating Texts**

   Marginal annotations
   - *Content notes: identify the meaning or purpose of the marked passages.*
   - *Organization notes: identify the major sections of the text.*
   - *Connection notes: identify links between readings and within a reading.*
   - *Questions: identify confusing, controversial, or questionable passages.*
   - *Response notes: identify your reactions to the reading.*

   End annotations
   - *Summaries: convey a brief overview of the reading.*
   - *Responses: convey your overall reaction to the piece.*
   - *Questions: convey your assessment of the reading's clarity, purpose, or effectiveness.*

Summary Chart

CRITICAL READING: NOTE TAKING

1. Before jotting down any notes, always write down the source text's full bibliographic information.
2. In your notes, carefully distinguish between material you quote and material you paraphrase.
3. Carefully list page numbers in your notes.
4. Pay attention to the punctuation in the source text.
5. In your notes, clearly differentiate between the author's ideas and your own.
6. Be consistent with your note-taking system.

Chapter 2

QUOTATION

DEFINITION AND PURPOSE

When you use someone else's words in your paper, you have to place them in quotation marks and supply proper documentation. Quoting and documenting material tells your readers where they can find that *exact* language in the source text. If you make any significant changes in a passage you are quoting, you need to indicate the alterations in your text with ellipses, brackets, or an explanation.

Generally, if you take more than three words in a row from a source text and incorporate them word-for-word in your essay, you need to place quotation marks around the passage. However, there are several exceptions to this general guideline. For example, if you repeat in your paper someone's official title as it appears in the source text (e.g., president of the school board), you do not need to quote the title, even if it is longer than three words. Also, if you use in your paper a *single* word or term from a source text that is significant or unusual, you *may* need to quote it. Learning what to quote and when to quote takes some time, practice, and thought. Making good decisions about quoting can be easier, though, if you keep in mind one of the main reasons for quoting material: you want to acknowledge an author's distinctive language.

When employed properly and judiciously, quotations can add color and credibility to your writing; they can help make your papers clearer, more entertaining, and more persuasive. If used improperly, quotations can give the impression that you cannot think through a topic for yourself or cannot articulate ideas in your own words. Therefore, knowing how to quote material properly is an extremely important part of writing from readings.

GUIDELINES ON WHEN TO QUOTE MATERIAL

You ought to have a good reason for quoting material in your paper. Do not quote material just to fill up space or to avoid thinking about your topic. Instead, you ought to consider how quoting material will help you support your thesis or explain important ideas to your reader. The next sections list some guidelines to help you decide when to quote a word or passage and suggestions on how to use that material in your paper. As you plan and draft a source-based paper, consider ways to integrate *a few* carefully selected quotations with your own writing to present your ideas as clearly and effectively as possible.

QUOTE PASSAGES WHEN THE AUTHOR HAS WRITTEN SOMETHING IN A DISTINCTIVE OR ESPECIALLY INSIGHTFUL OR INTERESTING WAY

Often an author will express an idea so well it is difficult or impossible for you to express it better by paraphrasing it. The author may have expressed the idea succinctly, employed especially effective adjectives or metaphors, or supplied an especially interesting example. In such cases, quote the word or passage—it may help make your paper more entertaining or persuasive.

QUOTE MATERIAL THAT LENDS SUPPORT TO A POSITION YOU ARE TRYING TO MAKE IN YOUR PAPER

Letting your readers see for themselves that an expert agrees with a position you are advocating can help persuade them to accept your argument or can help them better understand your position. You must be sure, though, that in your effort to find support for your position, you do not misrepresent an author's thoughts or findings. By leaving words out of a quotation or by adding language to it, you should not misrepresent what the author actually had to say. For example, several years ago a student of mine quoted an editorial writer as saying, "President Reagan's proposed budget cuts will . . . double the number of people living in poverty." I checked the original editorial; the actual sentence read, "President Reagan's proposed budget cuts will not double the number of people living in poverty." By leaving out the word *not*, this student clearly misrepresented the author's intended meaning. Such changes to a quotation are unethical.

Also, in an effort to find support for your thesis, do not limit your research to those authors who agree with the position you are advancing. For several reasons, this strategy is a mistake. First, in doing research, you should learn about a topic by studying many different views. Quite often writers change their position as they write and rewrite their papers; sifting through the material they have read frequently leads them to rethink and restate their thesis. Second, you may want to quote authors who present ideas that challenge your thesis: doing so can increase your credibility in the eyes of many readers. Finally, by seeking out alternative perspectives and learning more about the topic, you place yourself in a better position to defend your assertions, improving the likelihood that your readers will value what you have to say on the topic because of your expertise. Therefore, do not neglect opposing viewpoints when searching for material to quote in your paper.

When you use expert testimony to support a position in your paper, it is a good idea to mention the person's credentials in your paper:

> According to Helen Carter, former president of the First National Bank, ". . ."
> Milton Friedman, noted economist and winner of the Nobel Prize, contends that ". . ."

Citing the credentials of the experts you quote may help convince your readers to accept or at least seriously consider what they have to say. Again, you do not need to cite the credentials of every author every time you quote from his or her work. You also do not want to cite so many credentials that the sentence is hard to read. Variety is the key to using quotations well—cite the credentials when you think they are significant, and do so in a way that fits the overall tone of your paper.

QUOTE AUTHORITIES WHO DISAGREE WITH A POSITION YOU ARE ADVOCATING OR WHO OFFER ALTERNATIVE EXPLANATIONS OR CONTRADICTORY DATA

Often it is a good idea to quote authors who offer views or data that call into question the position you are advocating in your paper. Many beginning authors balk at this idea. They believe that introducing opposing views will only weaken the impact of their thesis. However, when you include in your paper a variety of perspectives, your readers are more likely to perceive you to be fair and thorough in your treatment of the subject: these quotations demonstrate that you recognize and understand alternative points of view. Second, such quotations allow you the opportunity to examine critically the other person's position, acknowledging its worth or value when needed and criticizing it when appropriate.

If you decide to quote authors who challenge your thesis, you must somehow address their ideas or findings, usually in one of four ways. You need to explain in your own words:

a. how that author's ideas do not seriously damage your thesis,
b. how that author's ideas or findings may actually support your contentions,

    c. how your thesis may be altered slightly to accommodate the author's ideas, or

    d. how that author's ideas are incorrect or at least questionable.

If you do not somehow address the opposing ideas you quote in your paper, your reader will likely be confused, wondering how that material fits your paper's thesis.

GUIDELINES ON WHEN NOT TO QUOTE MATERIAL

When writing from sources, students often rely too heavily on quoted material: their essays are a string of quotations. These papers more accurately represent the ideas and language of the source texts than they do the ideas and language of the student. To avoid producing a paper like this, consider these guidelines outlining when you should *not* quote material. Use quotations *selectively*; they should never make up the bulk of your paper.

DO NOT QUOTE PASSAGES MERELY TO FILL SPACE

Too often when writing from sources, students try to pad their essays with extensive quotations, and their final papers end up being a patchwork of quoted material. This is especially true when students are writing to meet a length requirement. If a teacher wants a paper eight to ten pages long, some students think the easiest way to reach that length is to keep piling on quotations. However, in college your readers will usually want to know what *you* think about your subject, what conclusions *you* have reached through your research, how *you* understand material. Do not substitute other people's views and voices for your own; use theirs to *support* your own.

DO NOT QUOTE PASSAGES AS A SUBSTITUTE FOR THINKING

In addition to using quotations to fill space, too often students rely on quotations alone to clarify, defend, or substantiate a finding or position. They may introduce an idea in a topic sentence, then string together two or three quotations to substantiate the point they want to make. Instead of presenting their own ideas in their own language, they rely on quoted material to present and defend their case.

    The better course to follow is to integrate selected quotations into your essay carefully: their purpose is to advance your argument or support your conclusions or findings. Do not expect a quotation alone to convince your readers to accept some contention you want to make. As you work through a writing assignment, find language that reflects and communicates the conclusions you have drawn and the assertions you want to make. When appropriate, support or illustrate your position with quoted material. Also remember that when you do quote material, in most cases you will need to comment on it, explaining in your own words the quotation's meaning, relevance, or importance.

Do Not Quote Passages Because You Do Not Understand the Author's Ideas Well Enough to Paraphrase Them

As you read material in college, you will often run into words you do not know, ideas that seem strange, arguments that are hard to follow, research methodologies and discussions of findings that seem to be written in a language of their own. If you have to write papers based on these readings, do not rely on quotations as a way to avoid thought. You need to understand the material you quote. As a general guideline, if you cannot paraphrase the material, do not quote it. That is, if you cannot convey that information in your own words, quoting it is probably a bad idea.

INTEGRATING QUOTATIONS INTO YOUR WRITING

There are several ways to place quoted material in your papers. You should study and practice several of these techniques because varying the way you integrate quotations into your writing can make your papers more interesting.

One of the real difficulties in learning to write from readings in college is the fact that different disciplines follow different rules concerning the proper way to document and punctuate quotations. Two primary style manuals used in your college courses are those published by the Modern Language Association (MLA), primarily used in humanities classes such as English and history, and by the American Psychological Association (APA), primarily used in social science classes such as psychology and sociology. Because each of these manuals offers its own set of rules concerning the proper punctuation and documentation of quotations, when you receive an assignment, always ask your instructor which style manual he or she expects you to follow. (See Chapters 12 and 13 for a complete discussion of the documentation guidelines suggested by each.)

Two Basic Types of Quotations

When you quote material, you will either set it off in a block quotation or integrate it into the body of your essay. Your choice depends on length: longer passages must be block quoted, while shorter quotations should be integrated.

Properly punctuating quotations can be tricky: again, the rules you follow depend on the academic stylebook your teacher wants you to follow. Although the two major style manuals generally agree on how to punctuate integrated quotations, they offer different guidelines for formatting, punctuating, and documenting block quotations. Pay close attention to how the following sample quotations are punctuated. All of the sample quotations will draw on passages from the following essay published in *America*.

Generation Text

The Dark Digital Age: 13 to 17

Mark Bauerlein

Mark Bauerlein *is a professor of English at Emory University and author of* The Dumbest Generation: How the Digital Age Stupefies Young Americans and Jeopardizes Our Future.

Children between the ages of 13 and 17 who have a mobile phone average 1,742 text messages each month, according to a report by the Nielsen Company in September 2008. That comes to nearly 60 per day. They also make 231 voice calls each month, close to eight per day. They play games on the device as well, and browse the Web, take pictures and log hours of social networking.

No wonder so many of them consider the cellphone (for some it is a BlackBerry or an iPhone) an essential part of their lives. Half of all young people between the ages of 8 and 12 own one such device, according to a Harris Interactive poll conducted in July 2008. The rate rises to around four out of five for teenagers; that's a 36 percent increase over the previous three years, which means that these tools have swept into young people's lives with the dispatch and coerciveness of a youth fad (like Pokemon and Harry Potter). The devices are more than just consumer goods. They are signs and instruments of status.

The age-old force of peer pressure bears down hard. Indeed, 45 percent of the teens that sport one agree that "Having a cellphone is the key to my social life"—not just helpful or useful, but "the key." If you don't own a cellphone, if you can't text, game, network and chat, then you are out of the loop. It is like not being picked to play kickball back in the primitive days of neighborhood sandlot gatherings. If a 16-year-old runs up 3,000 text messages in one month (and does not have a flat payment plan), mom and dad take the phone away. It's just a silly, expensive toy, they think.

But the 16-year-old thinks, "You have destroyed my life!" And for them, this seems true. Digital tools are the primary means of social contact. When they lose them, kids feel excluded and unpopular, and nothing hits a 16-year-old harder than the disregard of other 16-year-olds. They do not care what 40-year-olds think, and they do not worry about what happened at Thermopylae or what Pope John Paul II said about the "splendor of truth." They care about what other students in biology class think, what happened last week at the party and what so-and-so said about them.

It is an impulse long preceding the advent of the microchip, but digital devices have empowered that impulse as never before. Think about the life stage of adolescence. Teenagers stand at a precarious threshold, no longer children and not yet adults, eager to be independent but lacking the equipment and composure. They have begun to leave the home and shed the influence of parents, but they don't know where they are headed, and most of them find meager materials beyond the home out of which to build their characters. So they look to one another, emulating dress and speech, forming groups of insiders and outsiders, finding comfort in boyfriends and girlfriends, and deflecting more or less tenuously the ever-present risk of embarrassment.

Everyone passes through this phase, but this generation's experience marks a crucial change in the process. In the past, social life proceeded intermittently, all day at school and for a few hours after school. Kids hung out for an afternoon over the weekend and enjoyed a movie or party on Friday or Saturday night. Other than that, social life pretty much ended. They went home for dinner and entered a private space with only a "landline" as a means of contact (which appears to young people today a restricted connection—show them a rotary phone and watch them scowl). Teenage social life and peer-to-peer contact had a limit.

Teenagers did not like it. I certainly didn't want to listen to my parents when I turned 16. But the limit was healthy and effectual. Adolescents needed then and need now a reprieve from the tribal customs and peer fixations of middle school and high school. Wounds from lunchroom gossip and bullying, as well as the blandishments of popularity and various niche-crowd memberships, disable the maturing process. These form a horizon of adolescent triumphs and set the knowledge of history, civics, religion, fine art and foreign affairs beyond the pale of useful and relevant acquisitions. If a sophomore sat down on a bus with the gang and said, "Hey, did you see the editorial on school funding in *The Times* this morning?" the rest would scrunch up their faces as if an alien being sat among them.

Youthful mores screen out such things, which is all the more reason for parents to offer an alternative. A home and leisure life separate from teen stuff exposes youths to heroes and villains that surpass the idols of the senior class, to places beyond the food court and Apple Store, to times well before the glorious day they got their driver's license. It acquaints them with adult duties, distant facts and values and truths they will not fully comprehend until much later. They don't like them and rarely find them meaningful, but in pre-digital times teens had nowhere else to go after they entered the front door. They had to sit at the dining table and listen to parents talk about grocery shopping, vacation plans, Nixon, gas prices and the news.

No longer. In 1980, when an angry parent commanded, "Go to your room—you're grounded!" the next few hours meant isolation for the teen. Today, the bedroom is not a private space. It's a social hub. For many kids, the bedroom at midnight provides a rich social life that makes daytime face-to-face conversations seem tame and slow. Amid the pillows with laptop or BlackBerry, they chat with buddies in 11th grade and in another state. Photos fly back and forth while classmates sleep, revelations spill forth in tweets ("OMG, Billy just called Betty his ———"), and Facebook pages gain flashier graphics.

In this dynamic 24/7 network, teen activity accrues more and more significance. The events of the day carry greater weight as they are recorded and circulated. The temptation for teens to be self-absorbed and self-project, to consider the details of their lives eminently memorable and share-able, grows and grows. As they give in online, teenagers' peer consciousness expands while their historical understanding, civic awareness and taste go dormant before they have even had much chance to develop. This is the hallmark of what I have called the Dumbest Generation. These kids have just as much intelligence and ambition as any previous cohort, but they exercise them too much on one another. They are building youth culture into a ubiquitous universe, and as ever, youth culture is a drag on maturity. This time it has a whole new arsenal.

THE BLOCK QUOTATION

The APA and MLA style manuals both agree that longer quotations must be set off from the rest of the text, but they differ in how they define "longer":

- APA states that quotations of 40 words or more must be block quoted.
- MLA says to block quote passages that would be more than four typed lines in your paper.

Regardless of the style manual you follow, you should introduce a block quotation with a colon. You do not add quotation marks at the beginning or end of the passage, and all the punctuation in the source text stays the same in the block quotation.

APA Guidelines

According to the APA style manual, you should start a block quotation on a new line in your paper, setting the left margin of the quotation one-half inch in from the original left margin. Subsequent lines of the quotation align on that indent. (If you are quoting additional paragraphs in the source text, indent the first line of each an additional half inch.) The right margin stays the same, and the whole passage is double-spaced.

Example 1

In "Generation Text," Mark Bauerlein (2009) describes how the nature of "being grounded" has changed due to advances in technology:

> In 1980, when an angry parent commanded, "Go to your room—you're grounded!" the next few hours meant isolation for the teen. Today, the bedroom is not a private space. It's a social hub. For many kids, the bedroom at midnight provides a rich social life that makes daytime face-to-face conversations seem tame and slow. Amid the pillows with laptop or BlackBerry, they chat with buddies in 11th grade and in another state. Photos fly back and forth while classmates sleep, revelations spill forth in tweets ("OMG, Billy just called Betty his ——"), and Facebook pages gain flashier graphics. (p. 36)

Kids sent to their bedroom today do not face isolation. Thanks to modern technology, they can stay in constant contact with their friends.

Analysis

Notice that the period at the end of the quotation precedes the parenthetical citation. (If the quotation runs longer than one page in the source text, use "pp." to introduce the inclusive page numbers.) There are no quotation marks added at the beginning or end of the block quote. The words "Go to your room—you're grounded!" are quoted because they have quotation marks around them in the source text. If any words are italicized in the source text, they remain italicized in your block quote. Note also that the left-hand margin of the block quotation is indented a half inch.

MLA Guidelines

MLA says to begin a block quotation on a new line, indent the left margin one inch (and a quarter inch more for new paragraphs within the block quote), leave the right margin unchanged, and double-space the block quotation.

Example 2

In "Generation Text," Mark Bauerlein describes how the nature of "being grounded" has changed due to advances in technology:

> In 1980, when an angry parent commanded, "Go to your room—you're grounded!" the next few hours meant isolation for the teen. Today, the bedroom is not a private space. It's a social hub. For many kids, the bedroom at midnight provides a rich social life that makes daytime face-to-face conversations seem tame and slow. Amid the pillows with laptop or BlackBerry, they chat with buddies in 11th grade and in another state. Photos fly back and forth while classmates sleep, revelations spill forth in tweets ("OMG, Billy just called Betty his ——"), and Facebook pages gain flashier graphics. (36)

Kids sent to their bedroom today do not face isolation. Thanks to modern technology, they can stay in constant contacts with their friends.

Analysis

Note how the parenthetical documentation follows the period at the end of the quotation. No quotation marks are added to the block quote. The words quoted from the original passage retain their punctuation. There is a new left margin, but the right margin remains unchanged.

Example 3

Bauerlein introduces "Generation Text" by citing some interesting, and perhaps startling, statistics concerning children's use of technology:

> Children between the ages of 13 and 17 who have a mobile phone average 1,742 text messages each month, according to a report by the Nielsen Company in September 2008. That comes to nearly 60 per day. They also make 231 voice calls each month, close to eight per day. They play games on the device as well, and browse the Web, take pictures and log hours of social networking.
>
> No wonder so many of them consider the cellphone (for some it is a Black-Berry or an iPhone) an essential part of their lives. Half of all young people between the ages of 8 and 12 own one such device, according to a Harris Interactive poll conducted in July 2008. The rate rises to around four out of five for teenagers; that's a 36 percent increase over the previous three years, which means that these tools have swept into young people's lives with the dispatch and coerciveness of a youth fad (like Pokemon and Harry Potter). (34)

According to Bauerlein, this technology has spread quickly in the culture like so many other fads.

Analysis

Since this block quotation runs longer than one paragraph, note how the first line of the second paragraph is indented an additional quarter inch.

THE INTEGRATED QUOTATION

Short quotations should be integrated in the body of your essay rather than set off in a block quotation. As you will see, you have several ways to integrate quoted material into your paper. Try to use several of these techniques when writing an essay—such variety can help make your paper more interesting to read.

The APA and MLA style manuals generally agree on where to place quotation marks, how to use single and double quotation marks, and how to otherwise punctuate integrated quotations. Remember that all quotations must be documented. Again, see Chapter 12 for a detailed discussion on how to document quotations. In the following samples, I alternate between APA and MLA documentation conventions.

Introduce a Quotation with a Verb

Probably the most common way of introducing a quotation is to give the author's name, perhaps his or her credentials, maybe even the title of the work, followed by an appropriate verb—*says, notes, comments, contends, asserts,* and so on. Place a comma after the verb of saying.

Example 4 (MLA Documentation)

> Bauerlein, believing that owning a cell phone is a sign of social status and inclusion, writes, "Indeed, 45 percent of the teens that sport one agree that 'Having a cellphone is the key to my social life'—not just helpful or useful, but 'the key'" (34).

When you integrate material from a source text that already contains quotation marks, the regular quotation marks in the original (" ") are changed to single quotation marks (' ') in your paper.

Note the punctuation at the end of the sentence; the final period follows the parenthetical citation. If the last sentence of the quotation ends with an exclamation point or a question mark, include it before the closing quotation mark and place a period after the parenthetical citation. This punctuation guideline holds true for the APA and MLA style manuals.

Example 5 (APA Documentation)

> Bauerlein (2009) states that this generation of students, unlike others, expect to use only modern technology to communicate. In the past, he writes, children ". . . went home for dinner and entered a private space with only a 'landline' as a means of contact (which appears to young people today a restricted connection—show them a rotary phone and watch them scowl) (p. 35).

Again, note how a comma follows the verb (in this case, "writes"), how the material quoted in the source text is placed in single quotation marks, how the ellipsis indicates part of the passage was left out of the quote, and how the final period follows the documentation.

Example 6 (MLA Documentation)

> Bauerlein claims, "Children between the ages of 13 and 17 who have a mobile phone average 1,742 text messages each month . . ." (34).

Introduce a Quotation without a Verb

A more formal way of integrating a quotation into your paper is to introduce it with a colon. Commonly, quotations used as illustrations or elaborations of a point you have just made are introduced this way. Make sure that the colon comes at the end of a complete sentence; leave one space between the colon and the opening quotation mark.

Example 7 (APA Documentation)

> Toward the end of his essay, Bauerlein (2009) assumes a darker tone: "This is the hallmark of what I have called the Dumbest Generation. These kids have just as much intelligence and ambition as any previous cohort, but they exercise them too much on one another" (p. 36).

Example 8 (MLA Documentation)

> In generations past, teens needed a place to escape their peers: "Adolescents needed then and need now a reprieve from the tribal customs and peer fixations of middle school and high school" (Bauerlein 35).

Note that in this last example, because I did not use Baurerlein's name in the passage, I had to include it in the citation.

Run Your Sentence and the Quotation Together

This particular technique can be hard to master. Instead of separating your words from the quoted passage with a comma or colon, you run the two together seamlessly, relying on the quotation marks to let your reader know when you begin using someone else's language. Integrating quotations in this way, while sophisticated stylistically, can also lead you to misquote material if you are not careful. As students first learn to run their sentence and the quotation together, they tend to alter the quotation to fit the sentence they are writing rather than to alter their sentence so it fits the quotation. As you practice this method of quoting material, try to craft your sentence so it runs smoothly into the quotation. If you have to change the quoted passage in any substantive way, you must indicate the changes (see the section on "Altering Quoted Material and Avoiding Misquotations," which follows).

When you employ this technique properly and read your essay aloud, a listener would not be able to tell where the quotation started and ended. Note that you do not need to place a comma before the quoted material or insert an ellipsis if you are picking up the quotation in midsentence.

Example 9 (APA Documentation)

> Baurerlein (2009) believes that "the age-old force of peer pressure bears down hard" (p. 34).

In this example, note that the capital *T* in *The* can be changed to lowercase without the addition of brackets. Also, when using this approach, you do not need to include an ellipsis if you begin a quotation in midsentence.

Example 10 (MLA Documentation)

> Changes in education and technology have "set the knowledge of history, civics, religion, fine art and foreign affairs beyond the pale of useful and relevant acquisitions" (Baurerlein 35).

Pick Out Only Certain Words to Quote in Your Sentence

You do not always have to quote entire passages or sentences in your paper. Often you want to quote only a few key words or phrases. Be sure, though, to include proper documentation even if you quote only one word.

Example 11 (MLA Documentation)

> Bauerlein believes teens "stand at a precarious threshold" and that they are "eager to be independent" (35).

This particular example needs only one parenthetical citation because all the quoted material comes from the same page in the source text. If it came from different pages in the source text, parenthetical citations would follow each quoted word or phrase.

Example 12 (APA Documentation)

> According to Bauerlein (2009), because "peer pressure bears down hard" (p. 34), the children's use of social technologies "accrues more and more significance" (p. 36).

ALTERING QUOTED MATERIAL AND AVOIDING MISQUOTATIONS

When you place quotation marks around material in your essay and document that passage, you are telling your readers that if they turn to that page of that source text they will find that passage as it appears in your paper: the words and punctuation have not been changed. If that is not the case—if you have made any substantive changes to material you are quoting—then you need to acknowledge those alterations. Especially important is learning how to indicate that you left words out of a quotation, added words to a quotation, or changed the emphasis given words in a quotation.

Leaving Words Out of a Quotation

Use an ellipsis (. . .) to indicate that you left material out of a quotation. Add a fourth dot to act as a period if you omit the end of a sentence or leave out an entire sentence when block quoting. When you introduce a quotation with a colon, include an ellipsis if you pick up a quotation in the middle of a sentence in the source text.

Example 13 (MLA Documentation)

> Bauerlein observes, "No wonder so many of them consider the cellphone . . . an essential part of their lives" (34).

Example 14 (APA Documentation)

> Escaping the detrimental effects of social technologies, students will better learn adult behaviors: ". . . adult duties, distant facts and values and truths they will not fully comprehend until much later" (Bauerlein, 2009, p. 35–36).

Adding Words to a Quotation

When you add words to a quotation, use square brackets, not parentheses, around the words. Add material to quotations sparingly. Do it only when absolutely necessary to avoid confusing your readers.

Example 15 (MLA Documentation)

> Home life is devalued, "So they [teenagers] look to one another, emulating dress and speech . . ." (Bauerlein 35).

Noting Emphasis Added to a Quotation

If you want to emphasize a word or passage in a quotation, put it in italics. The stylebooks offer different guidelines on how to indicate the addition of emphasis to a quotation:

- APA style: immediately after the emphasized words, place in square brackets the words "emphasis added."
- MLA style: after the quotation itself, place in parentheses the words "emphasis added," after the page number (if any). Or place "emphasis added" in square brackets immediately after the emphasized words.

If you do not indicate otherwise, readers will assume any words italicized in a quotation appear in italics in the source text.

Example 16 (APA Documentation)

> Bauerlein (2009) notes that "everyone passes through this phase, but this generation's experience marks a *crucial change* [emphasis added] in the process" (p. 35)

Example 17 (MLA Documentation)

> English Professor Mark Bauerlein observes that "everyone passes through this phase, but this generation's experience marks a *crucial change* in the process" (35, emphasis added).

Summary Chart

GUIDELINES ON QUOTATIONS

1. **When to Quote Material**

   Quote passages when the author has said something in a distinctive or especially insightful or interesting way.

   Quote material that supports the assertions you make in your paper.

   Quote authorities who disagree with a position you are advocating or who offer alternative explanations or contradictory data.

2. **When Not to Quote Material**

   Do not quote passages merely to fill in space.

   Do not quote passages as a substitute for thinking.

   Do not quote passages because you do not understand the author's ideas well enough to paraphrase them.

Summary Chart

INTEGRATING QUOTATIONS INTO YOUR WRITING

1. **Block Quotations**

   Employ this method with longer quotations.

   Follow guidelines established by the style manual your instructor requires.

2. **Integrated Quotations**

   Introduce the quotation with an appropriate verb.
   - *precede with a comma*
   - *employ a verb of saying that fits the overall tone of your essay, such as:*

says	holds
states	maintains
asserts	contends
claims	explains

   Introduce the quotation without a verb.
   - *a more formal way of introducing the quotation*
   - *precede with a colon*

   Run your sentence and the quotation together.
   - *edit your sentence so it fits the tone and syntax of the quoted passage*

   Pick out only certain words to quote.
   - *quote interesting uses of language such as coined or controversial terms*
   - *quote terms to draw attention to them*

QUOTATION REVISION CHECKLIST

	Yes	No
1. Did you check your quoted passages against the original to make sure the wording is accurate?	_____	_____
2. Is the capitalization of words in the quotation proper and accurate?	_____	_____
3. Is the punctuation in the quotation proper and accurate?	_____	_____
4. Do you need to add italics, underline certain words, or use single quotation marks in the quotation?	_____	_____
5. Did you check the punctuation you employed to introduce the quotation?	_____	_____
6. Did you check the format of your block quotations?	_____	_____
7. If you added words to or deleted words from the source passage, did you confirm that you have not misrepresented the author?	_____	_____
8. Is the format of your documentation at the end of the quotation in the correct style?	_____	_____
9. Did you list the right page number or numbers in your documentation?	_____	_____

Chapter 3

PARAPHRASE

DEFINITION AND PURPOSE

When you paraphrase a passage, you express an author's arguments, findings, or ideas in your own words. Much of the writing you do in college will require you to paraphrase material. Some of these assignments will simply ask you to gather and convey information. To write this type of paper, you study the work of various authors, then paraphrase what they have written, trying to convey to your readers as clearly and accurately as possible what each has to say about the topic.

In other assignments you will rely on paraphrased material to help you develop and defend an argument. Paraphrasing the work of experts who agree with your position in a paper can be quite persuasive. Even paraphrasing the work of authors who *disagree* with a position you have assumed in your essay can be helpful: after you objectively present that opposing view, you can examine its strengths and weaknesses and adjust your position to accommodate ideas you can neither discredit nor dismiss. However, when paraphrasing information as a part of an argument you are advancing, you must fairly represent an author's views. It is always tempting to misrepresent what people say, especially when you disagree with them, either by oversimplifying their position or by employing misleading language. Try to resist these temptations; always try to be fair to an author when you paraphrase his or her work.

Finally, paraphrasing allows you to convey your unique understanding of a reading. Paraphrases of the same material written by different students are not likely to be exactly the same because writing a paraphrase involves a series of choices: each writer decides what information to include, what language to use, and what organization to employ. Though you should attempt to be objective in your paraphrase of a reading, the details you choose to include and the language you choose to substitute for the author's will be communicating your unique view of the passage.

QUALITIES OF A GOOD PARAPHRASE

Generally, a good paraphrase of a passage exhibits four characteristics. It is thorough, accurate, fair, and objective:

- *Thorough*—it will include all of the author's primary ideas or findings.
- *Accurate*—it will reflect what the author actually wrote.
- *Fair*—your choice of language will be as evenhanded as possible.
- *Objective*—you will avoid voicing your own opinion on the topic or on the quality of the source text.

THOROUGH

A paraphrase of a passage differs from a summary of a passage in its comprehensiveness. In a summary, you try to reduce the source material to its most essential message; in a paraphrase, you try to capture the entire content of the passage. Because you change words and sentence structure when paraphrasing material, your paraphrase of a passage may actually be longer than the original text. Summaries, however, will always be shorter than the original passage. Even though your goal is to be thorough, writing a paraphrase involves making some choices concerning content: you may leave out what you believe to be insignificant details, examples, or explanations found in the source text. Guiding these decisions, though, should be your desire to produce as complete a paraphrase as possible.

ACCURATE

Because you are not quoting authors when you paraphrase their work—because you are substituting your words for theirs—you must take care to be accurate in what you write. Your paraphrase should offer your reader a precise restatement of what the author wrote: though the language is different, your paraphrase should convey the same information or arguments found in the source text. However, accuracy can be hard to achieve. Even slight changes in language can drastically alter the meaning of a passage. Therefore, when writing and revising a paraphrase, check your work against your understanding of the source text. Have you at all misrepresented the *content* of the other writer's piece? Would the author read your paraphrase and agree that you have, indeed, captured what he or she wrote?

FAIR

Being fair in your paraphrase is related to being accurate. Writing a paraphrase involves putting into your own words someone else's ideas, arguments, or findings. When doing so, first you want to be fair to the author whose work you are paraphrasing. In exchanging your words for his or hers, you want to be as evenhanded as possible. Avoid language, for example, that implies a judgment on your part or makes an author's work appear more sophisticated or more simplistic than it actually is. Second, you want to be fair to your readers. When people read your paraphrase of an author's work, they expect you to give them a fair and accurate understanding of that material. They do not expect you to censure or praise the source text—that's the function of a critique, not a paraphrase.

For a number of reasons, paraphrases are often inaccurate or unfair. First, students often *misread source texts* and make flatly incorrect assertions about the author's work. This type of problem can be avoided through a careful, critical reading of the source text before you try to paraphrase it and by discussing the reading with others. Second, students often *paraphrase material out of context*. Their paraphrase of a passage is misleading because in the larger context of the work the passage has an entirely different meaning from the one reflected in the student's essay. This type of error frequently occurs if the author of the source text is summarizing opposing views in his work. Students who paraphrase this material out of context will frequently misrepresent the author's views, making it appear the author actually agrees with his critics. When you paraphrase someone else's ideas, be sensitive to the relationship between the passage you are working with and the meaning of source text as a whole. Finally, students often produce unfair paraphrases of a source text by *relying on emotionally charged or heavily connotative language*. If an article talks about "presidential aides" and you substitute "presidential cronies," "presidential lackeys," or "presidential co-conspirators," you probably are not being entirely fair in your paraphrase.

OBJECTIVE

A good paraphrase does not take sides. Students often fail to be objective in one of three ways. First, as discussed above, they may employ language that clearly editorializes. In writing a paraphrase, try to use language that fairly and accurately captures the meaning and intent of the source text, not language that reflects your views of the topic or the quality of the source text itself. Second, in writing a paraphrase, sometimes students want to comment directly on the topic the author is addressing. When paraphrasing an author's views on abortion rights, for instance, they may want to articulate their stand on the issue. That material does not belong in a paraphrase, where your goal is to communicate someone else's views. Finally, students sometimes want to include in their paraphrase comments on the quality of the author's work—that they found the argument convincing or faulty, that the author's style was cumbersome or flowing, that the article was "good" or "bad." These types of comments are appropriate for a critique, not for a paraphrase. Your goal in a paraphrase is to be as objective in your content and language as possible.

Before you try to paraphrase someone else's ideas, though, be sure you understand what he or she has written. Again, one of the most common causes of inadequate paraphrasing is failing to grasp the meaning of the source text. Therefore, whether you are paraphrasing a sentence, paragraph, chapter, or essay, you need to understand fully what the author has written before you attempt to put that person's ideas into your own words. Your paraphrase of that person's ideas or findings must be complete, accurate, fair, and objective. It cannot meet these standards if you are confused or at all uncertain about what the author has written.

However, paraphrasing a passage can also be an effective way of determining its meaning. If you are not sure what a passage means, try paraphrasing it. Putting someone else's ideas into your own words is often the best way for you to understand what the author has written. Always reread your paraphrase and the source text to be sure you have been thorough and fair, especially if the paraphrased material is going to be a part of a paper you are turning in.

HOW TO PARAPHRASE MATERIAL

Generally, you paraphrase material by changing words, changing sentence structures, or changing the order of ideas in a passage. More often than not, you will make all three types of changes each time you paraphrase someone's ideas.

CHANGING WORDS

One way to paraphrase a passage is to substitute your words for the author's. However, finding appropriate synonyms for words in the source text can often be challenging. Many students are tempted to turn immediately to a thesaurus for a list of possible replacement words. However, it is usually better to try to come up with appropriate synonyms on your own. Remember, writing a paraphrase involves putting someone else's ideas into *your* own words. If you can come up with replacement words that are fair, accurate, and appropriate for the tone of your paper, use them. If you cannot come up with a new word on your own, then turn to a thesaurus. However, after you look up a possible substitute word in the thesaurus, check its definition in a dictionary to see if the word accurately reflects the meaning you want to convey. The words you find in a thesaurus are not always interchangeable; there are often subtle differences in meaning you can determine by checking the definition of each term in a good dictionary.

Whether you rely on your own resources or on a thesaurus, using synonyms in a paraphrase raises similar concerns:

a. Does the new word convey the author's original idea accurately and objectively?
b. Does the new word fit the overall tone of the rest of your essay? Is it too formal or informal? Too technical or too general?

Often, it may be impossible to find an adequate substitute for a word or phrase in a passage: perhaps the author coined a phrase or used an unusual or shocking term. In such cases, it is appropriate for you to quote the language found in the source text (see Chapter 2 for guidelines on quoting material). When paraphrasing material, though, try to keep the number of quotations to a minimum. Also, remember that *all* paraphrased passages you include in your papers must be documented—even though you change the language of the source text when you paraphrase, you need to acknowledge through your documentation the source of the *ideas* you are discussing.

Below are examples of passages paraphrased primarily through word substitution. You will find the original passage, a rough-draft paraphrase, and a final paraphrase. The original passages in all of the following examples are drawn from the readings included in Chapters 1 and 2.

Example 1

A. Original

"Teenagers stand at a precarious threshold, no longer children and not yet adults, eager to be independent but lacking the equipment and composure."

B. Rough-Draft Paraphrase

Teenagers stand at a dangerous moment in their lives, between childhood and adulthood, wanting to be independent but not possessing the ability and maturity to do so.

C. Final Paraphrase (APA Documentation)

Teens face a dangerous time in their lives, between childhood and adulthood, wanting desperately to live on their own but not possessing the skills and maturity they need to enter the next phase of their lives (Bauerlein).

Discussion: In my rough draft, I changed a few words: "precarious threshold" became "dangerous moment in their lives," "no longer children and not yet adults" became "between childhood and adulthood," and "lacking the equipment and composure" became "not possessing the ability and maturity to do so." In places, my first attempt was still too close to the wording in the original passage, and I wasn't sure I captured the connotative meaning of several words. I liked "between childhood and adulthood," but I retained the word "independent" (which I thought I needed to change), "ability" did not seem like the right word to replace "equipment," "moment" wasn't the right word to replace "threshold," and I did not think the end of my paraphrase captured what the author meant in the context of the original. So in my next draft, I changed "moment in their lives" to "time in their lives," changed "ability" to "skills" (which I think comes closer to the author's word—"equipment"), and added the last part of the sentence to clarify what I think the author meant in the original. The basic sentence structure has remained the same; I've only tried to change some of the words.

Example 2

A. *Original*

"For many kids, the bedroom at midnight provides a rich social life that makes daytime face-to-face conversations seem tame and slow."

B. *Rough-Draft Paraphrase*

Many kids, even in their bedrooms in the middle of the night, have a richer social life electronically than they do talking one-on-one to their friends during the day.

C. *Final Paraphrase (MLA Documentation)*

Thanks to technology, many kids have a more exciting life electronically with friends overnight in their bedrooms than they have talking with them one-on-one during the day (Baurerlein 36).

Discussion: This was a difficult text to paraphrase out of context. In the original work, the author is clearly discussing the impact of technology on teenagers' social lives, but that word, "technology," does not appear in the passage. In my rough draft, I added the word "electronically" after "social life" to capture this meaning. The word "midnight" became "middle of the night," and "daytime face-to-face conversations" became "talking one-on-one to their friends during the day." I switched "rich social life" for "richer social life," which clearly needed to be changed or quoted. In my final draft, I opened the sentence with "Thanks to technology" to place the passage in context, changed "richer social life" to "more exciting life electronically." Again, I'm still not entirely happy with this paraphrase because I've only substituted words—it would be a better paraphrase if I also employed the techniques described below.

CHANGING SENTENCE STRUCTURE

Besides changing words, when composing a good paraphrase of material, you may also need to alter the sentence structure employed in the source text. Often such changes involve rearranging the order of ideas in a sentence or altering the order of dependent and independent clauses.

Example 3

A. Original

"Although communism and state socialism have failed to protect the environment, eco-extremists are basically anti-business."

B. Rough-Draft Paraphrase

"Eco-extremists" oppose business interests even though communism and state socialism have failed to protect the environment.

C. Final Paraphrase (MLA Documentation)

"Eco-extremists" oppose business even though communist and socialist governments have permitted environmental degradation (Moore 16).

Discussion: In my rough draft, I first changed the order of the ideas in the sentence. I could not think of an appropriate substitution for "eco-extremist" so I quoted it and changed "anti-business" to "oppose business." In my final draft, I had to find a better way of addressing the second half of my paraphrase. I started by changing "communism and state socialism" to "communist and socialist governments" and reworded the idea about failing to protect the environment to "have permitted environmental degradation." Looking at it now, I think "degradation" may not be the best word—some additional changes might be needed.

COMBINING SENTENCES

When you paraphrase longer passages, you will often have to "combine" sentences in the source text to paraphrase the material adequately. After you read the entire passage, you may feel that you can condense the information into fewer sentences while still being thorough and fair in your paraphrase. By changing words, altering sentence structures, and combining in one of your sentences information found in two or more source sentences, you can often achieve a smooth, effective paraphrase of material.

Example 4

A. Original

"In addition to choosing a dubious tactic, the environmental movement also changed its philosophy along the way. It once prided itself on subscribing to a philosophy that was 'transpolitical, transideological, and transnational' in character. Non-violent direct action and peaceful disobedience were the hallmarks of the movement. Truth mattered and science was respected for the knowledge it brought to the debate."

B. *Rough-Draft Paraphrase*

In recent years the environmental movement has adopted a new philosophy. It once believed its philosophy cut across political, ideological, and national lines. While its adherents believed in direct action and peaceful disobedience, truth also mattered, as did science, which brought knowledge to the debate.

C. *Final Paraphrase (APA Documentation)*

According to Patrick Moore (1995), the environmental movement has changed its guiding philosophy. They used to believe their ideas cut across political, ideological, and national lines. They also believed in peaceful protests, respected the truth, and valued science for the information it brought them.

Discussion: In my rough draft, I condensed the four sentences found in the source text into three sentences in my paraphrase. I was especially interested in combining the last two sentences. At the same time, I was trying to change some of the words. For example, I altered "transpolitical, transideological, and transnational" but let stand much of the language in those last two sentences. To begin my final draft, I added the author's name and dropped "in recent years," which I had added in the rough draft. In the next two sentences I tried to echo the term "philosophy" with the word "believed" and achieve parallel structure by using "They" twice. I continued to change some of the terms, substituting "peaceful" for "non-violent" and again tried to achieve some sense of parallel structure in my last sentence (which combines two sentences in the source text).

"UNPACKING" SENTENCES

Sometimes a sentence in a reading may be so densely written, so full of ideas, that in your paraphrase you may need two or three sentences to convey the same information. When "unpacking" a sentence like this, your goal remains to convey the author's ideas fairly and thoroughly in your own language. Be sure first, though, that you fully understand the source passage—densely written material is often hard to read.

Example 5

A. *Original*

"So they look to one another, emulating dress and speech, forming groups of insiders and outsiders, finding comfort in boyfriends and girlfriends, and deflecting more or less tenuously the ever-present risk of embarrassment."

B. *Rough-Draft Paraphrase*

Because many teenagers are still trying to define themselves, they look to each other for support. They end up dressing alike. They define who their friends are. They look to boyfriends or girlfriends. All the time, though, they are trying not to embarrass themselves.

C. *Final Paraphrase (MLA Documentation)*

Many teenagers look beyond their home and parents to define themselves. Instead, they look to each other for support. Ironically, in an effort to define their individuality, they end up dressing like their peers, forming cliques, and devoting themselves to girlfriends or boyfriends. All the time, though, they try, more or less successfully, to keep from embarrassing themselves (Bauerlein 35).

Discussion: This was a difficult passage to paraphrase. First, the original sentence makes little sense out of context, so in my rough draft, I paraphrased the sentence that leads up to this one in the source text: "Because many teenagers are still trying to define themselves." I then broke up the original sentence into five sentences, each covering one of the main ideas in the source text. This passage, though, was choppy and repetitive; I needed to combine them for better coherence. The final version has four sentences, and in the third sentence I added "ironically" to capture the tone and intent of the original sentence as I interpreted it. Even at this stage, though, I think the first two sentences could be combined to make the paraphrase even more concise— perhaps going back to the syntax I used in the rough draft.

COMBINING STRATEGIES: PARAPHRASING LONGER PASSAGES IN SOURCE TEXTS

There may be times when you have to paraphrase passages from a source text that are several sentences or even several paragraphs long. When this is the case, you will likely need to employ all of the strategies discussed in this chapter.

Example 6

A. *Original*

At the center of binge drinking on many campuses are fraternities and sororities. While they attract only a small percentage of students nationally, they continue to play a prominent role in campus life at many institutions. Our data shows that in fraternity houses, four of five residents binge, and more than half are frequent binge drinkers. And, fraternity parties are attended by many more students than just members. They attract even some high-school seniors—future college students who are introduced to binge drinking as a social norm. Not surprisingly, most of the alcohol-related deaths of college students recently reported in the media involved fraternity parties.

While some colleges have begun to address the drinking culture created by fraternities, many administrators are still hesitant to move strongly against fraternities, for fear of angering alumni donors who fondly remember their own college years of partying. But administrators have a responsibility to protect all of their students against alcohol-related disruptions and injuries, and should not wait for tragedy to strike before they revoke official recognition of fraternities that consistently cause problems. Colleges also can require all first-year students who live on campus to reside in dormitories, and not in fraternity or sorority houses. Of course, then those colleges must work to create interesting alcohol-free activities centered in the residence halls, to show students that out-of-control drinking need not be the focus of social life.

B. *Rough-Draft Paraphrase*

Even though only a small number of students join fraternities and sororities in college, they are responsible for much of the binge drinking on U.S. campuses. In fact, one study showed that four or five fraternity and sorority members binge drink, more than half, frequently. In addition, high-school students sometimes attend Greek parties, introducing them to binge drinking even before they enroll in college. Recently, several students have even died after becoming drunk at fraternity parties.

Although they know fraternities are often the site of binge drinking, college administrators are often reluctant to crack down on them because they are afraid of angering alumni donors who themselves were Greeks. However, in doing so, administrators fail to uphold their responsibility to protect all students. One way to attack the problem would be to require all freshmen to live in dorms, but schools would then also have to provide alcohol-free recreational opportunities to demonstrate that students do not have to get drunk to have fun.

C. *Final Paraphrase (MLA Documentation)*

In the United States, while only a small number of students join fraternities and sororities in college, they are responsible for much of the binge drinking. One study showed that four out of five fraternity and sorority members binge drink (over fifty percent, frequently) and often introduce binge drinking to high-school students who attend their parties. Although administrators know that fraternities are often the site of binge drinking (and that some students have died after getting drunk at fraternity parties), they are reluctant to crack down on them—many potential alumni donors were Greeks and may object to such action. To address the problem, administrators could prohibit freshmen from living in Greek housing, but they would also have to provide alcohol-free recreational opportunities to demonstrate that students do not have to get drunk to have fun (Wechsler 21).

Discussion: As I moved through the rough draft into the final paraphrase, I tried to condense and simplify the sentences in the source text while remaining comprehensive. I ended up with one paragraph instead of two, although the order of the ideas in my paraphrase still follows the order of ideas presented in the original. I'm still not sure that I like substituting "Greek" for "fraternities and sororities" in the paraphrase of the expression "crack down on them" (it may be too informal). To condense the material, I used parentheses twice to enclose material I thought was of secondary importance. Also note that I need to provide documentation only once, at the end of the paraphrased passage.

BLENDING YOUR WRITING WITH PARAPHRASED MATERIAL

Often in academic writing you will be blending your writing with material you're paraphrasing from source texts. Through documentation and attribution, you will guide your readers through the passage, clarifying which prose is yours and which is paraphrased. I have numbered the sentences in Example 7 below to make it easier to discuss the passage.

Example 7 (Using APA Documentation)

> [1]Clearly, binge drinking is a problem on many college campuses, but who is to blame? [2]Author Henry Wechsler (1998) lays part of the responsibility at the feet of fraternities and sororities. [3]According to Wechsler, although only a small number of college students actually "go Greek," fraternity and sorority members account for a disproportionate number of binge drinkers. [4]Fraternities, in particular, seem to promote binge drinking, since four out of five students living in a fraternity house report that they binge drink. [5]If college administrators know that fraternities and sororities are a major site of binge drinking on their campuses, why don't they act to stop that behavior? [6]Wechsler believes it comes down to money. [7]They are afraid to offend alumni donors who were themselves Greeks by cracking down on fraternities and sororities. [8]If these alumni feel that the administration is unfairly targeting Greeks, they will be less likely to donate money to the school.

Discussion: In this example, sentences 3, 4, and 7 are paraphrased from the source text and are therefore documented. Sentences 1, 2, 5, 6, and 8 are ones I wrote and therefore do not need to be documented. Note how citing the source text at the end of sentence 4 provides sufficient documentation for sentences 3 and 4.

DOCUMENTATION

Remember that any material you paraphrase from a source must be properly documented. Failing to document paraphrased material is a form of plagiarism. While the various forms of documentation you will encounter in college are discussed in Chapter 12, remember that every discipline expects writers to document all paraphrased material properly.

Summary Chart

HOW TO PARAPHRASE MATERIAL

1. **Read, reread, and annotate the material.**
   - *Use a dictionary to find the meaning of any words you do not know.*
   - *Form your own opinion about the meaning of the passage.*

2. **Change words in the passage.**
   - *Substitute synonyms for key terms in the passage.*
   - *Substitute pronouns for nouns when appropriate.*
   - *Change the verbs.*

3. **Change the sentence structure in the passage.**
   - *Rearrange the order of ideas presented in the source text.*

4. **Combine sentences found in the source text.**
   - *Combine into single sentences ideas presented in two or more sentences in the source text.*

5. **Unpack sentences found in the source text.**
   - *Convey in two or more sentences ideas presented in one sentence in the source text.*

Paraphrase Revision Checklist

	Yes	No
1. Have you provided the full title of the source and identified its author?	_____	_____
2. Have you employed a variety of methods to paraphrase the material?	_____	_____
3. Have you checked to be sure your paraphrase accurately captures the author's ideas?	_____	_____
4. Have you remained as objective as possible in choosing language for your paraphrase?	_____	_____
5. Have you avoided offering your opinions on the topic of the reading or on the writer's style?	_____	_____
6. Have you checked your language to make sure each word you have chosen means what you think it means, has the connotation you want it to have, and fits the general tone of your paraphrase?	_____	_____
7. Have you reviewed your sentence structure for clarity and variety?	_____	_____
8. Have you provided appropriate transitions between the ideas you paraphrase?	_____	_____
9. Have you provided proper and accurate documentation?	_____	_____
10. Have you properly punctuated your documentation?	_____	_____

Chapter 4

SUMMARY

DEFINITION AND PURPOSE

Summarizing a reading involves two separate processes: (1) identifying the important material in the text and (2) restating the material in your own words. Because part of your job when writing a summary is deciding what to include from the reading and what to leave out, summaries are always shorter than the source text. Like paraphrases, summaries are always written in your own words (you can use quotations in a summary, but only sparingly), and they should be as objective as possible (you do not include in a summary your own opinions, beliefs, or judgments, and you try to use neutral language).

The ability to summarize readings is fundamental to academic, source-based writing. You will likely be summarizing information when you prepare a lab report, review a movie, write a research paper, or take an essay test. Instructors will often ask you to summarize articles or book chapters to be sure you can read carefully and critically, identify key ideas and important supporting evidence or arguments, and express that information clearly in your own words.

Sometimes summaries are part of a longer work. In a history research paper, for example, you may summarize the work of several different theorists while presenting an argument of your own. Other times, though, summaries will be "freestanding"—graded as independent formal essays. Your goal in writing them is to convey in your own words only the most important ideas, arguments, or findings in a reading. To write these types of assignments, you need to form a clear understanding of the source text, decide what to include in your summary and what to leave out, and choose language that clearly and objectively conveys the author's ideas.

Other times, though, you will use summaries to support a larger argument you are advancing in an essay. First, you may summarize the arguments or findings of experts who agree with the position you have assumed in your thesis; readers may accept your position if they see that other authorities support it as well. Second, you may summarize the work of experts who call into question your thesis. Doing so will help your work appear informed and balanced, again improving your credibility in the eyes of many academic readers. Be sure, though, that if you do summarize opposing views in your essay you then somehow address them. For example, following your summary, you can critique that information—pointing out its strengths and weaknesses—and explain how the opposing ideas affect the validity of your thesis.

Whether your summary is part of a longer work or stands on its own, it must make sense to someone who has not read the source text. If, for example, you are working as a loan officer in a bank and your boss hands you a financial report to summarize, she wants to be able to understand your summary without having to read the report herself. She wants *you* to read the report carefully and distill from it the information she needs to know.

TYPES OF SUMMARIES

In college you will probably write two different types of summaries: informative and explanatory. An informative summary simply conveys the author's main ideas, data, arguments, and supporting material; an explanatory summary conveys this information as well, but also indicates the overall structure of the source text, explaining how the author develops his or her assertions. Informative summaries are shorter than explanatory summaries and are usually incorporated into longer works or take the form of an **abstract**. Explanatory summaries are longer than informative summaries, follow the organizational scheme of the source text, frequently refer to the name of the source text's author, and usually serve as independent, freestanding essays.

Below are two different summaries of the opening lines of the Gettysburg Address, one informative and one explanatory. As you read them, note the differences in content, structure, and word choice.

Example I

Source Text

> Four score and seven years ago our fathers brought forth on this continent, a new nation, conceived in Liberty and dedicated to the proposition that all men are created equal. Now we are engaged in a great civil war, testing whether that nation, or any nation so conceived and so dedicated, can long endure.

We are met on a great battlefield of that war. We have come to dedicate a portion of that field, as a final resting place for those who here gave their lives that that nation might live.

Informative Summary

Eighty-seven years ago the United States was founded on the idea that all people are created equal. Currently a civil war is testing whether such a nation can survive. A portion of this battlefield is to be designated as a cemetery for those who fought in the war.

Explanatory Summary

Lincoln opens the Gettysburg Address by remarking that eighty-seven years ago the United States was founded on the idea that all people are created equal. He next points out how the country is engaged in a civil war that will determine whether such a nation can survive, then acknowledges the occasion of the speech: to dedicate part of a great battlefield as a cemetery for the combatants.

Notice that the point of the informative summary is simply to capture in your own words the important ideas found in the source text. In an explanatory summary, though, you repeatedly refer to the author of the work and indicate how the piece was organized through your choice of verbs ("opens," "points out") and transition words ("next," "then").

QUALITIES OF A GOOD SUMMARY

Informative and explanatory summaries need to be comprehensive, brief, accurate, neutral, and independent.

- *Comprehensive*—it conveys all the important information in the reading.
- *Brief*—it conveys this information concisely.
- *Accurate*—it correctly conveys the author's ideas, findings, or arguments.
- *Neutral*—it avoids judgments concerning the reading's topic or style.
- *Independent*—it makes sense to someone who has not read the source text.

COMPREHENSIVE

Your summary needs to include all of the important ideas, assertions, or findings contained in the source text as well as the most significant information or arguments the author provides to support them. When you paraphrase a passage, you try to capture in your own language everything the author has written. However, when you summarize that same passage, you have to be more selective in choosing material to include. You need to identify what you believe to be the most important material in the passage and include only that in your summary. In this way your summary is comprehensive—you have not left out any important information.

Does that mean that if a number of people were summarizing the same article, all of their essays would be identical, at least in content? No. Determining what to include in a summary requires judgment. Each individual writer must decide what is most important in the source text. Some writers will make good choices; some will make poor choices. Even those making good choices may decide to include different information. Consequently, students assigned to summarize the same reading will likely produce slightly different essays. If you carefully and critically read the source text before you begin to write your summary, and if you check your work against the source text before you turn it in to be sure you have included all of the important information, you will probably produce a comprehensive summary.

BRIEF

In writing a summary, you have to balance two concerns: you want your summary to be comprehensive, but you also want it to be brief. The point of writing a summary is to *reduce* a text to its most essential information. In a summary, brevity is usually achieved through carefully selecting your content and words. First you need to include (1) the reading's primary ideas, arguments, or findings, and (2) the primary means of support the author offers for his or her contentions. Second, you must always be concerned about word count: if you can say something gracefully in four words rather than five, say it in four; if you can condense material by cutting unnecessary prepositions or adjectives, cut them. Composing a good summary requires disciplined writing.

ACCURATE

Your readers depend on you to be accurate in your summary. You have to be careful not to misrepresent—purposefully or accidentally—what the author wrote. Instead of reading the source text, your readers are depending on you to provide them a thorough, accurate, and fair overview of the piece. Misrepresenting an author in your summary is unfair to both your reader and the original author. However, accuracy can be hard to maintain. Because in a summary you are substituting your language for the author's, even slight changes in words can drastically alter the meaning of a passage. Therefore, when you review your summary, check it against the source to be sure you have accurately represented what the author wrote. Make sure you have not misrepresented the author's ideas or findings either by omitting some important information or by using inaccurate, slanted, or vague language.

NEUTRAL

Summaries should be objective. No matter how much you would like to praise or criticize an author's argument, interpretation of data, or style of writing, such comments do not belong in a summary. In a summary you do not present your views on the topic the author is addressing, you do not comment on the quality of the author's argument or writing, and you do not voice any of your opinions at all. Instead, you try to present what the author has written accurately and objectively. When reviewing your summary, make sure you have not included your own opinions and that you have used objective language. By avoiding highly charged or judgmental terms, you can help ensure that your summary is neutral, balanced, and fair.

When there are problems with objectivity in a summary, more often than not they appear in one of three places: at the beginnings of paragraphs, in the middle of long paragraphs, and at the very end of the piece. At the beginnings of paragraphs, students sometimes react to the material contained in the previous paragraph; instead of moving on to summarize the author's next point, they respond to the previous one. In the middle of paragraphs, students sometimes begin to debate the author. They may notice that the author has presented a weak argument, for example, and feel compelled to point that out. Such criticisms are appropriate for a critique, not for a summary. Finally, at the ends of summaries, students sometimes add the kind of concluding line commonly found in high school book reports, "Overall, I really liked this book because. . . ." or "Though I found the author convincing, sometimes I had a hard time. . . ." Such statements do not belong in an objective, neutral summary.

INDEPENDENT

Your summary ought to make sense to someone who has not read the source text. Keep in mind the purpose of a summary. If, for instance, your employer asks you to summarize a report, she wants to learn from your summary the main points of the report without having to read the original text. Your summary must be able to stand on its own—read independently, it has to make sense. To achieve this goal, you need to pay special attention to word choice when drafting your summary. For example, are there any terms that, taken from the context of the source text, will need to be defined in your summary? Have you included in your summary any pronouns that refer to an antecedent in the source, not to an antecedent in your summary? Have you referred to people who were identified in the source but are not identified in your summary?

To make sure your summary is independent, let someone read it who has not read the source text before you turn it in for a grade. Ask that person to mark any words or passages he or she finds confusing.

HOW TO SUMMARIZE A TEXT

READ, REREAD, AND ANNOTATE THE SOURCE TEXT

Obviously, the first step in writing a summary is to read the material you are summarizing. As you read through it for the first time, try to get a sense of the passage's main ideas and structure—a sense of what the author covers and the order in which the ideas are presented. Next, read the material again, only more slowly this time. As you reread, carefully mark the passage, highlighting important material and taking notes in the margin that identify the main points, key supporting information, and the structure of the piece.

If you are summarizing a paragraph, locate and mark the topic sentence. If there is no topic sentence, paraphrase the main point of the paragraph in the margin. If you are summarizing an entire essay or article, locate the thesis. If the author states the thesis, underline it and make a note in the margin. If the thesis is implied rather than stated, paraphrase the main point of the piece at the end of the passage. If the source text has headings and subheadings, note how they help structure the piece.

SUMMARIZE EACH SECTION OF THE SOURCE TEXT

Identify the major sections of the piece—where the author discusses one idea or develops one argument or explores one finding. These sections may consist of a single paragraph or a group of paragraphs. In the margin of the passage or on a separate sheet of paper, briefly summarize each section of the text. Using your own words, note the primary idea, assertion, or finding being developed in each section along with the primary supporting material the author provides—the most effective example, the most telling statistic, the most important authority cited.

CHECK THE SECTION SUMMARIES AGAINST THE SOURCE TEXT

The brief summaries you produce of each section of the source text will help you incorporate the material into a longer essay you are writing, compose an abstract of the source text, or produce an explanatory summary of the reading. Now is a good time to check these brief summaries against the source text to ensure they are accurate, neutral, comprehensive, and clear.

HOW TO WRITE AN ABSTRACT

As stated earlier, the goal of an informative summary is to convey as briefly and accurately as possible the primary content of a source text or perhaps just a certain section of that text. When you incorporate summarized material into a longer essay you are writing—a report or research paper, for example—you may introduce the material by referring to the author's name and/or the title of the piece before you add it to your essay. A special form of an informative summary in academic writing is an abstract. Abstracts are usually paragraph-long informative summaries of a reading and frequently accompany scholarly texts. Most often located under the title of the text, an abstract provides a succinct overview of the reading, informing readers of the text's primary assertions, findings, or arguments. When you are engaged in a research project, abstracts can be invaluable: when you locate a source text that looks interesting, by reading the abstract alone you can decide whether to read the entire piece or move on to the next one.

After you draft your abstract, be sure to check it against the original to ensure that the abstract is comprehensive and independent—it ought to make the main points of the reading clear to someone who has not read the text. Also be sure that you are paraphrasing the source text throughout your abstract: the language you use should be yours. Sometimes you might have to quote specific terms the author has used if they are particularly important or novel.

HOW TO WRITE AN INFORMATIVE SUMMARY ESSAY

An informative summary is longer and more detailed than an abstract, covering the author's primary assertions, findings, and arguments, as well as how they are supported. Informative summaries frequently follow the source text's organization—summarizing the text's first main point first, the second main point next, and so on. This is not necessary, however, if using a different organizational strategy would make your summary stronger. In the end, your informative summary should be comprehensive, brief, accurate, neutral, and independent.

In the *opening section* of your essay, introduce the topic or context of the reading, provide the source text's full title and the full names of its authors, and state your thesis. You might also want to provide the author's credentials or the publication information of the source text (where and when it was originally published). Your thesis will be a paraphrase of the source text's thesis.

In the *body* of your informative summary, paraphrase the primary content of the source text. You may want to use the one-sentence summaries of each section you composed earlier as a guide. Just paraphrase the content of the readings—do not embellish or editorialize. Your goal is to write a thorough summary of the source text that is both clear and neutral. Do not comment on the text's content, style, or structure. Plagiarism can be a problem with summarizing a text: be sure you paraphrase the material properly. You may quote material in an informative summary, but you should use quotations sparingly.

Informative summaries do not have conclusions like other forms of source-based essays. Instead, you close your paper by summarizing the source text's last key assertion, finding, or argument. Do not editorialize at the end of your summary—do not include any judgmental statements like "Overall, the author did a good job of presenting her ideas" or "The piece was extremely interesting and easy to read." Your summary should be neutral and objective.

As always, review your rough draft against the source text as you revise to ensure that your summary is comprehensive and that you have adequately covered the source text's primary content.

HOW TO WRITE AN EXPLANATORY SUMMARY ESSAY

As with an informative summary, an explanatory summary conveys the primary content of a text. However, it describes not only what the reading says but also how it is put together through frequent references to the author's organizational strategy. When a teacher asks you to write a summary of a text, this is the type of document he or she usually has in mind: an explanatory summary of the reading that is comprehensive, brief, accurate, neutral, and independent.

In the *opening section* of your summary—usually the first paragraph or two—introduce the topic of the source text, give the title of the piece you are summarizing, mention the name and credentials of the person who wrote the piece, and include your thesis. In a summary, your thesis will likely be a paraphrase of the source text's thesis.

In the *body* of your summary, present in your own words the author's primary assertions, conclusions, or findings, as well as the supporting examples or statistics you believe your readers will need to know to understand and appreciate the author's contentions. Use as a guide the brief summaries of each section of the text you wrote earlier. An explanatory summary is different from an informative summary because in the body of your essay you will make frequent references to the author of the piece and explain how the source text is structured through your use of transitions. Assume you are working with an article by Alice Smith. Your explanatory summary will include many passages such as these: "Smith opens her essay by . . . ," "Next, Smith discusses . . . ," "Smith's third main argument is . . . ," and "Smith concludes her essay with. . . ." All of these example passages include the author's name and some listing or transition word (e.g., "first," "next," "then"). You do not have to use the author's name in every sentence, just when you are moving from your summary of one section of the source text to another section so your reader has a clear sense of the source text's structure.

Generally, summaries do not need a *conclusion*; simply end your essay with a summary of the author's last point. If you want or need a formal conclusion, make it a brief restatement of the author's thesis.

Once you have finished the rough draft of your explanatory summary essay, reread the source text to ensure that you have captured all of the important content of the reading. To be sure that your summary is clear, ask someone who has not read the source text to read your summary and identify any passages he or she finds confusing. Remember: unless you are told otherwise by your teacher, assume your audience has not read the source text. Also check the tone of your summary. It ought to be objective and neutral.

DOCUMENTATION

Summarized material should be documented. Many students do not feel they need to document summaries because they are using their own language to convey the author's ideas. However, when you write a summary, you still need to give the author credit for those ideas, arguments, or findings. Documentation also tells your readers where they can locate the source text if they want to read the whole piece themselves.

Reading

Following are three summaries—an abstract, an informative summary, and an explanatory summary—of the following article, "From *Animal House* to *Big Brother:* Student Privacy and Campus Security in an Age of Accountability" by Ron Chesbrough. It originally appeared in *Student Affairs Leader*.

From *Animal House* to *Big Brother:* Student Privacy and Campus Safety in an Age of Accountability

Ron Chesbrough

Ron Chesbrough is the vice president of student affairs at Hastings College in Nebraska. He is also a member of Student Affairs Leader's editorial board.

Two Scenarios: A student at a large university spots a gun on the desk of a fellow student during class. Frightened, the student sends a text message to someone outside of the classroom, who in turn contacts the University Police Department. Members of the University Police respond immediately, going to the classroom and removing the student and the gun. In the process, they learn that the gun is a toy gun used in the popular game "Assassin." They seek out the other students engaged in the game and confiscate their toy guns. A notice is sent to the university community describing the incident in detail and announcing the prohibition of this game on university property.

A student at a small private college reports to the dean of students that she has read disturbing poems on the Facebook page of another student. The dean reviews the postings, which contain references to being unhappy and questioning the purpose of life. The dean calls the student in and requires that he undergo a full psychiatric evaluation based on the poems.

Background

We have learned recently many times over, and with crushing severity, what we have long known—that college campuses are risk-inherent environments. We have also been tragically reminded of a corollary fact—that one of our greatest challenges in creating and preserving safe environments on our campuses is the ability to find and strike a proper balance between our students' rights to privacy and their rights to a safe and healthy living and learning community. This is not a new imperative for us; it is simply one that has gained importance in recent years and with recent events on our campuses.

In the wake of the tragedy of the Virginia Tech shootings of nearly a year ago and those that have followed, the intersection of student privacy rights and community safety is, now more than ever, one where the traffic light is changing erratically. With the lights blinking red, green, and yellow on all sides, institutions and professionals are left largely to their own interpretations and intuitions about when to go, stop, or proceed with caution when it comes to student privacy rights.

From emergency alert text messaging systems to patrols of Facebook and MySpace and all things in between, colleges and universities are searching for the new right relationship with students in the interest of campus safety.

Take, for example, a recent article in the *Wall Street Journal*, featured in the February 1 issue of *Student Affairs Leader*, [that] described Cornell University's new "alert team" and related university-wide training to recognize and report signs of student emotional distress and behavioral concerns ("Bucking Privacy Concerns, Cornell Acts as Watchdog," *WSJ*, December 28, 2007). These practices place Cornell "squarely in the center of a debate over the rights of American college students," according to the article. Just what is the debate, we should ask, and how have we arrived here?

FERPA in Transition

The Family Education Rights and Privacy Act (FERPA) has long governed the treatment of student privacy rights in higher education. Its protections and allowances are familiar enough by now to not bear detailed repeating here, although a refresher on the various amendments to FERPA, particularly over the past decade, is not a bad idea.

It is also useful to gain some familiarity with the shifting ground of case law in matters concerning student privacy rights and our duty to protect students from harm—whether from themselves or others.

Two recent cases worth reading again in this regard are *Shin v. Massachusetts Institute of Technology* and *Schieszler v. Ferrum College*. In both cases the courts found a special duty to care (in these cases to prevent self-harm) based on the unique relationship between students and their academic institutions.

If we set aside the legitimate and compelling question of an institution's ability to "prevent" harm to all students at all times, we can see that the real central issue here is one of discernment and disclosure.

In other words, how do we maximize our ability to detect or discern threats to safety on our campuses? And once a possible or plausible threat is discerned, to what end and to whom do we disclose this information? And finally, what are the implications of this discernment/disclosure puzzle for our relationships with students?

Disclosure

To begin, we might begin to rethink our definition of "privacy" in this scenario. We might also question the original intent of FERPA—asking who and what it was originally intended to protect, and from whom. Here it seems clear that the original and ongoing intent of FERPA is to provide reasonable protections against undue intrusions into the education records of students by those not determined under law to have legal rights to such access, and to provide students with their own due process rights to the same information pertaining to them and being held by the institution.

Where institutions keep information of a disciplinary nature, and where such records do not constitute criminal records, the same protections and rights have applied, with notable recent amendments allowing disclosure of information to certain others (e.g., parents, victims) when in relation to certain types of potentially noncriminal records (e.g., campus drug/alcohol violations, sexual violence).

Similarly, allowances exist for disclosure of certain medical or treatment records held by the college to both parents and others as directed by FERPA. Finally, the Jeanne Clery Act not only allows but also requires both annual reporting and timely warning (in cases of an ongoing threat) of criminal activity on our campuses.

Given these provisions for disclosures under FERPA and what some would argue is a gross historic misunderstanding of more general parental disclosure rights of the institution under FERPA, it is fair to say that we have often overstated protections afforded to students under this law.

It is safe to say, historically speaking, that we have often erred on the side of overprotecting these rights, especially in the grey areas of FERPA, that many would argue still exist after more than four decades and numerous amendments to the legislation. But are we moving too far, too fast into this new intersection of student privacy rights and campus safety?

Who Bears Responsibility—and to Whom

In their recent look at critical issues for student affairs professionals, Arthur Sandeen and Margaret J. Barr had this to say about the rising complexity of the question of student safety on our campuses: "Legal requirements, institutional missions, parental expectations, chronic psychological problems of students, and student behaviors require both the profession and institutions to answer this fundamental question" (Sandeen & Barr, 2006, p. xii). Their chapter entitled "Who Has the Responsibility for the Lives of Students?" is an attempt to answer this question.

I would argue, as perhaps they would, that this is not a new question, but an old one posed in a new context, with new and literal meaning imbued by recent events on our campuses nationwide. It is not the "who" in this question that has changed, but the "how."

How are we differently responsible for the lives of our students in the current era, and as importantly, how do we best fulfill that responsibility when faced with the kinds of scenarios posed at the outset? Put differently, how do we begin to rebalance the right of all students to a safe learning environment with the rights of those whom Sandeen and Barr refer to as our "disturbed" students, students whom they suggest are coming to us in increasing numbers (Sandeen & Barr, pp. 155–180)?

A Beginning Attempt

To begin, we need to revisit this concept of the disturbed student, first coined by Ursula Delworth, two decades ago in a definition that has almost eerie accuracy in today's environment of high-stakes disturbance on campus. These students, according to Delworth, can demonstrate an outward (anger and lashing out) or inward (depression and withdrawal) focus, and hold the potential to harm themselves or others (Delworth, 1989). Of particular importance, according to Delworth, is our recognition and response to those students who are both disturbed and disturbing of the campus environment.

We should refresh ourselves in the clear communication roles and responsibilities among campus administrators and health professionals established by Hollingsworth and Dunkle (2005) in our coordinated response to these students. And in this we should heed Arthur Sandeen's (1989) reminder that "an institution that decides it can not afford the resources required to address the problems of the disturbed and disturbing student may discover the costs of ignoring them are too great" (p. 61).

We should set clear behavioral expectations of our students in the classroom, in residence halls, and in the campus community at large. These are simply those norms that we insist should exist for the emotional and physical comfort of all members of the learning community, and they should be indexed to those instances where a certain behavior might reasonably be seen as imposing on or limiting the rights of other members of the community to a safe, healthy, and positive living and learning environment.

We should anticipate both the reasonable accommodations that might be made to students unable to meet certain behavioral requirements consistently or in all settings, and the absolute limits of behaviors that fall outside of the pale of the learning community. And we should clearly state what our responses would be in either case.

If we intend to not allow play guns on campus, or if concerning posts to a Facebook page are cause for college response, then students should be aware of this and the consequences of behaving in these ways. This takes hard and deliberate thought and imagination, and ought to involve a hearty dose of student and faculty input. It will lead to debate, discussion, and disagreement—but it is precisely this debate that needs to occur, in anticipation of difficult campus events rather than in response to them.

Students, and their parents, should be made to understand that college officials will exercise their full rights under FERPA to share information deemed necessary between college health officials and administrators; between administrators and parents or appropriate outside officials; and between members of the faculty, staff, and administration of the college or university as allowed by law—to ensure the safety of all members of the community to the best of their ability. And the mechanisms for said sharing should be transparent and readily understood by all members of the learning community and its constituents.

Implications

Some will point to a chilling effect of a learning environment so characterized. I would argue the opposite. What is chilling in the present environment is the relative lack of these types of safeguards in the face of clear and repeated evidence of our need for them. What is discomforting is the unease we feel at the intersection of student privacy rights and community safety—and it is discomforting not just for student affairs practitioners, but also for students, staff, faculty, and parents alike.

In this environment, it falls most logically to student affairs professionals to take the steps necessary to police this intersection and to work with others to develop the proper new traffic signals for this new environment.

It can also be said that this new posture poses new legal liability threats to institutions that may be claiming, by making such clear statements of intent, to be able to prevent bad things from happening on their campuses. Arguably, due diligence does in fact take on a new meaning in light of commitments like those described to attempt to discern and report potential threats to safety.

At the same time, we enter an environment wherein the lack of such stepped-up attempts may soon be discerned as a failure of due diligence, particularly as institutions move individually in these directions and as findings from various reports raise the question for legislators, parents, and others as to what our due diligence ought to, in fact, entail.

Still others may find such measures to have a discriminatory or dampening effect on admission for those students disclosing in that process a pre-existing diagnosis that may make them more prone to "concerning" exhibitions of behavior. All the better that college officials have more knowledge about the support needs of incoming students from the outset in order to put in place appropriate accommodations and to take the "handoff" from those who have provided supports and accommodations up to that point.

We might ask ourselves which student with special needs has the better chance of success in a college environment: the student who has disclosed what has helped him or her to succeed, or the student with special needs who is silent?

Finally, to those who herald this as a return to an even more extreme version of *in loco parentis* in our relationships with our students than we have so recently congratulated ourselves on shedding, I would say not quite, and perhaps the opposite. If we look closely at the legal doctrine of *in loco parentis*, we find that it describes a circumstance in which one assumes responsibility for a child without formally adopting the child. Applied to schools and colleges, this has typically meant that, by our actions, policies, and formal statements we agree to accept responsibility for our students "in the place of" their parents. Here I am arguing for something different.

I am arguing that we find new ways to hold our students accountable for their own actions, and that we involve parents as active partners and appropriate outside professionals whenever the need is evident. Staying with the Latin, we might call this the doctrine of *modestus pateo,* or, loosely translated, orderly openness. More simply, we might think of where we have arrived in higher education in this and many other regards as the *age of accountability*—to our students, their parents, our colleagues, and our many constituencies—in all that we do.

If campus safety at your institution is still something that the student affairs professionals are left to figure out and stew over, then it is time for change. The issues raised here about student privacy, campus safety, and our right relationship with our students in this age are not student affairs issues; they are issues of concern and importance to every member of the college community. Everyone must join the conversation. We are all standing at the same intersection, and the lights are still flashing red, green, and yellow.

References

Delworth, D., (1989). Dealing with the Behavioral and Psychological Problems of Students. New Directions for Student Services, no. 45. San Francisco: Jossey-Bass.

Hollingsworth, K. and Dunkle, J. "Dealing with Disturbed and Disturbing Students: Best Practices and Their Implications." Paper presented at the National Association of Student Affairs Personnel Administrators Annual Conference, Tampa, FL, 2005.

Sandeen, A., (1989). "A Chief Student Affairs Officer's Perspective on the AISP Model," in U. Oelworth (Ed.), <u>Dealing with the Behavioral and Psychological Problems of Students</u>. New Directions for Student Services, no. 45. San Francisco: Jossey-Bass.

Sandeen, A. and Barr, M. J., (2006). <u>Critical Issues for Student Affairs: Challenges and Opportunities</u>. San Francisco: Jossey-Bass.

Wall Street Journal, <u>Bucking Privacy Concerns: Cornell Acts as "Watchdog,"</u> 12/28/2007.

<u>Schieszler v. Ferrum College</u>, 233 F.Supp.2d 796 (W.D.Va. 2002). <u>Shin v. MIT</u>, 2005 Mass. Super. LEXIS 333, *32.

SAMPLE ABSTRACT

The author discusses a dilemma facing campus administrators: keeping students safe while protecting their privacy rights. The author argues that administrators may be reading FERPA restrictions too narrowly, failing to collect and share information that might protect students. He states that student safety is the responsibility of the entire campus community and that students' parents may play a more expanded role in forming a viable solution to the problem.

SAMPLE INFORMATIVE SUMMARY ESSAY

Ron Chesbrough's "From *Animal House* to *Big Brother*: Student Privacy and Campus Safety in an Age of Accountability" examines the tension that exists between college administrators' desire to keep students safe while at the same time protecting their privacy rights. After the fatal shootings at Virginia Tech, administrators have had to reconsider their existing policies.

Difficulties arise due to the Family Education Rights and Privacy Act (FERPA), legislation that has long served to protect student privacy. FERPA may prevent college authorities from addressing potential threats because doing so might violate a student's right to privacy. On the other hand, courts have held that colleges have a special obligation to protect the safety of students.

To address this dilemma, school administrators need to revisit the intention of the FERPA act, which was to ensure the privacy of student academic records and provide students due process rights. Allowances in the law enable schools to contact parents and other appropriate authorities about student health or disciplinary problems. In the past, schools have erred on the side of caution and have generally not communicated their concerns about particular students to off-campus authorities.

Particular attention needs to be paid to how schools address "disturbed" students who for medical or non-medical reasons pose a possible threat to other students. Schools must employ health care professionals who can help these students, convey to all students the school's standards of behavior, develop plans for accommodating students who need extra help coping with school, ban firearms from campus, and inform parents and students that school administrators will use all the powers FERPA provides to protect the safety of everyone on campus.

Some may find these actions too severe or opening colleges up to litigation should a tragedy occur. However, proper due diligence on the school's part is required to ensure student safety and privacy. Central to this effort is holding students accountable for their actions and enlisting the help of students and parents when formulating new school policies.

SAMPLE EXPLANATORY SUMMARY ESSAY

In "From *Animal House* to *Big Brother:* Student Privacy and Campus Safety in an Age of Accountability," author Ron Chesbrough explores how to make college campuses safer. Reacting to recent tragedies such as the killings at Virginia Tech, Chesbrough questions how best to balance the needs for student safety and student privacy, especially in light of safeguards guaranteed by the Family Education Rights and Privacy Act (FERPA). He argues that college administrators may need to operate out of a more liberal reading of FERPA regulations and enlist the aid of parents to meet the needs of students who may pose safety issues for a school.

Chesbrough opens his essay by defining a problem all college administrators face: how to ensure student safety while maintaining the privacy rights of students who may exhibit threatening or concerning behavior or actions. Central to the debate is how administrators interpret the restrictions placed on colleges through FERPA. While agreeing that FERPA has many

benefits, Chesbrough notes how two recent court cases have
redefined schools' responsibilities to protect students from
themselves and their peers. He then poses an additional question
to consider: under these new interpretations of FERPA, how do
college administrators know when to release information about
students who might pose a risk to the school and when to keep
such information confidential?

To answer this question, Chesbrough examines the original
intent of FERPA: who was it intended to protect and from what?
He concludes that the act was passed primarily to protect student
academic records and to ensure students due process rights
concerning the release of those records. However, Chesbrough
notes, FERPA allows for the release of some student medical
information to parents while the Clery Act compels college
administrators to act in a timely manner and with due diligence
to address campus threats.

Chesbrough then offers a number of initial steps that might
be taken to improve campus safety within FERPA restrictions:
better define what a school means by a "disturbed" student,
establish a clear communication protocol across campus to respond
to any dangerous situations, share with students what constitutes
acceptable and unacceptable behavior, and clarify university policy
regarding firearms and Facebook postings.

Closing his essay, Chesbrough contends that taking these steps
will make campuses safer while still maintaining student privacy
rights. While there is a threat to privacy in identifying students
who have potentially harmful mental or emotional conditions,
administrators can enlist the aid of parents to help ensure that
these students receive the assistance they need and that the safety
of other students is protected.

Summary Chart

HOW TO SUMMARIZE TEXTS

1. **Read, reread, and annotate the material.**

   Carefully read the material, paying particular attention to the content and structure of the piece.

   Reread and annotate the material, being sure to note:
   • *the thesis;*
   • *the primary assertions, arguments, or findings; and*
   • *the primary means of support for each point.*

2. **Write one-sentence summaries of each section of the text.**

   Identify the major sections of the reading, in which the writer develops one idea before moving on to the next.

   In your own words, restate the main point developed in each section of the text and primary means of support the author provides.

3. **Write the first draft of your summary.**

   Introduce the topic of the reading.

   Include, early in your essay, the author's full name and the full title of the piece.

   In the body of your summary, elaborate on the one-sentence summaries, clearly explaining the important content of the reading.

4. **Check the rough draft of your summary against the source text. As you review your work, make sure your summary is:**

   Comprehensive—you have included in your summary all of the author's important ideas, assertions, or findings.

   Accurate—in choosing words and selecting material for your summary, you have not misrepresented the author's positions or findings.

   Neutral—in choosing words and selecting material for your summary, you have attempted to be objective and fair.

   Independent—your summary will make sense to someone who has not read the source text.

5. **Rewrite your summary.**

   Based on your evaluation of your rough draft, make any needed changes in the content, organization, or language of your summary.

   If you are writing an explanatory summary, include any transition words you need to guide your reader through your work.

Summary Revision Checklist

	Yes	No
1. In the opening section of your summary have you:		
• introduced the topic of the essay?	_____	_____
• given the full title of the source text?	_____	_____
• given the full name of the author?	_____	_____
• included *your* thesis?	_____	_____
2. In the body of your essay do you summarize only one point at a time?	_____	_____
3. Have you accurately and fairly put into your own words all of the author's important findings, arguments, or ideas?	_____	_____
4. Have you identified the primary means of support the author provides for each finding, argument, or idea?	_____	_____
5. By cutting material or words, have you tried to make your summary as brief as possible while still being comprehensive?	_____	_____
6. To be neutral, have you avoided comments on the:		
• topic of the piece?	_____	_____
• author's ideas?	_____	_____
• author's style?	_____	_____
7. To help ensure that your summary will make sense to someone who has not read the original work, have you:		
• defined any unusual or technical terms?	_____	_____
• identified any people you refer to in your work?	_____	_____
• provided a sufficient context for understanding the author's assertions or findings?	_____	_____
8. Do you have adequate paragraph breaks and transitions?	_____	_____
9. Have you supplied proper documentation?	_____	_____

Chapter 5

RESPONSE ESSAYS

DEFINITION AND PURPOSE

Response essays ask you to examine, explain, and often defend your personal reaction to a reading. In this type of essay you explore why you liked the reading, agreed with the author, found the piece informative or confusing—whatever your response might be. There are no necessarily "right" or "wrong" reactions to material; instead, response essays are usually evaluated on the basis of how well you demonstrate an understanding of the reading and how clearly you explain your reactions.

Sometimes teachers grade response essays the same way they grade any other assignment. Other times they assign ungraded response essays—usually as a way to help students develop material for graded essays. Still other teachers combine response essays with other types of papers; for example, they might ask students to summarize and then respond to a reading, or to respond to a reading and then critique it. Sometimes teachers will specify which aspects of the text they would like you respond to in your essay (for example, the author's thesis or use of figurative language); other times they will leave the choice of content up to you. In short, the response essay is a very flexible assignment employed widely by teachers in college. Writing this type of paper helps you understand your personal reaction to what you read: what you think about the topic, how you judge the author's ideas, and how the words on the page affect you as a reader.

Effective response essays demonstrate a strong connection between the source text and your reaction. Your responses are triggered by what you read, by certain words on the page. It is important to keep that connection strongly in mind as you compose your response essay. First, you need to put into words your responses to the source text. Second, you need to identify which words on the page triggered those responses. Third, you need to determine, then explain for your reader, why and how those words triggered those responses.

In writing this type of essay, you cannot simply state your response and move on: "I liked this. I didn't like that." "This interested me; that puzzled me." Instead, you must develop and explain your response: what, *exactly*, is your response; what part of the text triggered it; what, *exactly*, is the relationship between the words on the page and your reactions to them? While the idea of "developing" your response may seem odd, remember that you are writing for a reader, not just for yourself. You want your reader to be able to understand and appreciate both your response and what led you to have it. Clearly, writing a response essay is more difficult than it might first appear.

QUALITIES OF A GOOD RESPONSE ESSAY

Part of what makes a good response essay difficult to write is that it must be honest, informed, clear, and well supported.

- *Honest*—it reflects your true responses.
- *Informed*—it reflects an accurate and thorough understanding of the source text.
- *Clear*—it makes sense to your readers.
- *Well supported*—it demonstrates a close link between your responses and the source text itself.

HONEST

A response essay should focus on your sincere, thoughtful reactions to what you read. You want to identify your responses to the material and explore their relationship to the text itself: What gives rise to your reactions? How do they affect your reading of the author's work? These essays are highly subjective—you focus on *your* reactions to the text. Consequently, you should not pretend your responses are other than what they truly are. If you found a work boring, for example, do not claim that you found it intriguing simply because you think that is the way you are *supposed* to respond.

INFORMED

Can your responses, then, ever be "wrong"? In one sense, they cannot—your responses are your responses. That does not mean, though, that all responses to a reading are equally informed. If, for example, your response is based on a misunderstanding of the source text—if you criticize an author for saying something she never said—then your response is misguided. Responses can also be naive, shortsighted, or biased. These responses are not, in a sense, "wrong," but neither are they very insightful. Informed response essays are based on a clear understanding of the source text: the more you know about a topic, author, or reading, the more likely your response will be informed.

Take, for example, an experience I had a few years ago. I asked a group of students to respond to a satirical political essay before we discussed the piece in class. The students who recognized the satire produced fine response essays. However, the students who did not understand that the author was being satirical terribly misread the piece and produced misguided essays. Their responses were honest—the responses accurately reflected their reading of the text—but they were not informed.

CLEAR

When your readers finish your response essay, they should understand (1) how you reacted to the reading and (2) how your reactions are tied to the source text. Problems with clarity often arise from weak content, weak organization, or poor word choice.

Problems with clarity involving **content** occur when the person writing the response essay fails to state clearly the nature of his or her response, fails to identify which aspect of the source text gave rise to that response, or fails to explain the relationship between his or her response and those aspects of the text. Unless all three are clearly stated and explored, readers can be left confused about the nature of your response to the reading.

Other problems with clarity involve **organization**. Be sure that your essay has a fully developed opening and closing section and a clearly stated thesis. A good response essay also explores only one reaction at a time and provides clear transitions between the various sections of the paper. Problems with clarity can occur when you shift too quickly from discussing one response to discussing another—without a good transition, the change of focus might not be clear to your reader.

Finally, problems with clarity often involve the **language** used in response essays. Too often students use vague language to explore their reactions—words that mean something to them but nothing to their readers. Though response essays are highly subjective, when you turn them in for a grade, they must be addressed to a more public audience. Good response essays can be difficult to write for just this reason: you have to find language that clearly and efficiently communicates to others your subjective responses to a reading.

WELL SUPPORTED

In good response essays, students support and explain their reactions to the text with specific, elaborated examples. If, for example, a student claims that she was offended by an author's illogical assertions, she should quote some of those passages and explain why she finds them illogical. If another student reads the same work and finds the same passages convincing because they match his experiences, he should also quote some examples and explain why he finds them convincing. In either case, the student supports her or his responses by citing from the source text examples that gave rise to them and then clearly explaining the relationship between those examples and their responses.

WRITING THE RESPONSE ESSAY

CAREFULLY READ THE MATERIAL

The problem with many response essays is that the students have not *fully* understood the source text before they begin to write. Some students respond to only part of the reading, without indicating they understand how the material fits into the author's overall thesis. As a result, their responses often seem limited or even biased; their work tends to ignore important issues raised in the source text. Other students simply misread the source text—basing their response on something the author neither wrote nor intended.

Therefore, when you are assigned to respond to a reading, read it several times and briefly summarize it before you write your essay (see Chapter 4 for advice on writing summaries). Summarizing the piece first can help ensure that your response will be based on a full and accurate understanding of the text's content, structure, tone, and thesis.

Explore Your Responses to the Reading as You Annotate the Text

To develop material for your response essay, as you read and annotate the text, note your responses briefly in the margin of the piece. Sometimes just jotting down a key word or two will do; other times you may need to write out a question you have. Even punctuation marks, such as exclamation points or question marks, can help you keep track of your reactions. When you are finished, expand on these notes at the end of the reading or on a separate sheet of paper. Your goal is to capture in a few sentences your overall response to what you have just read. These notes will form the basis of your response essay. In deciding what to mark and what kinds of comments to write as you read the source text, try answering the following questions.

How Do You React Emotionally to What the Author Has Written?

Your subjective, emotional reaction to a reading is a good place to start generating material for a response essay. Does the text make you angry? Excited? Bored? To explore these reactions, ask yourself several questions:

1. What, exactly, has the author written that makes you feel this way?
2. At what point in your reading did you have these reactions?

3. Which words on the page or ideas caused this response?
4. In short, what has the author done to make you respond this way? Examine the choices the writer made concerning content, organization, and style. What aspects of the text contribute to your response?

As you try to capture your responses in writing, carefully examine your reactions and, when possible, tie them to specific words, passages, or graphics in the text.

How Do the Ideas Offered in the Reading Compare with Your Experience or Your Sense of Reality?

We have all had the experience of hearing or reading something that has a ring of truth or falsehood. Something in a reading makes sense to us because it squares with our experience; it sits right with what we have come to understand about the world. As you reread and annotate a reading, note which of the author's ideas you tend to agree with or question based on their match to your own experience.

There is a real danger, though, in judging what others say by the standards of our experience alone. All of us bring to a reading important but limited experiences. When an author's statements do not match our sense of reality, we should not act defensively and immediately dismiss her ideas. Likewise, simply because we tend to agree with an author does not mean we ought to accept her ideas uncritically. Writing a response essay will give you the chance to question what you believe in light of what the author writes and to understand how your experiences influence the way you react to new ideas.

How Do the Ideas Offered in the Source Match What Others Have Had to Say on the Topic?

When you read a source, you bring with you not only what you think and feel based on your own experience, but also what you know, what you have already learned from your reading and education. There is no reason to ignore this knowledge when you write your response essay. In fact, whether the source text confirms or contradicts what you already know about the topic may be one of the reasons for your reaction to the piece. Be sure to note any reactions you have based on the match between the author's ideas and those proposed by other authors you have read.

COMPOSE YOUR ROUGH DRAFT

When you write your response essay, you will need to introduce the source text, provide your reader with a brief summary of its content, and then develop and clarify your reactions.

Introduce Your Topic, Source Text, and Thesis

When composing the opening of your response essay, you have four goals: introduce the topic of your essay, introduce your source text, state your thesis, and capture reader interest. Once you introduce the source text's topic, provide its title and its author's full name. Your thesis for this type of essay will be a statement of your overall response to the reading and, if you like, an indication of how you will develop or explore that response in the body of your paper. If you employ an "open" thesis statement for your essay, you will indicate your overall response to the piece:

- I found parts of the essay confusing.
- Reading this essay proved to be an emotional challenge.

If you employ a "closed" thesis statement for your essay, you will indicate your overall response to the source text and also indicate how you will develop that response in the body of your paper:

- I found parts of the essay confusing, especially its structure and many of its allusions.
- Because members of my family have been touched by the issues the author discusses, reading this essay proved to be an emotional challenge.

Either type of thesis can work equally well.

Finally, to capture reader interest you may want to use one of the following strategies:

- Open your essay with a provocative or interesting question raised by the reading or your response to it.
- Open your essay with an interesting quotation from the reading.
- Open your essay with a personal anecdote or hypothetical story related to the topic of the reading.
- Open your essay with a reference to a current controversy or public issue related to the topic of the reading.

Summarize the Source Text

After introducing the source and stating your thesis, give a brief summary of the reading. Generally, this summary will be only a paragraph or two long, highlighting the reading's most important findings, conclusions, or arguments. In the summary, anticipate what you will address in the body of your response. For example, if you know you will be questioning the validity of some of the author's claims, summarize his claims in this part of your essay. When they come up again in the body of your response, your reader will remember them and will be able to follow your assertions more easily.

State and Explain Your Responses Clearly and Concisely

In the body of your essay, you explore your responses, clearly and thoroughly, one at a time. This process might sound simple, but clearly and thoroughly stating and explaining your response to a reading can be difficult primarily because it is *your* response. The language you use when describing your reaction may make perfect sense to you but might well be unclear to your reader. For instance, if you were reading someone else's response essay and the writer complained that the source text made her feel "wheezy," would you really know what the person meant? Perhaps her explanation would make it clear, but the language she uses to characterize her response may hinder her readers' ability to understand her reaction. Therefore, a first step in clarifying your response for a reader is to choose language that others can understand. Likewise, explain the terms you use. For example, if you contend that a source is "confusing," explain whether you had difficulty understanding the writer's language, findings, structure, or some other aspect of the text.

Next, be sure to provide specific examples from the source text to help your reader understand each response. When you have a particular response to a reading, something on the page triggered it. In your essay, identify those "triggering" passages before you explain the dynamics of your response. For example, if you contend that a source text is confusing, identify and perhaps quote a passage you cannot understand, then explain what it is about the writing you find difficult to follow (the logic of the passage? the wording? the structure?).

WRITE YOUR CONCLUSION

With a response essay, your conclusion should restate your overall response to the source text, echoing your thesis. To give a sense of closure to your essay, you should also try to mirror the strategy you employed to capture reader interest in the opening of your essay. For example, if you opened your essay with a question, return to that question in your conclusion and provide an answer. If you opened with an anecdote or story, refer back to it in your conclusion, perhaps indicating how that anecdote or story turned out. If you opened with a quotation from the source text, consider closing with a quotation as well.

REVISE YOUR ROUGH DRAFT

As you revise the rough draft of your response, pay particular attention to your assertions, organization, language, and support.

Review Your Assertions

When you review the assertions you make in your response essay, your primary concern is accuracy:

- Have you truly captured your reactions to the reading?
- Have you openly, honestly, and thoroughly explored your response to the material?
- Does your essay offer an accurate representation of your reaction?
- When other people read your essay, will they be able to understand and appreciate your reaction?

To check your assertions, first reread the source text and see whether you still feel the same way about it. Even a short time away from a reading may enable you to reconsider your reactions—maybe your views have changed. If they have changed, revise your essay. Also, in reviewing the source text, be sure you reread the annotations you originally made. Have you addressed the concerns, questions, and reactions you noted as you earlier annotated the piece?

Review Your Support and Explanations

As you revise your response, examine the way you illustrate and explain each of your responses. Remember that your responses should be tied to specific aspects of the source text, such as words, images, and graphics. When you compose your response, you need to explain for your reader the link between the source text and your reaction. In the body of your essay, you should state a response, point out what aspect of the reading led to that reaction (perhaps quoting the passage), and then explain clearly and thoroughly how that material led you to that response. As you revise your draft, make sure you accomplish all three goals in each section of your essay.

Review Your Organization

Next, when you review the organization of your rough draft, check to be sure you have fully developed opening and closing sections and have a clearly stated thesis. In the body of your essay, be sure that you are developing only one response at a time. Often when you write your rough draft, examining one reaction will lead you to a new response, one you have not previously considered. That is one of the real powers of writing: it not only helps you capture ideas in words but often will help you generate new ideas as well. When this happens, some writers will follow that new idea even if it does not belong in that part of the essay, knowing that in the next draft they can place it elsewhere. Other writers prefer to write a note to themselves to explore that new idea later, not wanting to lose track of the idea they are currently exploring. When you review your rough draft, check to see that you are developing only one response at a time in your essay.

Finally, be sure you indicate to your reader—through paragraph breaks and transition words—when you shift focus from one response to the next. Adding these signals to your paper makes it easier for your reader to follow your line of thought. Since you are writing about *your* responses, you know when you have changed focus; your readers, though, may have a harder time recognizing the structure of your essay. Adding appropriate paragraph breaks and transitions can help.

Review Your Language

As indicated earlier, word choice—finding and choosing appropriate terms to express your reactions—can be truly problematic when you are writing response essays. First, your initial reactions to what you read may be so emotional or so abstract that you cannot put them into words. You may struggle to find appropriate language. Second, your first efforts at finding words may result in highly "private" writing; since they arise from your own knowledge and experience, the terms you use may make sense only to you. In this case, you need to find terms that can communicate your responses to others. Before you turn in the final draft of your response essay, be sure to have someone else read your work, someone you trust to give you an honest appraisal of your language. Ask that person to indicate any part of the response he or she does not understand because of the words you are using.

SAMPLE RESPONSE ESSAY

This sample essay is responding to "From *Animal House* to *Big Brother*: Student Privacy and Campus Safety in an Age of Accountability" by Ron Chesbrough, found in Chapter 4 of this book. If you are unfamiliar with the article, read it before you read the following response essay.

A Response to "From *Animal House* to *Big Brother*: Student Privacy and Campus Safety in an Age of Accountability"

As Ron Chesbrough notes in his essay "From *Animal House* to *Big Brother*: Student Privacy and Campus Safety in an Age of Accountability," violent episodes, like the shootings at Virginia Tech a few years ago, have raised serious concerns about campus safety. Though my roommates and I have discussed this issue a few times and we had a floor meeting to talk about emergency evacuation plans at the beginning of the term, Chesbrough's essay offers a perspective on the problem I hadn't considered: what policies can the administration at a school adopt to keep students safe? As a first-year college student, I found Chesbrough's essay informative but not very helpful. In the end, he fails to offer very satisfying answers to the problems he raises.

Campus safety happens to be an issue I deeply care about. When the shootings took place at Virginia Tech, my sister was attending Redford College, which is not far from Blacksburg. When I saw the news coverage on television, I started texting my sister immediately to be sure she was safe. She told me the students at her school were also keeping up with the story and were a little nervous, but that I shouldn't worry because nothing like that had ever happened at her school. I felt better, but when I thought about it, what happened at Virginia Tech could happen at any college in the country.

In his article, Chesbrough explores why the violence erupted at Tech and offers a few explanations I had not considered. For example, I had not realized the kinds of restrictions administrators face due to FERPA (the Family Education Rights and Privacy Act). From orientation, I knew that my school could not release my grades to anyone without my permission, even to my parents. I was surprised to learn that FERPA regulations might have kept the administrators at Virginia Tech from acting to prevent the attack. According to news reports, the shooter, Seung-Hui Cho, had a history of mental illness and had received treatment while a high school student. Virginia Tech officials were not informed of Cho's past problems, and when they started to emerge on campus, FERPA regulations kept administrators from telling his teachers or others because Cho did not authorize the release of that information.

This whole scenario is just frustrating, especially for college students like me who could be facing similar dangers and not know it. Respecting a student's privacy is important, but should privacy concerns override safety concerns? I think they should not, but Chesbrough explains why Tech officials did not act. "Due diligence" requirements would seem to mandate that school officials step in to restrain students whose behavior is dangerous. Not acting could open them to lawsuits should something terrible happen. However, if the officials act and nothing happens, they can be sued for violating the student's privacy. I agree with Chesbrough that parents should inform the administration of any pre-existing emotional problems a student has when he or she enters school. Instead of using this information to keep these students from enrolling at the school, administrators can use it to provide the students the help and support they need.

Chesbrough's ideas all seem reasonable, but I do not think they offer a satisfying response to the problem. When balancing the privacy needs of potentially dangerous students against the safety of the entire student body, schools should take greater action to protect the campus. Simply knowing up front which entering students have emotional and psychological problems does not guarantee that the students will seek appropriate treatment on campus. Instead, schools should consider provisional admission for these students— they can stay enrolled on campus as long as they verify that they are getting appropriate treatment. The treatment can remain private, but the administration has to make sure it is taking place. The campus health center could be charged with monitoring the students' treatment, ensuring that they are taking the medicines or receiving the counseling they need. If these students do not keep up with the treatments prescribed by their physician or therapist, they are expelled from school. This solution is not perfect because treatments are not perfect, but it would help ensure that troubled students are receiving help while maintaining their privacy.

Most of the time I do not worry about campus safety. If students take the right precautions on our campus (like never going out alone at night, staying with groups of people, locking doors and windows at night), they can avoid problems. After reading this article though, I am more concerned. How many students on campus have severe emotional or psychological problems? How many of them are getting help so that our school does not become another Virginia Tech?

Summary Chart

HOW TO WRITE A RESPONSE ESSAY

1. Carefully read the material.

Your goal is to form a clear understanding of what the writer has to say.

Identify and be able to paraphrase the writer's thesis and main assertions or findings.

2. Reread and annotate the text.

As you reread the material, begin to examine your responses by asking yourself the following questions:
- *How do I react emotionally to what the author has written?*
- *How do the ideas offered in the source text match my experience and my sense of reality?*
- *How do the ideas offered in the text match what others have had to say about the topic?*

Note in the margin your responses to these questions using some combination of the following:
- *key words*
- *questions*
- *statements*
- *punctuation marks*

When you are finished, write out in a few sentences your response to the material.

3. Compose your rough draft.

Introduce the topic, your source text, and the full name of the author or authors.

Summarize the source text.

State and explain your responses clearly and concisely one at a time.
- *State your response. (For example, the material made you angry.)*
- *Explain the terms you are using. (What do you mean by "angry"?)*

SUMMARY CHART: HOW TO WRITE A RESPONSE ESSAY *(CONTINUED)*

- *Tie that response to some aspect of the source text.*
  What material in the reading made you feel that way?
- *Explain how that material gave rise to that response.*
  Why or how did that material make you feel angry?
- *Write your conclusion.*
  What was your overall response to the material?

4. **Revise your rough draft.**

   Review your assertions about your reactions.
   - *Are they honest?*
   - *Are they informed?*
   - *Are they clear?*
   - *Are they well supported?*

   Review your organization.
   - *Are your opening and closing sections constructed well?*
   - *Are you addressing one response at a time?*
   - *Are there clear transitions between the responses you explore?*
   - *Are your responses tied to some guiding thesis?*

   Review your language.
   - *Are you using terms your readers are likely to understand?*
   - *Are you invoking a consistent tone, not becoming too informal, too angry, or too satiric when that does not match the tone of your response as a whole?*

   Review your support.
   - *Have you tied each response to some aspect of the text?*
   - *Have you added enough textual references to make clear the connections between the reading and your response?*
   - *Have you attempted to explain those connections?*

RESPONSE ESSAY REVISION CHECKLIST

	Yes	No
1. In the introductory section of your essay, have you: • introduced the topic of the reading? • included the full and exact title of the reading? • included the full name of the author?	_____ _____ _____	_____ _____ _____
2. Have you included a thesis statement that captures your overall response to the reading, a response you develop in the body of your essay?	_____	_____
3. Have you considered the accuracy and honesty of the responses you include in your essay?	_____	_____
4. Have you clearly stated each of these responses?	_____	_____
5. Have you explained the terms you used to characterize each of your responses?	_____	_____
6. Have you tied each of your responses to some aspect of the source that gave rise to it?	_____	_____
7. Have you explained how the material in the source text gave rise to your response?	_____	_____
8. Have you developed only one response at a time in each section of your essay?	_____	_____
9. Have you used language that helps your reader understand when you are moving from your discussion of one response to the next?	_____	_____
10. Have you explained the connection between each response you explore and your overall thesis?	_____	_____
11. Have you reviewed the language you use to make sure your word choice is clear and accurate?	_____	_____

Chapter 6

CRITIQUE

DEFINITION AND PURPOSE

While response essays focus on your personal reactions to a reading, critiques offer a more formal evaluation. Instead of responding to a reading in light of your experience and feelings, in a critique you evaluate a source text's quality or worth according to a set of established criteria. Based on your evaluation, you then assert some judgment concerning the text—whether the reading was effective, ineffective, valuable, or trivial. Critiques, then, are usually argumentative. Your goal is to convince your readers to accept your judgments concerning the quality of the reading.

These judgments will be based on certain criteria and standards. **Criteria** are certain aspects of a reading that serve as the basis of your assessment—for example, the text's style or use of evidence. **Standards** serve as the basis for evaluating a criterion—what makes a certain "style" good or bad, acceptable or unacceptable? What counts as "valid" evidence in a reading? When you critique a reading, you will employ either **general** academic criteria and standards (those used to evaluate source material in many fields) or **discipline-specific** criteria and standards (those used by scholars in a particular field of study and generally not applicable to material studied in other disciplines).

In college composition courses you may learn how to critique a source text using general evaluative criteria—for example, how to assess the quality of a reading based on its structure, style, or evidence. These criteria can help you evaluate source material in a variety of classes. In your other college courses you may learn discipline-specific evaluative criteria typically used to assess source material in that field of study. For example, in an English literature course you may learn the criteria used by scholars to critique a poem or a play; in an accounting class, you may learn to employ the criteria and standards experts in that discipline use to critique a financial report or prospectus.

Students often find the idea of writing a critique intimidating: they are not sure what the assignment is asking them to do, how to generate material for their paper, what to include in their essay, how to support their assertions, or what tone to assume. However, you are probably more familiar with this type of writing than you realize since you are often exposed to one special form of critique: the movie review. If you ever listened to movie critics argue over a film, you are familiar with the basic structure of a critique. If you ever discussed the strengths and weaknesses of a movie and tried to get a friend to go see it (or to avoid it), then you have already engaged in critique. Examining how a film critic writes a review of a movie can help you understand how to write a critique of a reading.

THE FILM REVIEW AS CRITIQUE

First, consider the nature of a movie critic's job: he watches a film, analyzes and evaluates what he sees, forms some judgment based on that analysis and evaluation, then writes his review, trying to clarify and defend his judgments with specific references to the film and clear explanations of his assertions. In writing his review, the critic does not address every aspect of the film; he addresses only those aspects of the movie that best support his judgment of it. If, for instance, he thought a film was wonderful, he would address in his review only the aspects of the film that, in his opinion, made it exceptional— for example, the direction, the photography, and the acting. If he thought the film was uneven—some parts good, other parts weak—he would offer in his review examples of what made the film effective (maybe the plot or the lighting) and examples of what made it ineffective (maybe the musical score and the special effects).

Think about the way you discuss a film with someone. Maybe the conversation runs something like this:

> "So, did you like the movie?"
>
> "Yeah, pretty much. I wasn't too sure about some of the dialogue— sounded pretty lame sometimes—but the special effects were good and the acting was ok."
>
> "The acting was just 'ok'? What didn't you like? I thought the acting was great."
>
> "Well, there was that scene early in the film, right before he shot the guy; I just didn't buy it when he . . . ."

In this conversation, one friend asserts a position about the film, is challenged, then begins to defend or explain her view. To convince her friend to accept her judgment, she will likely discuss specific aspects of the film she believes best illustrate her views.

Most of us are accustomed to talking about movies, television shows, or CDs this way—we form and defend judgments about what we see, hear, and read all the time. However, we are usually more comfortable evaluating movies than we are critiquing arguments, book chapters, or lab reports. First, when it comes to movies, we are probably familiar with many of the source texts—we have seen lots of films—and most of us feel we can knowledgeably discuss what we have seen. We can generate, fairly easily, lots of examples from a movie to support our views. Second, we know *how* to talk about films: we know how to identify and discuss particular aspects of a movie—certain criteria—that influence our judgment. We know that when we analyze a movie we can address the dialogue, the acting, the special effects, and so forth. Finally, we know the standards usually applied to evaluate various aspects of a film; we know what passes for good dialogue, good acting, good special effects, and so on. In short, when we discuss a movie, we know how to *analyze* it (what parts to focus on for review), *evaluate* it (what kinds of questions to ask of each part when assessing its quality), and *defend* our assertions (how to examine specific scenes from the film that support our judgments).

These are the same basic skills you employ to critique readings in college. To critique readings, you need to engage in:

- *Analysis*—break readings down into their essential parts.
- *Evaluation*—assess the quality of those various parts.
- *Explanation*—link your judgments to specific aspects of the readings and make those connections clear and convincing to your reader.

Even though you have probably engaged in this process quite often when discussing movies or television shows, you may have a hard time using these skills to critique readings. First, you are probably less familiar with how critiques look and sound than you are with how movie reviews look and sound. When you are assigned to write a critique, no model may come to mind. Second, the readings you are asked to critique in college can be hard to understand. You cannot critique a reading until you are certain you know what it has to say. Finally, you are probably less familiar with the criteria and standards used in college to analyze and critique readings than you are with the criteria and standards used to review films. When you are asked to critique a philosophical essay on the nature of knowledge, do you know how to break that reading down into its key parts and what kinds of questions to ask of each part to determine its quality? When asked to critique a chapter of your history book, do you know what to look for, what questions to ask? Learning how to critique readings such as these is a central goal of your college education, a skill you will obtain through practice in many different disciplines.

Examining how a movie critic organizes a review can also help you understand how to structure a critique. For example, a critic typically opens her review with a "thesis" that captures her overall assessment of the film. This thesis may take the form of a statement early in the review, a graphic placed beside the review—for example, five stars or two stars—or frequently a comment at the end of the review. Sometimes the critic will love the film; she will give it five stars and a rave review. Sometimes she will hate the movie; she will give it one star and a terrible review. Still other times she will have a split decision; she will give it two and a half stars and in her review acknowledge the strengths and weaknesses of the movie. Next, the critic will typically offer a brief summary of the film so her readers can follow what she has to say in the review. Then, in the body of the review, she will address only the aspects of the film that best illustrate or defend her thesis: she will introduce a particular element of the film (for example, the special effects), comment on its quality (claim they were especially effective), describe a specific example or two from the film (perhaps the climactic battle scene), and explain how that specific example illustrates or supports her judgment (what made the special effects in that battle scene especially good).

Writing a critique involves much the same process. After reading the text, you'll form a judgment of its quality or worth based on some set of criteria and standards. This judgment will form the thesis of your critique, which you will explain or defend in the body of your essay, with specific references to the reading. As you draft your thesis, keep in mind the range of judgments open to the film critic. To critique a reading does not necessarily mean only to criticize it. If you honestly think a reading is weak, based on your evaluation of its various parts, then say so in your thesis. If, however, you think the writing is quite strong, say that. If your judgments fall somewhere in the middle—some parts are strong while others are weak—reflect *that* in your thesis. Your thesis should reflect your carefully considered opinion of the reading's overall quality or worth, whatever that judgment may be.

Next, you will offer a brief summary of the text so your reader can follow what you later have to say about the piece. In the body of your critique, you will choose for examination only the parts of the reading that best illustrate or defend your thesis: you will introduce a particular aspect of the reading (for example, its use of statistical evidence), describe a specific example or two from the reading (perhaps the way statistics are used to support the author's second argument), and explain how that specific example illustrates or supports your judgment (what makes the statistical evidence especially compelling in this section of the text).

Your goal, then, in writing a critique mirrors in many ways the goal you would have in writing a movie review. Your task is to analyze and evaluate a reading according to a set of established criteria and standards, pass judgment on the reading's quality or worth, then assert, explain, and defend that judgment with specific references to the reading.

WRITING A CRITIQUE

Writing a critique typically involves five steps:

1. Read and annotate the text.
2. Analyze and evaluate the piece: break it down into its primary parts and judge the quality of each part.
3. Write your thesis and decide which aspects of the reading you will focus on in your essay.
4. Compose your rough draft.
5. Rewrite your critique.

This is only a general guide. Throughout college you will learn much more specific, specialized ways to critique readings.

STEP 1—CAREFULLY READ AND ANNOTATE THE SOURCE TEXT

Before you start to write a critique, you first need to develop a clear understanding of the reading you are about to analyze and evaluate. The material you read in college is often challenging; you have to work hard to understand exactly what the author is asserting. However, this work is unavoidable; it makes little sense to evaluate a piece of writing when you are not completely sure what point the author is attempting to make. As you annotate a reading for a critique, keep in mind the following suggestions.

Note the Author's Thesis, Primary Assertions, and Primary Means of Support

Be sure that you mark the author's thesis, highlight and summarize each major point the author makes, and highlight and summarize how the author supports each idea, argument, or finding. Are the thesis and primary assertions clearly stated? Does the thesis direct the development of the paper? Are the assertions supported?

Note the Author's Use of Graphics, Headings, and Subheadings

What graphics does the author provide? What is their function? How do the headings and subheadings organize the piece? Are the headings and graphics effective? How so?

Note the Author's Diction and Word Choice

Consider the kind of language the writer is employing. Is it formal or informal? Is it overly technical? Is it appropriate? Do you notice any shifts in diction? Are some sections of the text more complicated or jargon laden than others? Note any strengths or weaknesses you see in the author's language.

Note the Author's Tone

What seems to be the author's attitude toward the topic? Is he being serious, comical, or satiric? Does the tone seem appropriate, given the writer's topic and thesis? Are there any places in the text where the tone shifts? Is the shift effective?

Note the Author's Audience

When you finish the piece, determine what the writer seemed to assume about his readers. For example, is the writer addressing someone who knows something about the topic or someone likely reading about it for the first time? Is the author assuming readers agree or disagree with the position being forwarded in the piece? Judging from the content, organization, diction, and tone of the piece, which type of reader would tend to accept the author's position and which would tend to reject it?

Note the Author's Purpose

Decide, in your own mind, the primary aim of the piece. Is the author attempting to entertain, inform, or persuade readers? Where in the text has the author attempted to achieve this aim? How successful are those attempts? Note at the beginning or end of the reading your comments concerning the author's purpose.

Summarize the Piece

After you have read and studied the text, write a brief summary of the piece, either at the end of the reading or on a separate sheet of paper (see Chapter 5 for tips on summarizing a reading).

When you have finished reading, rereading, and annotating the source text, you should have a clear understanding of its content, organization, purpose, and audience. Try to clear up any questions you have about the reading before you attempt to critique it. You want your critique to be based on a thorough and clear understanding of the source text.

STEP 2—ANALYZE AND EVALUATE THE READING

Think back to the process of putting together a movie review. When a movie critic watches a film, she forms a judgment of its quality based on certain things she sees or hears. As she watches the movie, she will examine and judge certain aspects of the film, including its

acting	scenery	lighting
direction	costuming	plot
special effects	dialogue	action
theme	pacing	makeup
cinematography	stunts	music

Her evaluation of these various elements of the film, either positive or negative, will form her overall judgment of the movie—her thesis.

What, then, should you look for when analyzing a reading? What parts of a text should you be isolating for evaluation as you read and reread the piece? In part, the answer depends on the course you are taking: each discipline has generally agreed-on ways of analyzing a reading. As you take courses in anthropology or physical education, you will learn how experts in those fields analyze readings. However, analyzing certain general aspects of a reading can help you better understand material in a wide variety of classes. Regardless of the course you are taking, you might start to analyze a reading by identifying its:

- thesis and primary assertions or findings,
- evidence and reasoning,
- organization, and
- style.

Once you have analyzed a reading, isolating for consideration its essential elements, your next task in writing a critique is to evaluate the quality of each element. Here, writing a critique differs from writing a response essay. In a response essay, your goal is to articulate your personal, subjective reaction to what you have read. In a critique, though, you are expected to evaluate the reading according to an established set of standards. Think about the movie critic's job again. Most reviewers employ similar criteria and standards when evaluating a film. If a reviewer decides to critique the musical score of a film, she knows the types of evaluative questions one usually asks about this aspect of a movie: How did the music contribute to the overall mood of the film? Was it too intrusive? Did it add humor or depth to the scenes? Did it heighten drama? Was it noteworthy because of the performers who recorded it? Her answers to these questions will lead to her final assessment of this particular aspect of the film. (Of course, another reviewer employing the same criteria and applying the same standards could come to a different judgment concerning the quality of the music in the film; for example, one reviewer might think it heightened the drama in a particular scene while another might think that it did not.)

In college, you will quickly discover that the criteria and standards used to evaluate readings vary from discipline to discipline. Teachers often employ evaluative criteria unique to their field of study, especially in upper-level courses in which the professor is preparing students to enter a profession. In lower-level courses designed to introduce you to a field of study, you may encounter a different sort of problem. Teachers in different fields may be asking you to employ the same or similar criteria, but their standards are very different. Suppose, for example, you are asked to evaluate the style of a particular reading in both an education and an English course. Your job is the same—determine, stylistically, whether this is a well-written essay. Your answer might be different in each class. According to the stylistic standards advocated by the school of education, you might have before you a well-written essay. According to the standards advocated by the English department, however, the same piece of writing might not fare so well. As always, work closely with your teacher when evaluating a reading to be sure you are applying an appropriate set of criteria and standards.

Below is a series of questions you can ask to begin your analysis and evaluation of a reading's thesis, assertions, evidence, reasoning, organization, and style. The questions are meant to serve only as general guidelines. Your teacher may have much more specific questions he would like you to ask of a reading or evaluative criteria he would like you to employ. Together, analysis and evaluation enable you to critique a reading. After breaking a reading into its essential parts and judging their effectiveness, you will form the thesis of your critique—a judgment of the reading's quality or worth—which you will develop and defend in your essay.

Analyzing and Evaluating a Reading's Thesis and Primary Assertions or Findings

Sometimes identifying an author's thesis can be relatively easy—you can point to a specific sentence or two in the text. Other times, though, an author will not state his thesis. Instead, the thesis is implied: some controlling idea is directing the development of the piece even though the author never puts it into words. If this is the case, you will need to identify and paraphrase this controlling idea yourself and evaluate it as if it were the thesis.

Many times, identifying the author's primary assertions or findings can be easy, too. For example, if the author has made effective use of paragraph breaks, topic sentences, headings, or graphics, you can usually locate his primary assertions fairly easily. However, do not rely on these means alone to identify the author's main ideas. Not every source text is well written. Often, important assertions get buried in an article; key findings may be glossed over. As you analyze a reading, make up your mind about its primary assertions or findings independently of what the author may indicate. Also, be sure to distinguish between primary assertions and their evidence or support. Very often a student will identify as a primary argument of a reading some statistic or quotation that the author is using only as a piece of evidence, something to support the actual assertion he is trying to make. In short, to analyze a reading's thesis and primary assertions, consider the following questions:

- What is the author's thesis? Is it stated or unstated? If stated, highlight it; if unstated, paraphrase it.
- What are the primary assertions in the reading? Highlight each one and paraphrase it in the margin of the text.
- What is the primary means of support offered to illustrate or defend each assertion? Again, highlight this material.

In determining the quality of a reading's thesis and primary assertions or findings, you can begin by questioning their clarity, effectiveness, and organization. The thesis, whether stated or implied, should direct the development of the piece. Each major finding or assertion should be clearly stated and linked to that thesis through the effective use of transitions, repetition of key terms, or headings. To evaluate an author's thesis and findings, you might begin by asking the following questions. If your answers are positive, you can likely claim that the author has effectively presented and developed his thesis; if your answers are negative, be sure to articulate exactly where the problems exist.

- Is the thesis clearly stated? Does it control the organization of the piece? Is it consistently held or does the author shift positions in the essay?
- If the thesis is implied rather than stated, does it still serve to direct the organization of the piece? Are you able to paraphrase a comprehensive thesis on your own, or does the material included in the piece preclude that?
- Are the author's assertions or findings clearly stated?
- Are the author's assertions or findings somehow tied to the thesis?

Analyzing and Evaluating a Reading's Evidence and Reasoning

Here you identify two separate, but related, aspects of a reading: (1) the evidence an author provides to support or illustrate her assertions and (2) the author's reasoning process or line of argument.

First, try to identify the types of **evidence** the author uses to support her thesis. (At this point do not try to evaluate the effectiveness of the evidence—that comes later.) The types of evidence used to support a thesis vary greatly in academic writing, so again be cautious when using these guidelines to analyze the readings in any particular course. However, to begin your analysis of the evidence an author employs, you might try asking yourself this series of questions:

- In supporting her assertions or findings, what kinds of evidence has the author employed? Has the author used any of these forms of evidence:

statistics	empirical data	precedent
expert testimony	emotional appeals	case histories
personal experience	historical analysis	analogies

- Where in the article is each type of evidence employed?
- Is there a pattern? Are certain types of evidence used to support certain types of claims?
- Where has the author combined forms of evidence as a means of support?

Analyzing an author's **reasoning process** is more difficult because it is more abstract. First, you identify how the author uses evidence to support her thesis and how she develops and explains her ideas, her line of reasoning. Second, you examine the assumptions an author makes concerning her topic and readers. As she wrote the piece, which aspects of the text did she decide needed more development than others? Which terms needed clarification? Which argument or explanation needed the most support? In analyzing the author's reasoning process, these are the kinds of questions you might ask:

- In what order are the ideas, arguments, or findings presented?
- What are the logical connections between the major assertions being made in the piece? How does one idea lead to the next?
- What passages in the text explain these connections?
- What assumptions about the topic or the reader is the author making?
- Where in the text are these assumptions articulated, explained, or defended?

Standards used to assess the quality of an author's evidence and reasoning will vary greatly across the disciplines. For example, you might want to determine whether an author offers "adequate" support for his or her thesis. However, what passes for adequate support of a claim will be quite different in an English class from what it will be in a physics course or a statistics course: these fields of study each look at "evidence" and the notion of "adequacy" very differently. In other words, a good general strategy to employ when critiquing a reading is to determine the adequacy of its evidence; however, how that strategy is implemented and what conclusions you reach employing it can vary depending on the course you are taking. Part of learning any subject matter is coming to understand how scholars in that field evaluate evidence; therefore, answer the following questions thoughtfully:

- Does the author support her contentions or findings?
- Is this support adequate? Does the author offer enough evidence to support her contentions?
- Is the evidence authoritative? Does it come from legitimate sources? Is it current?
- Does the author explain *how* the evidence supports or illustrates her assertions?
- Has the author ignored evidence, alternative hypotheses, or alternative explanations for the evidence she offers?
- In developing her position, are there any problems with unstated assumptions? Does the author assume something to be the case that she needs to clarify or defend?
- Are there problems with logical fallacies such as hasty generalizations, false dilemmas, or appeals to false authorities?
- Has the author addressed the ethical implications of her position?
- Is the author's reasoning a notable strength in the piece? Is it clear and convincing?

Your answers to these questions will help you determine whether there are serious problems with the evidence and reasoning employed in the reading.

Analyzing and Evaluating a Reading's Organization

Here you want to identify how the author orders the material contained in the reading. As the author develops a set of findings or ideas, lays out his reasoning for the reader, and offers examples and explanations, what comes first? Second? Third? How has the author attempted to mold these parts into a coherent whole? When analyzing the organization of a reading, you might begin by considering the following questions:

- In what order are the ideas or findings presented?
- How has the author indicated that he is moving from a discussion of one point to the discussion of another point?
- What is the relationship between the thesis of the piece (stated or unstated) and the order in which the assertions or findings are presented?
- How has the author tried to help the reader understand the organization of the reading? Identify where in the text the author has used any of the following to help guide his readers through the text:

headings and subheadings	repetition of key terms
transition words or phrases	repetition of language from the thesis
transition paragraphs	repetition of names or titles

If any aspect of a reading's organization makes it difficult for you to understand the author's message, you may want to examine it in your critique. Clearly explain the nature of the problem and how it damages the reading's effectiveness. Likewise, if the organization is especially strong, if it significantly enhances the reading's clarity or effectiveness, you can point that out in your critique and explain how it helps the text. Here are some questions to consider when evaluating the source text's organization:

- Is there a clear connection between the major assertions of the essay? Does there seem to be some reason why one idea precedes or follows another?
- Are all the assertions clearly related to the overall thesis of the piece?
- Has the author provided headings or subheadings to help readers follow his line of thought? How effective are they?
- Has the author provided adequate transitions to help readers move through the writing and see the logical connection between the assertions he is making? How effective are they?

Analyzing and Evaluating a Reading's Style

Stylistic analysis is a complicated process—an academic specialty in and of itself within the field of English studies. In most of your college courses, though, when analyzing style you will likely focus on issues of clarity and convention. First, when you critique a reading, you might comment on its clarity. You will want to identify which aspects of the writer's word choice and sentence structure help you understand what she has to say or which serve to complicate your reading of the text. Other times, you may ask a different set of questions concerning style, especially in upper-division courses. Your assignment will be to assess how well an author adheres to the stylistic conventions of a discipline. For example, you might explore whether the author's language, tone, and syntax are appropriate for a particular type of writing or field of study. To begin your analysis of style, here are some questions you might ask about a reading:

- What level of diction is the writer employing (how formal is the prose)?

  formal   conversational
  informal   a mixture

  Identify which words or passages lead you to this conclusion.
- What is the tone of the piece (what is the author's apparent attitude toward the topic)?

  serious   satiric   involved
  humorous   angry   detached

  Identify which words or passages lead you to this conclusion.
- What kind of language is used in the piece? Identify any passages using specialized language, emotional language, or jargon.
- What types of sentences are used in the reading?

  simple, compound, complex, complex-compound
  long or short
  active or passive
  a mixture of types

When critiquing a reading's style, you evaluate elements of the author's prose such as diction, tone, word choice, and syntax. Again, stylistic standards vary greatly across the disciplines. While teachers in various disciplines may use similar terms when describing "good" style in writing—that it should be clear and concise, for example—how they define their criteria is likely to vary. Clear and concise writing in a chemistry lab report may have little in common, stylistically, with clear and concise writing in a philosophy research report. Below are some questions that might help you begin to evaluate certain aspects of an author's style. Remember, though, that your answers may well depend on the stylistic standards accepted by a particular discipline:

- How would you characterize the diction of the piece: formal, informal, or somewhere in the middle? Is it consistently maintained? Is it appropriate? Does it contribute to the effectiveness of the piece?
- How would you characterize the tone of the piece? Is it inviting, satiric, or humorous? Is it appropriate, given the topic and intent of the piece? Does the tone enhance or damage the effect of the writing?

- Is the author's word choice clear and effective? Or does the writer rely too heavily on jargon, abstractions, or highly technical terms?
- Is the author's word choice needlessly inflammatory or emotional? Or do the words convey appropriate connotations?
- Are the sentences clearly written? Are any of the sentences so poorly structured that the source is difficult to read and understand?
- Are the sentence types varied? Is the syntax appropriate given the audience and intent of the piece?

STEP 3—WRITE YOUR THESIS AND DECIDE WHICH ASPECTS OF THE READING WILL BE THE FOCUS OF YOUR ESSAY

At this point you need to develop your thesis and decide which aspects of the reading you will use to develop your critique. To formulate your thesis, you need to decide which elements of the source text best illustrate or defend your judgment. You want your reader to understand and accept your thesis, but this acceptance can come about only if you clearly explain each claim you make about the reading and offer convincing examples from the text to illustrate and defend your contentions.

In your critique, you do not need to address every aspect of the source text. Remember how the movie critic supports her assertions about a film. No review addresses every aspect of a movie. Instead, the critic chooses to discuss in her review only those elements of the movie she thinks most clearly and effectively illustrate her judgment. Maybe she will address only the acting and direction, perhaps only the dialogue, plot, and special effects. Perhaps she will choose to mention, only briefly, the costuming and musical score, then concentrate more attention on the film's cinematography.

Follow the same line of thinking when you decide which aspects of the reading to address in your critique. To illustrate and defend your thesis, you may choose to look only at the logic of the piece and its structure. However, you may choose to ignore both of these and concentrate, instead, on the writer's style. Maybe you will decide to look briefly at the evidence the author offers, then concentrate most of your attention on the organization of the piece. Your decisions should be based on two fairly simple questions: (1) Which aspects of the reading most influenced your judgment of its quality and worth? (2) Which aspects will best illustrate and support your thesis? Choose only those aspects of the reading for examination in your critique.

Your thesis in a critique is a brief statement of what you believe to be the overall value or worth of the source text based on your analysis and evaluation of its parts. In stating your thesis, you have several options. You can say only positive things about the reading, only negative things, or some mixture of the two. Your main concern at this point is that your thesis honestly and accurately reflects your judgment.

Also, your thesis statement can be either open or closed. In an open thesis statement, you offer your overall judgment of the piece and nothing else. In a closed thesis statement you offer your judgment and indicate which aspects of the reading you will examine when developing your essay. Below are some sample open and closed thesis statements for a critique—positive, negative, and mixed.

Positive Thesis Statement

Open

Jones presents a clear, convincing argument in favor of increased funding for the school district.

Closed

Through his use of precise examples and his accessible style, Jones presents a clear and convincing argument in favor of increased funding for the school district.

Negative Thesis Statement

Open

Jones's argument in favor of increased funding is not convincing.

Closed

Due to numerous lapses in reasoning and problems with the organization, Jones's argument in favor of increased funding is not convincing.

Mixed Thesis Statement

Open

Although uneven in its presentation, Jones's argument in favor of increased funding for the school district is, ultimately, convincing.

Closed

Even though there are some problems with the organization Jones employs in his report, his use of expert testimony makes his argument for increased funding for the schools convincing.

STEP 4—WRITE YOUR ROUGH DRAFT

While there are many ways to structure a critique, the suggestions that follow can serve as a general guide.

Introductory Section

- Introduce the topic of the reading.
- Give the title of the piece and the name of its author.
- Give your thesis.
- Summarize the source text.

In the opening section of your critique you should introduce the topic of the reading and give your reader its exact title and the full name of its author. You will also include here your thesis and a brief summary of the reading (one or two paragraphs long). The exact order you choose to follow when covering this material is up to you. Some writers like to begin with the summary of the source text before giving their thesis; some prefer to give their thesis first. Overall, though, your introductory section should only be two or three paragraphs long.

Body

- Examine one element of the reading at a time.
- Cite specific examples of this element from the reading.
- Explain your evaluation of each example you offer.

State the Criteria and Your Judgments

In the body of your critique you will explain and defend the judgment you made in your thesis, focusing on one aspect of the reading at a time. Topic sentences in a critique usually indicate the element of the reading you will be examining in that part of the essay and whether you found it to be a strength or liability—for example, "One of the real strengths of the essay is the author's use of emotional language."

Offer Examples

Whatever aspect of the reading you are examining—logic, word choice, structure—give your readers specific examples from the source text to clarify your terms and demonstrate that your judgment is sound. For example, the student who hopes to prove that the author's use of emotional language is one of the reading's strengths will need to quote several examples of language from the text he believes are emotional. Offering only one example might not be convincing; readers might question whether the student isolated for praise or criticism the single occurrence of that element in the text.

Explain Your Judgments

After you have specified the aspect of the reading you are examining in that part of your critique and have offered your readers examples from the text, you will need to explain and defend your judgment. After the student mentioned above cites a few specific examples of the author's emotional language, he will need to explain clearly and convincingly *how* that language strengthens the author's writing. Simply saying it does is not good enough. The student will have to explain how this type of language helps make the author's article clearer or more convincing.

In this section of the critique you will likely develop and explain your unique perspective on the reading. Suppose you and your friend are critiquing the same reading. You could both agree that it is effective and could even choose to focus on the same elements of the reading to defend and illustrate this judgment; for example, you could both choose to focus on the author's use of evidence. The two of you will probably differ, though, in your explanation of how and why the author's use of evidence is strong. You will offer your individual assessments of how the writer effectively employed evidence to support his thesis.

Conclusion

- Wrap up the paper.
- Reassert the thesis.

In your concluding section, try to give your reader a sense of closure. Consider mirroring in your conclusion the strategy you used to open your critique. For example, if you opened your essay with a question, consider closing it by answering that question; if you began with a quotation, end with a quotation; if you opened with a story, finish the story. You might also consider restating your thesis—your overall assessment of the piece—to remind your readers of the judgments you developed in the body of your essay.

STEP 5—REWRITE YOUR CRITIQUE

In rewriting your critique, check to make sure your work is accurate, thorough, organized, and clear.

- *Accurate*—it reflects your true assessment of the source text.
- *Thorough*—you completely explain your assertions.
- *Organized*—readers can easily follow the development of your critique.
- *Clear*—you have explained all the terms you need to explain and supported any assumptions that might reasonably be questioned.

Check for Accuracy

When reviewing your work, first check for accuracy. You want to be sure that your essay reflects your honest assessment of the source text. Starting with your thesis, look through your essay to make sure the assertions you make, the supporting material you employ, and the explanations you offer accurately reflect your point of view.

Check the Development of Your Assertions

Next, make sure you have been thorough in developing your critique. Check to be sure you have offered examples from the source text to support and illustrate your claims and that you have explained your reasoning clearly and completely. Add material—quotations, examples, and explanations—where you think it is needed.

Check the Organization

As you review the organization of your critique, make sure your thesis guides the development of your essay. Are you examining only one aspect of the reading at a time? If not, move material around to improve the organization in your essay. Have you provided adequate transitions to help your reader move through the piece? Do you repeat key terms or provide transition words that remind your reader of your thesis or signal the relationship between the various assertions you make?

Check for Clarity

Check your critique for clarity. Have you used any terms that need to be defined? Have you made any assertions that readers would find unclear? Have you made any assumptions that need to be explained or defended? When necessary, change the content, word choice, or sentence structure of your essay to make your ideas more accessible to your readers.

READINGS

The essay "Zero Tolerance and Student Dress Codes" by Nathan Essex was published in *Principal*. "A Uniform Look," by Yasmine L. Konheim-Kalkstein, appeared in the *American School Board Journal*. Following the readings is a sample critique essay.

Zero Tolerance and Student Dress Codes

Nathan L. Essex

Nathan L. Essex is a professor of law and president of Southwest Tennessee Community College.

In recent years, zero-tolerance policies have emerged in public schools as a means of reducing and preventing violence. From their inception, most of these policies were aimed at deterring serious student offenses involving possession of firearms and other weapons, drugs, tobacco, and alcohol.

However, zero-tolerance is taking a different twist in a small Texas school district where over 700 students were suspended in a single month last year for violating a zero-tolerance dress code policy. Under its policy involving student dress, the suburban Duncanville Independent School District in Texas penalizes students in grades 7–12 with a one-day suspension for the first violation, two days for a second violation, and two days plus loss of school privileges for a third violation.

These suspensions, which attracted national attention and threats of lawsuits by parents, raise four fundamental questions:

- How far should school officials go in enforcing zero-tolerance policy relating to student dress?
- Does the student dress in question pose a health or safety hazard?
- Does student dress create material or substantial disruption?
- Is there an educational justification for zero-tolerance dress code restrictions?

There is little debate that school officials are vested with broad and implied powers designed to protect the health and safety of students and maintain a peaceful school environment. Consequently, school officials may promulgate *reasonable* rules and regulations necessary to address health and safety concerns and orderly conduct among students (Essex 2002). A central issue involving zero-tolerance in the Texas district is whether the dress code policy is reasonable. Emphasis on reasonableness centers around the well-established fact that students have protected constitutional rights and that those rights must be weighed against a compelling need to restrict them.

Courts have generally supported the view that school boards have the authority to regulate student dress and appearance if they become so extreme as to interfere with the school's favorable learning atmosphere (Alexander and Alexander 2001). Challenges to dress code enforcement have relied on a number of legal issues, including First Amendment freedom of speech and Fourteenth Amendment rights to due process and liberty. However, the courts have not consistently agreed upon application of these rules regarding dress code enforcement. For example, they have upheld regulations prohibiting excessively tight skirts or pants and skirts more than six inches above the knee, while disallowing regulations prohibiting Freda trousers, tie-dyed clothing, and long skirts.

Justifying Dress Codes

Codes that place restrictions on student dress are not unusual in public schools. However, they must be justified by demonstrating that the students' attire materially or substantially disrupts school operations, infringes on the rights of others, creates health and safety concerns, or focuses too much attention to students' anatomy. According to the *Tinker* ruling, disruption must be viewed as more than a mere desire to avoid the discomfort and unpleasantness that always accompanies an unpopular view or an unidentified fear or apprehension (*Tinker v. Des Moines Independent Community School District*, 393 US 503 at 511.89 S. Ct. 733, 21 L. Ed. 2nd, 731 1969).

However the courts provide broad latitude to school officials on matters involving dress so long as they provide a justification for invoking restrictions. Dress is generally viewed as a form of self-expression reflecting a student's values, background, culture, and personality. Thus, students must be provided opportunities for self-expression within reasonable limits. Student rights regarding dress must be balanced with school officials' responsibility to provide a safe, secure, and orderly educational environment for all students.

Therefore, while students have a responsibility to conform to reasonable dress standards, school officials have a responsibility to ensure that rules do not unduly restrict the personal rights of students. As school officials implement zero-tolerance policies, they are expected to do so in a thoughtful and deliberate fashion, ensuring that their approach is fundamentally fair and legally defensible. Dress codes that do not weigh the severity of the infraction, the student's history of past behavior, the process, and First Amendment rights are at best highly risky.

A Drastic Dress Code

In the Duncanville District, the dress code forbids Capri pants, overalls, sweat pants, athletic jerseys, tank tops, and tube tops. Students are not permitted to wear low-riding, hip-hugging pants or display body piercing. No hats or hooded sweatshirts may be worn. Belts are required unless pants or skirts lack belt loops. Shirts and blouses must be tucked in at all times and should be long enough to stay in. No dress or grooming is permitted that, in the principal's judgment, is "startling, unusual, immodest, disruptive, or brings undue attention to the student's anatomy."

As can be seen, many of these requirements are highly subjective and may create confusion for students. For example, what constitutes unusual or startling dress? School rules should not be so broad and nebulous as to allow for arbitrary and inconsistent interpretation. Fundamental fairness requires that students know precisely what behaviors are required of them by school officials.

It is important to remember that schools must exercise fair and reasonable administrative authority that will withstand court scrutiny. For example, there is a question as to whether the suspension of a 13-year-old honor student for having her shirt untucked was reasonable, even though she immediately tucked it in after she was pulled aside by an administrator. Another student was suspended when her shirt had come untucked when she sat down, and she was not allowed to tuck it back. All students were asked to stand up in their classrooms so that an administrator could determine whether shirts were tucked in and belts worn. If these practices were challenged in court, there would likely be a question of fairness, particularly if no disruption occurred, the student had no history of misbehavior and, did in fact, attempt to conform to the school's policy.

The Key Element: Fairness

School officials should proceed with caution as they develop dress codes, especially those that involve zero-tolerance. Student dress may be restricted if school officials can provide concrete evidence that it communicates a message that appears to invite disruption. However, if student dress does not communicate such a message, school officials must demonstrate a reasonable justification for restrictions. The burden of proof rests with them, although community representatives—parents, community leaders, and citizens—should be involved in the policy development to ensure that it reflects community values and sentiments.

Policies that do not take into account the seriousness of the infraction, the student's record of behavior in school, and the immediate need to act are very risky, as are dress codes that provide no flexibility in enforcement and result in suspension for very minor infractions. When challenged in these cases, the burden will fall on school officials to justify the rules on the basis of past disruption or a legitimately based expectation of disruption.

School officials should always be guided by fundamental fairness and a regard for the individual rights of all students. The Supreme Court's *Tinker v. Des Moines* case reminded all of us that students do not shed their constitutional rights at the schoolhouse door. In formulating dress codes, school officials should demonstrate fairness not because the court requires it, but because it is the right thing to do.

References

Alexander, Kern and David Alexander. *American Public School Law,* 5th ed. Belmont, Calif.: West/Thomson Learning. 2001.

Essex, Nathan. *School Law and Public School: A Practical Guide for School Leaders,* 2nd ed. Boston: Allyn and Bacon. 2002.

A Uniform Look

Yasmine L. Konheim-Kalkstein

Yasmine Konheim-Kalkstein *is a doctoral student in educational psychology at the University of Minnesota.*

Since the 1990s, the practice of having public school students wear uniforms—like their private school peers—has been credited with some amazing results. School uniforms, proponents have said, can lead to improved discipline and classroom behavior, increased school attendance, respect for teachers, better school performance, higher student self-esteem and confidence, lower clothing costs, promotion of group spirit, reduction in social stratification, and lower rates of violence and crime. Uniforms, in short, seem like the solution to all of education's problems.

Of course, there have also been naysayers. They argue that requiring school uniforms violates students' rights, that uniforms are not responsible for decreased violence, that students will find other ways to compete, and that uniforms have no direct bearing on academic achievement.

Which side is correct? Like so many other educational issues, the truth probably lies somewhere between the two extremes. For answers, we can look to the research on and articles about school uniforms, particularly in the areas of violence prevention, school climate, and finances.

Early Signs of Success

Schools have always had dress codes, of course. But in 1986, Baltimore's Cherry Hill Elementary School became the first U.S. public school to adopt a school uniform policy. The policy was an attempt to reduce clothing costs for parents and to help curb social pressures. According to a 1996 issue of *Communicator,* a newsletter published by the National Association of Elementary School Principals, Cherry Hill Principal Geraldine Smallwood reported increased attendance, reduced suspensions, less frequent fighting, increased test scores, and improved school performance after students began wearing uniforms.

A similar success story was reported when, in 1995, Long Beach, Calif., became the first large urban school district to require uniforms for all students in kindergarten through eighth grade. Five years later, overall crime in the school district had dropped by 91 percent. Suspensions were down 90 percent, sex offenses had been reduced by 96 percent, and vandalism had gone down 69 percent.

New York City adopted a policy in 1999 that allowed schools to vote on whether to opt out of a new school uniform policy. About 70 percent of the city's elementary schools adopted school uniforms. In 2000, the Philadelphia School Board unanimously adopted a district-wide policy requiring some type of uniform. That same year, 60 percent of Miami public schools required uniforms, as did 80 percent of public schools in Chicago. Also, 37 state legislatures enacted legislation empowering local districts to determine their own uniform policies.

With so many school districts adopting such policies, it seemed as though uniforms were doing something to prevent violence, improve school climate, or help parents out financially. A look at the research and literature on the effect of school uniforms on these areas is revealing and can help you decide if such a policy would be useful in your district.

Reducing Violence

Proponents suggest that school uniforms can reduce violence in schools by diminishing gang influence and easing competition over clothing as a source of conflict.

In fact, gang violence is one of the most influential reasons for adopting uniform policies. In urban schools, fashion trends are often characterized by gang-related clothing. In theory, then, school uniforms would prevent gang activity by not allowing students to wear gang colors or gang insignia. And in practice, there is some evidence that this is true.

For example, a 1999 *Education World* article by Glori Chaika reported a significant drop in gang violence in Chicago schools that adopted school uniforms. Similarly, in a 2003 *Education and Urban Society* article, Kathleen Wade and Mary Stafford reported that teachers at schools with uniforms perceived lower levels of gang presence than teachers at schools with no uniforms. This difference was significant, despite the fact that the uniform schools were in areas with slightly higher numbers of gang-related crimes. However, students in both types of schools perceived gang presence at the same level. Students may see other signs besides clothing that hint of gang activity.

Clothing has caused other school conflicts as well. After introducing uniforms, the Birmingham, Ala., schools reported a drop in weapon and drug incidents, and Houston schools noted a decrease in violent crime. Interestingly, however, Miami-Dade counties report that fights nearly doubled at their middle schools after schools adopted a uniform policy.

How valid are the findings linking school uniforms to decreased violence? There is substantial criticism on that point. In many of these school districts, other changes in policy were being promoted at the same time—such as having more teachers patrolling the hallways. These additional variables confuse the issue and must be controlled for statistically in the research before drawing conclusions.

Improving School Climate

Obviously, less violence in schools translates to a better school climate, another area that is said to be affected by school uniforms. And indeed, there is some evidence that school uniforms may improve a school's environment by reducing competition, improving student self-esteem, and improving academic achievement.

Writing in the *NASSP Bulletin* in 1997, Richard Murray reported on the results of a survey of 306 middle school students in Charleston, S.C. Murray found that students in a middle school with a uniform policy had a significantly better perception of their school's climate than did students in a school without a uniform policy. Similarly, in Charleston secondary schools, a South Carolina State University doctoral student found in 1996 that a school with a uniform policy reported higher attendance, self-esteem, and academic scores.

Winston Tucker, a University of Minnesota researcher, investigated the perceptions of St. Paul teachers in 1999. He found that in schools where uniforms were worn, teachers perceived more positive behavior and peer interactions. They also reported fewer cliques, less teasing, and better self-esteem. On the other hand, Wade and Stafford's survey of teachers and students revealed no difference between perceptions of school climate in schools with and without uniforms.

Research on school uniforms and test scores is equally mixed. For example, a 1998 study by David Brunsma and Kerry Rockquemore, published in *The Journal of Educational Research,* refuted the belief that uniforms will result in higher test scores. Using data from the National Educational Longitudinal Study of 1988, they found that in Catholic schools, school uniforms had no direct effect on substance abuse, behavioral problems, or attendance. More recently, however, researcher Ann Bodine criticized the inferences drawn from this study. In a 2003 article in the same journal, she contended that examination of public schools shows a positive correlation between uniforms and achievement.

Like the research on a possible relation between school uniforms and reduced violence, findings on uniforms and school climate have yielded no clear conclusion.

Saving Money

Advocates of school uniform policies argue that uniforms will save families money. But Pamela Norum, Robert Weagley, and Marjorie Norton, writing in the *Family and Consumer Sciences Research Journal* in 1998, concluded that families who buy school uniforms spend more on clothing than families who are not required to do so. However, a subsequent paper, presented by Michael Firmin, Suzanne Smith, and Lynsey Perry at the 16th Annual Ethnographic and Qualitative Research in Education Conference, points out that many parents believe a policy requiring school uniforms lowers clothing costs, and others believe it would do so in the long run.

It seems clear that introducing a uniform policy results in more expense in the beginning, but more research is needed to determine whether school uniforms save families money. The experience of families at different socioeconomic levels should be compared, rather than averaging across socioeconomic levels. It is possible that families who struggle financially might depend on hand-me-downs or thrift stores to begin with, and the cost of a new uniform substantially increases their clothing costs.

If a uniform policy is adopted, it will be important to take into account how to provide uniforms for students whose families can't afford them. Some school districts collect outgrown uniforms to distribute to needy families. Some give out donated money so parents themselves can select their children's uniforms. California requires school districts to subsidize the cost of uniforms for low-income students, and the U.S. Department of Education's "Manual on School Uniforms" suggests that some type of assistance should be given to needy families.

In some cases, school uniforms could save money, but it's clear that uniforms could be a financial burden for many families.

Legal Considerations

Legal issues have surrounded the school uniform debate for two primary reasons: claims that the school has infringed on the student's First Amendment right to free expression and claims under the 14th Amendment that the school has violated the student's liberty to control his or her opinion.

The 1998 case of *Canady v. Bossier Parish School Board* addressed the constitutionality of student uniforms. In this landmark case, the Supreme Court upheld a school's right to implement a school uniform policy, given four conditions:

- First, that the school board has the power to make such a policy;
- Second, that the policy promotes a substantial interest of the board;
- Third, that the board does not adopt the policy to censor student expression; and
- Fourth, that the policy's "incidental" restrictions on student expression are not greater than necessary to promote the board's interest.

The American Civil Liberties Union has taken a stance against school uniform policies and cautions schools against omitting an opt-out provision from such policies. "For a public school uniform policy to be legal, it has to have an opt-out provision," wrote the ACLU's Loren Siegel on the organization's website in 1996. "Every child in this country has the right to a public school education, and that right cannot be conditioned upon compliance with a uniform policy. Some parents and children will have religious objections to uniforms. Others won't want to participate for aesthetic reasons."

As we can see, powerful quantitative evidence suggests that uniforms can reduce school violence, but these studies have not accounted for confounding variables. Perceptions of teachers, parents, and administrators seem to strongly support the idea that school climate is affected positively by school uniforms. They have reported more positive learning environments and peer interactions after the introduction of uniform policies. There remains, however, a lack of research on student's perspectives on school uniforms.

The research is not conclusive, but the testimonials from teachers, parents, and administrators alike are hard to ignore. Whether to require school uniforms should be a school or district decision, and guidelines should be followed to make sure students' rights are not violated. That is particularly important in cases where religious practice calls for clothing or head covering that is not consistent with the accepted school uniform. Provision should also be made for those families who can't afford to purchase uniforms.

When these concerns are addressed—and when the idea is supported by the community—school uniforms can be successful.

SAMPLE CRITIQUE

An Unconvincing Argument concerning School Uniforms

As author Yasmine Konheim-Kalkstein notes in the opening line of her essay, "A Uniform Look," over the past few decades schools across the country have debated whether to require high school students to wear uniforms. However, are school uniform requirements effective in meeting their goals: reducing school violence, raising school attendance, bolstering student grades, and reducing the cost of school for parents, just to name a few? On a first reading of the essay, it may appear that Konheim-Kalkstein's goal is to answer these questions impartially by surveying the research published on the topic. However, she withholds her thesis until the last sentence of the piece, revealing her true intention: "When these concerns are addressed—and when the idea is supported by the community—school uniforms can be successful" (119). A close reading of her essay, though, shows that Konheim-Kalkstein fails to support even this assertion.

In the opening section of her essay, Konheim-Kalkstein acknowledges two sides in the debate over the effectiveness of school uniforms, yet she consistently emphasizes arguments and research findings that favor the pro-uniform position. For example, she cites statistics from schools in New Jersey, Long Beach, California, New York City, and Chicago that all demonstrated positive results from requiring elementary school students to wear uniforms and concludes, "With so many school districts adopting such policies, it seemed as though uniforms were doing something to prevent violence, improve school climate, or help parents out financially" (116). Konheim-Kalkstein terms the research on school uniforms "revealing" (116) and states that they can "help you decide if such a policy would be useful in your district" (116). Since this article was published in *American School Board Journal*, one can assume that "you" in the previous sentence refers to school board members.

Indeed, at first glance, the figures Konheim-Kalkstein presents concerning the link between uniform requirements and school violence are impressive. She cites an *Education World* article that reported a drastic drop in gang violence at schools that required uniforms and another article from *Education and Urban Society* that says these results were replicated at other high schools as well. Yet, Konheim-Kalkstein must admit that these statistics may reveal only a correlation between uniform requirements and drops in school violence. She offers no proof that requiring students to wear uniforms actually caused a drop in violence or gang activity; in fact, she states that "other changes in policy were being promoted at the same time—such as having more teachers patrolling the hallways" (117). Any one factor, or any combination of factors, could be responsible for the drop in violence, yet Konheim-Kalkstein wants to attribute it to school uniforms. In fact, from the students' perspective, the uniforms had no effect on violence-related gang activity (117). In the end, Konheim-Kalkstein states that these "additional variables confuse the issue and must be controlled for statistically in the research before drawing conclusions" (117). On this first point—that uniform requirements help reduce gang activity and violence—Konheim-Kalkstein actually offers only testimonial evidence in support of her thesis that "school uniforms can be successful," evidence countered by the experiences of students at those schools.

Konheim-Kalkstein next examines the relationship between uniform requirements and "school climate" (117), indicating some

evidence exists that schools requiring student uniforms benefit
from reduced competition, higher self-esteem, and higher grades
and test scores (117). After citing several studies that reported
a link between uniform requirements and better school climates,
Konheim-Kalkstein cites only one that showed no such relationship.
Moving on to focus on the relationship between uniforms and higher
academic achievement, she cites several studies which showed no
link between the two, but ends that section of her essay by referring to more recent research that demonstrates "a positive correlation between uniforms and achievement" (118). In the end, though,
Konheim-Kalkstein must concede: "Like the research on a possible
relation between school uniforms and reduced violence, findings
on uniforms and school climate have yielded no clear conclusion"
(118). This concession again calls into question Konheim-Kalkstein's
thesis, that school uniform policies can be successful.

Konheim-Kalkstein next turns her attention to arguments that
requiring school uniforms saves families money by reducing clothing
costs for the children. She cites a conference paper in which the authors found that parents "believe" (118) requiring uniforms will save
them money in the long run, but again the evidence she examines
leads to a different conclusion. A study published in *Family and Consumer Sciences Research Journal* "concluded that families who buy
school uniforms spend more on clothing than families who are not
required to do so" (118). In fact, Konheim-Kalkstein concludes that
school uniform requirements may prove too expensive for students
in lower socioeconomic classes. After reviewing all the evidence,
Konheim-Kalkstein is forced to admit that "it's clear that uniforms
could be a financial burden for many families" (118).

Konheim-Kalkstein closes her essay by examining primarily
legal issues involved in requiring students to wear uniforms in
school, starting with the Supreme Court case (*Canady v. Bossier
Parish School Board*) that affirmed the constitutionality of such
programs so long as they met four criteria:

- first, that the school board has the power to make such a
  policy;
- second, that the policy promotes a substantial interest of the
  board;
- third, that the board does not adopt the policy to censor student expression; and
- fourth, that the policy's "incidental" restrictions on student
  expression are not greater than necessary to promote the
  board's interest. (119)

However, school uniform laws have been opposed by the American Civil Liberties Union (ACLU), which asserts that any school
uniform policy must have an "opt out" provision for children and
families who believe the requirements inhibit their freedom of
religion or free speech, objections that Konheim-Kalkstein does
not address (119). American courts have long held that freedom of

expression extends to people's clothing, including that of students. Konheim-Kalkstein does not offer a clear position on this question. Instead, she implies that if a school uniform policy meets the four criteria outlined above, it would be legal.

Despite all of the contradictory research and gaps in her argument, Konheim-Kalkstein still wants to maintain that requiring school uniforms "can be successful" (119). To do so, she puts the best possible spin on the evidence she presents in her essay:

> As we can see, powerful quantitative evidence suggests that uniforms can reduce school violence, but these studies have not accounted for confounding variables. Perceptions of teachers, parents, and administrators seem to strongly support the idea that school climate is affected positively by school uniforms. They have reported more positive learning environments and peer interactions after the introduction of uniform policies. (119)

However, these positive assertions can be seriously questioned by the information and arguments Konheim-Kalkstein presents. For example, she provides ample reason to question each of the positive claims she makes for school uniforms, admittedly basing her claim for their efficacy on teacher or parent testimonials (119). Read as a whole, the article actually offers a strong argument against the institution of school uniform policies because there simply is no preponderance of evidence to support any of the benefits such a move is supposed to bring about. Konheim-Kalkstein's "A Uniform Look" casts great doubts on whether school uniform policies can successfully achieve the benefits supporters ascribe to them.

Summary Chart

HOW TO WRITE A CRITIQUE

1. **Carefully read and annotate the source text.**
   - *Read and reread the text.*
   - *Identify the author's intent, thesis, and primary assertions or findings.*
   - *Write an informal summary of the piece.*

2. **Analyze and evaluate the reading, breaking it down into its parts and judging the quality of each element.**

   Identify and evaluate the author's logic and reasoning.
   - *Is the thesis clearly stated, and does it direct the development of the text?*
   - *Are the author's primary assertions reasonable and clearly tied to the thesis?*
   - *Are there problems with logical fallacies?*
   - *Are the author's positions or findings logically presented?*

   Identify and evaluate the text's evidence.
   - *Does the author support his or her assertions or findings?*
   - *Is the support offered adequate to convince readers?*
   - *Is the evidence authoritative?*
   - *Is the evidence current?*
   - *Does the author explain how the evidence supports his or her assertions or findings?*
   - *Has the author ignored evidence or alternative hypotheses?*

   Identify and evaluate the text's organization.
   - *Is there a clear connection between the assertions developed in the essay?*
   - *Are the assertions or findings tied to a guiding thesis?*
   - *Does there seem to be a reason for one assertion following another, or do they seem randomly organized?*

   Identify and evaluate the text's style.
   - *Is the author's diction consistently maintained?*
   - *Is the author's word choice clear and effective?*
   - *Is the author's tone consistent and effective?*
   - *Are the author's sentences clear?*

SUMMARY CHART: HOW TO WRITE A CRITIQUE *(CONTINUED)*

3. **Formulate your thesis and choose the criteria you will include in your essay.**
   - *Draft a thesis, a brief statement concerning the overall value or worth of the source text.*
   - *Choose which elements of the reading you will focus on in your critique.*

4. **Write your rough draft.**
   - *Introduce the topic, source text, and your thesis.*
   - *Establish your evaluative criteria and your judgments of them.*
   - *Offer examples to substantiate each of your criteria and judgments.*
   - *Explain your judgments, clarifying how the examples you provide support your assertions.*

5. **Rewrite your critique.**

   Check to make sure your writing is accurate.
   - *Does your writing honestly reflect your judgment?*
   - *Does your writing misrepresent the author?*

   Check to make sure your writing is thorough.
   - *Do you cover all the aspects of the source text you need to cover?*
   - *Do you clearly and thoroughly explain and support your assertions?*

   Check to make sure your writing is organized.
   - *Does your thesis statement guide the development of your essay?*
   - *Have you provided transitional devices to help lead your reader through your work?*

   Check to make sure your writing is clear.
   - *Is your terminology clear?*
   - *Are your sentences clear?*
   - *Are your examples and explanations clear?*

CRITIQUE REVISION CHECKLIST

	Yes	No
1. Have you included the title of the reading and the author's name in your introduction?	_____	_____
2. Does your thesis make clear your overall assessment of the reading?	_____	_____
3. Toward the beginning of your critique, have you provided a brief summary of the reading?	_____	_____
4. In the body of your critique, do you examine only one element of the reading at a time?	_____	_____
5. Do you clearly state a judgment concerning each element of the reading you explore?	_____	_____
6. Do you provide examples from the reading to support and illustrate your judgment of each element you examine?	_____	_____
7. Do you clearly and thoroughly explain your judgments concerning each example you provide from the reading?	_____	_____
8. Have you employed proper evaluative criteria and standards?	_____	_____
9. Have you provided clear transitions between the major sections of your paper?	_____	_____
10. Is there a clear relationship between each section of your paper and your thesis?	_____	_____
11. Have you provided proper documentation for all quoted, paraphrased, and summarized material?	_____	_____
12. Have you revised your paper for accuracy? In other words, does the final draft reflect your honest appraisal of the reading?	_____	_____
13. Have you reviewed the language in your paper to make sure your words adequately capture and communicate your judgments?	_____	_____
14. As you review your work, do your judgments still stand? Do you need to change your thesis or any part of your paper?	_____	_____

Chapter 7

RHETORICAL ANALYSIS OF WRITTEN TEXTS

DEFINITION AND PURPOSE

A rhetorical analysis essay is a special form of critique (see Chapter 6). In a critique essay, you determine a source text's overall value or worth by critically examining a set of relevant criteria; in a rhetorical analysis essay, you determine a source text's rhetorical effectiveness by examining how the author employs language and/or visual images to achieve a particular effect on an audience. This chapter addresses how to compose a rhetorical analysis of a written text; the following chapter offers instruction on how to compose a rhetorical analysis of a visual text.

Writing a rhetorical analysis of a reading requires you to answer three related questions:

- What response is the author of the reading trying to elicit from his or her readers?
- How does the author employ language to elicit that response?
- How well does the author succeed in achieving this response?

Composing a rhetorical analysis requires you to examine a source text from the perspective of both a reader and a writer, assessing how well an author achieves certain rhetorical goals in a text.

Rhetorical analysis of print texts is based on certain assumptions about how writers write and the way writing works. First is the assumption that writing is purposeful, that every text is written by someone who directs it toward some audience to achieve some purpose. To accomplish their ends, writers make a series of strategic choices—they choose this approach to the topic instead of that approach, this set of arguments rather than that set of arguments, this evidence instead of that evidence, this thesis rather than that one, this organizational plan in place of another, this word rather than that word. In a rhetorical analysis essay, you critically examine this series of choices, identifying and critiquing the strategies a writer employs to achieve his or her rhetorical goals.

A second assumption is that text and context are intimately connected, that text is fundamentally influenced by the context in which it is written. Writers work within a set of givens, a rhetorical context or situation that includes their reasons for writing the text, their purpose or aim, their audience's needs or interests, and their knowledge of the topic they are addressing. To be effective, writers must adapt their writing to meet the needs of the given rhetorical situation. If they ignore or misconstrue any element of the rhetorical situation, their writing will be less effective than it might otherwise be. Because writers typically want to produce the most effective text possible, they take particular efforts to ensure that their language suits the text's audience, purpose, message, and occasion. Therefore, to evaluate a text's rhetorical effectiveness, you must understand the context in which it was written.

A final assumption is that no rhetorical analysis is definitive. Readers often disagree about a text's purpose, intended audience, rhetorical strategies, and effectiveness. Because readers always bring their own knowledge, experiences, sensitivities, and biases to a text, they will form unique, individualized responses to even the most fundamental questions concerning how a reading communicates its meaning. Consequently, when you write a rhetorical analysis essay, you must explain your conclusions as clearly as you can, supporting them with thorough explanations and specific references to the source text.

THE RHETORICAL SITUATION

When you compose a rhetorical analysis essay of a written text, you must examine how an author uses language to achieve a particular response from readers. However, your task is a little more complicated than it might appear at first. You will actually be examining how an author uses language to achieve a particular response from readers *given the specific context in which the writer produced the text*. This "specific context" is called the text's **rhetorical situation**, which includes the author's audience, subject matter, purpose, and occasion for writing. In your paper, you will assess how the writer manipulates language to meet the needs of the rhetorical situation and achieve his or her goals for the text.

A brief example may help explain why understanding the rhetorical situation of a source text is essential to composing an effective rhetorical analysis essay. Suppose your source text is a set of instructions for installing a new hard drive on a computer. Your task is to evaluate how well the instructions achieve their intended purpose. The first thing you notice is that the instructions are full of undefined technical terms—IDE cables, jumper selectors, drive rails, boot drives. Are the instructions effective? Upon consideration, you would have to conclude that the answer is, "It depends." If the instructions are written for someone who is already well versed in computer technology, they may be fine; if they are written for a novice computer owner, they may not be so effective. Composing an effective rhetorical analysis of the instructions requires that you evaluate the writing in light of its purpose and intended audience, two crucial elements of the text's rhetorical situation.

Because understanding a text's rhetorical situation is so fundamental to writing this type of essay, it is worthwhile to examine each element in isolation. The next section contains definitions of various elements of a text's rhetorical situation and a series of questions writers frequently ask of each element as they prepare to write a rhetorical analysis essay.

ELEMENTS OF THE RHETORICAL SITUATION

Author—the person or people who wrote the text

- Who wrote the piece?
- What is the author's background in terms of race, sex, education, political affiliation, economic status, or religion?
- What are the author's possible or likely biases?
- What perspective does the author bring to the topic?
- How does the author "sound" on the page—angry, detached, confused, funny?
- What has the author written about the topic in the past?

Topic—what the text is about

- What is the person writing about?
- Is the author addressing a particular aspect of the topic or the topic as a whole?
- Which aspects of the topic receive the most attention and which receive the least?
- What, exactly, is the author stating about the topic?
- What have others said about this subject matter?
- What is the relationship between what others have written about the topic and what the author is writing about it?

Audience—who the writer is addressing

- To whom is the text addressed?
- If the text is not written to a specific person or group of people, what kind of reader did the author seem to have in mind when writing the piece?

For example, does the author seem to be assuming he or she is addressing a friendly audience or a hostile audience? An expert audience or a novice audience? An academic audience or a popular audience?

- What is the audience's likely knowledge of or attitude toward the author and/or subject matter?
- What assumptions does the author make about the audience? Are these assumptions accurate?

Purpose or Aim—what the author is trying to accomplish in writing the text

- If the author states a purpose or aim for the piece, what is it? To inform, persuade, entertain, educate, provoke to action, draw attention, ridicule, shock?
- If it is not stated, what is the author's implied purpose or aim for the text?
- Is there more than one purpose or aim for the text? If so, what are they? Does one purpose seem more dominant than the others? Which one?
- How does the author's purpose influence the text's content, structure, or language?

Occasion—what prompted the writer to write the piece

- Why did the author feel compelled to write this text?
- What is the historical context of the piece?
- Is the author adding to a debate over a particular political issue or social question? Is the author responding to another writer or text? Is the author responding to a particular historical event or cultural phenomenon?

Writing a rhetorical analysis essay usually requires you to examine the complex interrelationships that exist among these elements. For example, how does the author's audience influence what she writes about the topic or the language she employs? What is the relationship between a text's purpose and the time or place it was written? How effective is the author in producing a text that is appropriate for both the audience and the occasion?

RHETORICAL STRATEGIES

Once you understand the text's rhetorical situation, you are ready to turn your analysis to the author's rhetorical strategies—the way the author manipulates the text's content, structure, or style to achieve his or her aim. **Content** concerns the material an author includes in the text, **structure** concerns the order in which the author presents that material, and **style** concerns the language and sentence structure an author uses to convey that material. A rhetorical analysis essay is unlikely to address every aspect of a text's content, structure, or style. In fact, it may address just one or two of the author's rhetorical strategies. As the person writing the analysis, you will determine which strategies you wish to examine. They will likely be the ones you think are most essential to the author achieving his or her aim.

CONTENT

When composing a rhetorical analysis essay, most writers analyze a text's content in one or two related ways: by examining its arguments, evidence, and reasoning or by examining its persuasive appeals. Because both approaches are closely related, writers will often examine aspects of each in their essays. Both are discussed below.

Arguments, Evidence, and Reasoning

When analyzing a text's rhetorical strategies in terms of its arguments, evidence, and reasoning, you are primarily concerned with examining the claims or assertions a writer makes, the way that writer supports those claims, and the way he or she explains them. You need to ask yourself, given the text's rhetorical situation, why the writer would choose those particular arguments. Are they the best arguments for the writer to make? Why did the writer choose to support those claims the way he or she did? Again, was this the best choice of evidence? How effective were the writer's decisions? Does the writer explain his or her reasoning in the piece, exploring or defending the link between his or her claims and supporting evidence? Are there certain assumptions or leaps of reasoning the writer leaves unstated? Why might the writer have made that choice? Was it a good decision? Below are some questions that can help you analyze and evaluate a text's rhetorical strategies in terms of its arguments, evidence, and reasoning.

Arguments or Assertions

- What arguments or assertions does the author make and how are they related to the rhetorical situation?
- How does the audience, purpose, and occasion of the text influence the author's arguments or assertions?
- Given the audience and purpose of the text, are these the most effective arguments? If so, what makes them effective? If not, why not? What arguments might be more effective?
- What arguments or assertions are emphasized the most? Why did the author decide to emphasize those assertions instead of others?
- What relevant arguments or assertions are ignored or slighted? Why do you think the author chose not to address them?
- How might the intended audience respond to the arguments offered? How well does the author seem to anticipate and perhaps address these likely responses?

Evidence or Examples

- How does the author support his or her assertions? Are they supported by primary or secondary research? By personal experience? By statistics or expert testimony?

- What is the source of the author's evidence for each assertion or argument? Are they particularly effective sources, given the text's rhetorical situation?
- Is the evidence offered appropriate, given the text's rhetorical situation? Does the evidence offered effectively support each claim?
- How might the intended audience respond to the evidence or examples offered? How well does the author seem to anticipate and perhaps address these likely responses?
- Is the presentation balanced or one-sided? In either case, is that choice appropriate given the rhetorical situation?
- How does the author address possible counterarguments or evidence that does not support his or her assertions?
- Are there obvious arguments the author chooses to ignore or gloss over? What are the effects of these omissions? How might they be explained, given the text's rhetorical situation?

Reasoning

- Does the author present a clear and cogent line of reasoning in the text?
- How well does the author move from one assertion to the next?
- How compelling is the connection the author makes among assertions? Between assertions and their supporting evidence?
- Does the text lead logically and convincingly to its conclusion?
- Are there clear connections between the text's thesis and its primary assertions?
- Are there any important assumptions the author leaves unstated? Does leaving them unstated and undefended make the text any less successful?
- Is the reasoning fair and balanced? Should it be, given the text's rhetorical situation?
- Are there any logical fallacies or flaws in reasoning that might hinder the text's effectiveness, given its audience, purpose, and occasion?

Persuasive Appeals

Another set of strategies authors often employ to achieve their rhetorical goals involves appealing to their readers' rationality (logos) or emotions (pathos) or establishing their own credibility as an authority on the topic (ethos). Though one of the three appeals may dominate a particular reading, most effective persuasive texts use elements of all three. In brief, when authors try to persuade readers by presenting a reasonable series of arguments supported by evidence and examples, they are relying on **logos** to achieve their goal; when they try to persuade readers through emotional language or examples or by appealing to the reader's needs or interests, they are relying on **pathos**; when they try to persuade readers by appearing fair, balanced, and informed or by establishing their own credibility and authority on the subject, they are relying on **ethos**. Below are some questions you can ask about a text's persuasive appeals if you are analyzing its rhetorical effectiveness.

Logos

- How reasonable and appropriate are the author's claims, given the rhetorical situation?
- How clear are the author's claims?
- Are the author's claims broad and sweeping or does the author limit or qualify them?
- How well does the author use facts, statistics, and expert testimony to support his or her claims?
- Are the author's claims adequately explained?
- Does the author avoid lapses in reasoning or logical fallacies?
- Does the author address opposing or alternative viewpoints?
- Are there relevant claims the author fails to address?
- Are the author's claims convincing?

Pathos

- Does the author attempt to convince his or her readers through appeals to their emotions?
- To which emotions is the author appealing? To the readers' personal fears or concerns? To the readers' economic or social self-interests? To the readers' desires for acceptance, love, or beauty? To the readers' sense of justice or social responsibility?
- Does the author appeal to his readers' emotions through his choice of arguments, evidence, language, or some combination of the three?
- How are appeals to emotion balanced with other appeals in the text?
- Does the author try too hard to appeal to readers' emotions? Are the appeals to emotion too clumsy or awkward to be effective?
- Is an appeal to the readers' emotions an effective strategy to employ given the rhetorical situation?

Ethos

- How does the author attempt to establish her credibility or authority?
- What level of expertise does the author demonstrate when writing about the topic of her text?
- Does the author's own experience or expertise lend credibility to the text?
- Does the author demonstrate or document the validity of the source texts used to support her assertions?
- Does the author present a balanced or a one-sided argument? Is that approach appropriate, given the rhetorical situation?
- Does the author demonstrate a sufficient understanding of the topic's complex or controversial nature?
- Does the text's tone or the author's voice contribute to or detract from her credibility?

STRUCTURE

While many rhetorical strategies are related to a text's content, others involve its structure. Once writers decide what information or arguments they will include in their essays, they need to decide the order in which to present them. Structure also involves the way a writer introduces and concludes a text and draws connections among parts of the text. Following are some questions you can ask about a text's structure as you evaluate its rhetorical effectiveness.

- In what order does the author present information or claims?
- What purpose might lie behind this order?
- How might the text's structure influence an audience's response to the author's ideas, findings, or assertions?
- Does the text present a clear and consistent line of reasoning?
- Are there clear connections between the text's stated or implied thesis and its topic sentences?
- Does the text's structure enhance its appeal to logic? Does the author draw clear, logical connections among the text's ideas, findings, or assertions?
- Does the structure of the piece enhance its appeal to emotion, particularly in its introduction or conclusion?
- Does the structure of the piece enhance its appeal to credibility? Does the author seem in control of the writing? Does the text hold together as a whole? Are there any obvious flaws in structure that might damage the author's credibility?

STYLE

Finally, when analyzing an author's rhetorical strategies, consider his or her style. Among other elements of writing, style concerns the text's sentence structure, word choice, punctuation, voice, tone, and diction. Here are some questions that can help you assess how style contributes to a text's rhetorical effectiveness:

- What type of syntax does the author employ? How does the author vary sentence length (long or short) and sentence type (simple, compound, complex, and compound-complex; cumulative, periodic, and balanced)? How is syntax related to the audience, purpose, or occasion of the text?
- What types of figurative language does the author employ (for example, metaphors, similes, or analogies)? Are the choices of figurative language appropriate and effective given the text's rhetorical situation?
- What types of allusions does the author employ? Are they appropriate and effective?
- How appropriate and effective is the author's voice, given the text's rhetorical situation?
- How appropriate and effective is the author's tone, given the text's rhetorical situation?
- How appropriate and effective is the author's diction, given the text's rhetorical situation?

ANALYZING A TEXT'S RHETORICAL STRATEGIES—AN EXAMPLE

To better understand how to analyze a text's rhetorical strategies in terms of its content, structure, and style, carefully read the following speech, Abraham Lincoln's Second Inaugural Address. Lincoln delivered this speech on March 4, 1865, in Washington, D.C. Though the Civil War was not yet over, the struggle had turned in the Union's favor, and the end of the conflict was in sight. In this address, Lincoln acknowledges the price the nation has paid for the war and argues that lasting peace and reconciliation will come only through mercy and forgiveness. Many historians and rhetoricians consider this Lincoln's greatest speech.

Lincoln's Second Inaugural Address

Fellow-Countrymen:

At this second appearing to take the oath of the Presidential office there is less occasion for an extended address than there was at the first. Then a statement somewhat in detail of a course to be pursued seemed fitting and proper. Now, at the expiration of four years, during which public declarations have been constantly called forth on every point and phase of the great contest which still absorbs the attention and engrosses the energies of the nation, little that is new could be presented. The progress of our arms, upon which all else chiefly depends, is as well known to the public as to myself, and it is, I trust, reasonably satisfactory and encouraging to all. With high hope for the future, no prediction in regard to it is ventured.

On the occasion corresponding to this four years ago all thoughts were anxiously directed to an impending civil war. All dreaded it, all sought to avert it. While the inaugural address was being delivered from this place, devoted altogether to *saving* the Union without war, urgent agents were in the city seeking to *destroy* it without war; seeking to dissolve the Union and divide effects by negotiation. Both parties deprecated war, but one of them would *make* war rather than let the nation survive, and the other would *accept* war rather than let it perish, and the war came.

One-eighth of the whole population were colored slaves, not distributed generally over the Union, but localized in the southern part of it. These slaves constituted a peculiar and powerful interest. All knew that this interest was somehow the cause of the war. To strengthen, perpetuate, and extend this interest was the object for which the insurgents would rend the Union even by war, while the Government claimed no right to do more than to restrict the territorial enlargement of it. Neither party expected for the war the magnitude or the duration which it has already attained. Neither anticipated that the *cause* of the conflict might cease with or even before the conflict itself should cease. Each looked for an easier triumph, and a result less fundamental and astounding. Both read the same Bible and pray to the same God, and each invokes His aid against the other. It may seem strange that any men should dare to ask a just God's assistance in wringing their bread from the sweat of other men's faces, but let us judge not, that we be not judged. The prayers of both could not be answered. That of neither has been answered fully. The Almighty has His own purposes. "Woe unto the world because of offenses; for it must needs be that offenses come, but woe to that man by whom the offense cometh." If we shall suppose that American slavery is one of those offenses which, in the providence of God, must needs come, but which, having continued through His appointed time, He now wills to remove, and that He gives to both North and South this terrible war as the woe due to those by whom the offense came, shall we discern therein any departure from those divine attributes which the believers in a living God always ascribe to Him? Fondly do we hope, fervently do we pray, that this mighty scourge of war may speedily pass away. Yet, if God wills that it continue until all the wealth piled by the bondsman's two hundred and fifty years of unrequited toil shall be sunk, and until every drop of blood drawn with the lash shall be paid by another drawn with the sword, as was said three thousand years ago, so still it must be said "the judgments of the Lord are true and righteous altogether."

With malice toward none, with charity for all, with firmness in the right as God gives us to see the right, let us strive on to finish the work we are in, to bind up the nation's wounds, to care for him who shall have borne the battle and for his widow and his orphan, to do all which may achieve and cherish a just and lasting peace among ourselves and with all nations.

A RHETORICAL ANALYSIS OF LINCOLN'S SPEECH

In terms of the speech's content, notice how Lincoln makes several related arguments designed to persuade his audience that after the Civil War ends, the North must treat the South with charity and compassion. He opens his address by asserting that he will not detail a course of action for the country's future—clearly everyone in the nation has been and continues to be consumed by the war. Next, Lincoln asserts that the primary cause of the war was slavery. Four years earlier, the Union sought to halt the spread of slavery peacefully. However, the Confederacy, he asserts, would not accept this position and turned to armed conflict instead. Neither side, though, anticipated the duration and ferocity of the war. While both sides in the conflict call on God for victory, Lincoln questions whether any divine power would support the perpetuation of slavery. Interestingly, he sees *both* sides in the war being chastised for their involvement with slavery and hopes that the suffering all are undergoing can purge their collective guilt and set the stage for a more just nation. Lincoln closes his speech by asserting that reconciliation will only succeed if it is based on mercy, forgiveness, and justice, not revenge and recrimination.

Both Lincoln's position as president and the occasion of the speech lend credibility to his address. However, Lincoln enhances his credibility by articulating the North's perspective on the war's causes, a position most of his audience would presumably endorse. Making numerous references to God and God's will also serves to enhance his ethos but serves as an emotional appeal as well: Lincoln hopes the citizens of the North will be swayed to extend mercy to the South after the war by ascribing such a position to divine will. By speaking mercifully and understandingly about the suffering of the South during the war, Lincoln models the behavior and attitudes he hopes the members of his audience will adopt themselves.

Structurally, Lincoln opens his address by commenting on the previous four years of his presidency and acknowledging the country's current struggle before laying out the North's view of the war's cause. Having articulated a position his audience would accept, Lincoln then changes the direction of the speech. Instead of attacking the Confederacy for its secession from the Union, he speaks about the suffering the war has brought to *all* Americans, how neither side in the conflict accurately anticipated the terrible nature of the war, and how the South has already suffered severely for its actions. Audience members might expect Lincoln to call for revenge against the South; instead, he argues that both sides have suffered enough. At the end of his speech, he urges his audience to treat the South with charity.

Stylistically, the speech is remarkable for its somber tone. Though this is an inaugural speech, Lincoln is not celebrating. Instead, his tone reflects the suffering the nation has endured over the previous four years and the hard work that lies ahead of it. Syntactically, he employs balanced sentences to create memorable phrases—"All dreaded it, all sought to avert it," "Fondly do we hope, fervently do we pray," "With malice toward none, with charity for all"—and to emphasize the balanced view he takes concerning the war's consequences. The North and South have both suffered and reconstruction must be based on an understanding of their shared humanity. Lincoln repeatedly employs language from the Old Testament to emphasize his view of the war as a form of divine judgment against the nation for its past offenses. Underlying this argument is the notion that justice lies in the hands of God: if God has scourged the nation for its transgressions, there is no need for humans to further the South's punishment following the war.

This brief rhetorical analysis of Lincoln's speech gives you some idea of how an author can manipulate a text's content, structure, and style to achieve a particular aim.

WRITING A RHETORICAL ANALYSIS ESSAY

STEP 1—CAREFULLY READ THE ASSIGNMENT

As you read the assignment, be sure you understand who *your* audience is for your essay. What can you assume your reader knows about the source text, its author, or the context in which it was written? How much information do you need to provide so your reader will understand your analysis of the text? Also, what can you assume your reader knows about rhetoric? What terms, if any, will you need to define in your essay?

STEP 2—ESTABLISH THE SOURCE TEXT'S RHETORICAL SITUATION

First, establish the rhetorical situation of the source text (see "The Rhetorical Situation" previously). Following are some of the questions you should answer either before or as you carefully read the source text:

- Who is the author?
- What is the writer's message?
- Who is the writer addressing?
- What is the writer's purpose or goal?
- Why is the writer composing this text?
- When was the text produced?
- Where was the text published?

To establish the text's rhetorical situation you might need to do a little research, but writing a rhetorical analysis essay requires that you understand the context in which the text was produced.

STEP 3—DETERMINE THE AUTHOR'S GOAL

In a sentence or two, paraphrase what you think the author is trying to accomplish in the text. What effect does she want to have on the audience? Is the author trying to persuade her readers to adopt a particular position? Does the author want to influence what her readers believe? Is the author trying to elicit a particular emotional response from people who read the text? State the author's purpose or goal, as you understand it, as clearly and specifically as you can.

STEP 4—IDENTIFY AND EVALUATE THE TEXT'S RHETORICAL STRATEGIES

Once you have a clear sense of the text's rhetorical situation, read through it again to identify the strategies the author employed to achieve his goal. Examine the text's content, structure, and style in relation to its rhetorical situation. How has the author manipulated various elements of the text to achieve a particular response from his readers? Spend as much time on this step in the process as you need—the ideas and insights you develop now will help you form a thesis for your essay. Remember that in your essay, you will not address every rhetorical strategy the writer employed. Instead, you will focus on the strategies you think most significantly contribute to the text's ability or inability to achieve its rhetorical goal. As you reread the text, make a list of the ways the author employs content, structure, and style to achieve his purpose, noting specific examples of each from the reading. Based on this list, decide which strategies help the writer achieve his goals and which do not, given the text's audience, topic, purpose, and occasion. State in one or two sentences what makes each strategy successful or unsuccessful.

STEP 5—DETERMINE YOUR THESIS

In your thesis, you will state how successful you think the author is in achieving his or her rhetorical goal and indicate which of the author's rhetorical strategies you will examine in your essay. Your thesis may indicate that the author succeeds in achieving his or her rhetorical goals, fails to achieve them, or succeeds in some ways but fails in others. Whatever your assessment, state it clearly in your thesis, along with the rhetorical strategies you will examine to explain and defend your judgment.

Sample Thesis Statement 1: Author succeeds in achieving his or her rhetorical purpose

> Lincoln's Second Inaugural Address effectively establishes the North's moral imperative for successful Reconstruction by making repeated appeals to authority and emotion.

Sample Thesis Statement 2: Author fails to achieve his or her rhetorical purpose

> Lincoln's Second Inaugural Address fails to establish the North's moral imperative for successful Reconstruction because he relies too heavily on religious allusions and does not adequately address the North's desire for revenge after the war.

Sample Thesis Statement 3: Author has mixed success in achieving his or her rhetorical purpose

> Lincoln's attempts to establish the North's moral imperative for successful Reconstruction in his Second Inaugural Address are aided by his repeated appeals to authority, but they are hindered by his overreliance on religious allusions.

Whatever stand you assume, your thesis statement should establish the purpose and focus of your essay.

STEP 6—WRITE YOUR ROUGH DRAFT

While every rhetorical analysis essay will be structured a little differently, the following outline may help you determine how to organize your paper.

Introductory Section

- Indicate the topic of the source text.
- Introduce the text you are analyzing or evaluating.
- State your thesis.
- Capture reader interest.

In this part of your paper, you need to indicate the topic of your essay, introduce the source text (provide the author's full name and the title of the reading), and state your thesis. One of the real challenges in writing the introductory section of a rhetorical analysis essay is to capture reader interest as well. You may be able to develop reader interest in your essay by opening with a question raised by the source text, starting with an exciting quotation from the reading or providing some interesting information about the reading's author or historical significance.

Summary of Source Text and Overview of the Rhetorical Situation

- Briefly summarize the source text.
- Explain the source text's rhetorical situation.

In one or two paragraphs, summarize the reading and its rhetorical situation. In addition to stating what the author wrote, explain the audience, purpose, and occasion of the piece. Your analysis will depend on readers understanding the source text's rhetorical situation, so explain it carefully in this part of the paper. You will be making frequent reference back to this information in the body of your essay.

Body Paragraphs

- Examine the text one rhetorical strategy at a time (content, structure, or style).
- Cite specific examples from the source text to support any assertion you make.
- Explain the link between the examples you provide and the assertions you make.

As you draft the body of your rhetorical analysis essay, carefully critique the text one rhetorical strategy at a time, explaining whether employing that strategy helps the author achieve his or her rhetorical goal. You will need to illustrate and support your assertions with specific examples from the source text. Generally, each of your body paragraphs will contain (1) an assertion regarding whether a particular rhetorical strategy helps the author achieve his or her rhetorical goal, (2) examples from the source text that illustrate that particular rhetorical strategy, and (3) an explanation of how each example you cite supports your assertion.

Do not make the mistake of thinking that the examples you cite will "speak for themselves," that you do not need to explain how the examples support your assertion because the link will be obvious to anyone who has read the text. Instead, always explain the link between your evidence and your assertion. In fact, the success of your rhetorical analysis essay often depends on the clarity and logic of this explanation: your readers need to understand how the examples you cite support your assertion.

Conclusion

- Wrap up the essay.
- Remind readers of your thesis.
- Maintain reader interest.

In the conclusion of your rhetorical analysis essay, provide your readers with a sense of closure and remind them of your thesis. The conclusion should flow naturally from the body of your essay and recapture your readers' interest. One strategy you might employ is to echo your paper's introduction. For example, if you open your essay with a question, you might want to come back to it in your conclusion; if you open with a quotation, consider concluding your essay with one. This repetition will help give your essay a sense of balance and closure.

STEP 7—REVISE YOUR ESSAY

When revising your rhetorical analysis essay, make sure your work is accurate, developed, organized, clear, and documented.

- *Accurate*—your essay accurately captures your analysis and accurately represents the source text.
- *Developed*—you thoroughly develop and explain your assertions.
- *Organized*—the assertions in your essay are easy to follow and are interconnected.
- *Clear*—you have provided your readers with the information they need to understand your essay and have presented your ideas using clear, accessible language and sentences.
- *Documented*—all quoted and paraphrased material is documented as needed and your readers can easily discern which information comes from the source texts and which information you provide.

Check the Accuracy of Your Assertions and Examples

As you revise, start by checking your essay's content. First, make sure you have covered everything you intended to cover in your paper and that your essay accurately reflects your views. Second, be sure you have not misrepresented the author of the source text—any material you quote or paraphrase from the source text must accurately capture what the author actually wrote. Finally, be sure you fairly and accurately represent the text's rhetorical situation.

Check the Development of Your Essay

All of your assertions need to be fully explained and supported. Because your rhetorical analysis essay will reflect your individual response to and evaluation of the source text, you have to explain all of your assertions thoroughly. Readers need to know not only what you think but also why you think it. Do not expect readers to draw connections between your assertions and evidence on their own.

Check the Organization

First, be sure your thesis statement offers an accurate overview of your essay. The thesis statement should help guide your reader through your rhetorical analysis, previewing assertions you will develop in the body of your essay. Next, check the topic sentences in the body of your essay. Each topic sentence should relate back to the thesis statement, introduce a new idea, and provide a transition from the previous section of your essay. Be sure that you employ effective transitions within your body paragraphs as well, highlighting the logical relationship of one sentence to the next. Finally, check the opening and closing sections of your essay to be sure each accomplishes what it is supposed to accomplish.

Check for Clarity

Are there any terms that need to be defined? Any references drawn from the source text that need to be explained? Any sentences that could be more clear? Check to see that all quoted and paraphrased material will make sense to someone who has not read the source text and that any technical terms that need to be defined are defined.

Check Your Documentation

Because you are working with a source text, be sure that all quoted and paraphrased material is properly documented.

SAMPLE RHETORICAL ANALYSIS ESSAY

The following is a rhetorical analysis of Lincoln's Second Inaugural Address.

RHETORICAL ANALYSIS OF LINCOLN'S SECOND INAUGURAL ADDRESS

When President Lincoln stepped up to the podium to deliver his second inaugural address, he knew the Civil War was reaching its end. Though victory was not certain, events on the battlefield suggested that Union forces would soon put down the Southern rebellion and reunite the country. Lincoln knew he would soon be presiding over a deeply divided country, with many in the North demanding revenge against the southern states, including the arrest and execution of the Confederacy's leaders. A close analysis of Lincoln's address makes clear, however, that he envisioned a reconstruction based on mercy and forgiveness rather than vengeance, a message he forcefully conveys though the somber tone of the speech and its many religious allusions.

Since the Union forces were nearing victory after four years of brutal warfare, one might assume that Lincoln would deliver a joyful second inaugural address. Instead, the speech's tone is somber and reserved. While he states that the war's progress has been "reasonably satisfactory and encouraging to all" (135), Lincoln makes no prediction about its final outcome. He asserts that both sides in the conflict "deprecated" (135) war and that neither "expected for the war the magnitude or duration which it has already obtained" (135). Lincoln claims that "American slavery" (136) was the primary cause of the war, and though he states that the South was at fault for maintaining and spreading the practice, Lincoln claims that God "gives to both North and South this terrible war as the woe due to those by whom the offense came ..." (136). Instead of celebrating the North's impending victory in the war, Lincoln claims that both the North and the South are paying a terrible price for their moral transgressions.

In his speech, Lincoln soberly assesses the causes and consequences of the war and indicates how the nation should proceed once peace comes. The final paragraph of his speech begins with the famous phrase "With malice toward none, with charity for all" (136), summing up Lincoln's message of mercy and forgiveness. The needed course of action now, Lincoln contends, is "to bind up the nation's wounds, to care for him who shall have borne the battle and for his widow and orphan" (136). This statement embraces both sides in the conflict: the nation's obligation is to care for both Yankee and Rebel soldiers, for all widows and orphans. Such mercy is the only way to obtain "a just and lasting peace among ourselves and with all nations" (136). Again, "ourselves" is inclusive: Lincoln is including the people of both the North and South in this statement, pointing the way to a reunited country. Lincoln's reflective, restrained tone in this speech indicates how he would like every citizen of the United States to respond to war's conclusion: with forgiveness, introspection, and understanding.

Lincoln's message of mercy and forgiveness is also furthered by his many religious allusions. Rather than claiming that the North's coming victory in the war has been ordained by God, Lincoln believes that God is neutral in the conflict, that the North and South are united by a common religious heritage: "Both read the same Bible and pray to the same God ..." (136). Though Lincoln doubts that any deity would support human slavery, he warns his listeners, "judge not, that we be not judged" (136). Lincoln's repeated invocations of God strike a note of humility, reminding his audience that their fate is not in their own hands, that Providence dictates the course of history. The North has no reason to gloat in its victory or to judge the South severely after the war. Both sides have suffered judgment already; now is the time to act "with firmness in the right as God gives us to see the right ..." (136).

Lincoln's Second Inaugural Address establishes a somber, reflective tone and employs numerous religious allusions to convey successfully his central message that, in victory, the North must act with mercy, forgiveness, and humility during reconstruction. Revenge and retaliation is not the path to reestablishing a peaceful, united, just nation. "With malice toward none, with charity for all," the nation could be reunited. Unfortunately, one of those attending the speech that day was John Wilkes Booth, who would soon assassinate the president at Ford's Theater. Lincoln never had the chance to put his philosophy of merciful reconstruction to the test.

Summary Chart

HOW TO WRITE A RHETORICAL ANALYSIS ESSAY

1. **Carefully read the assignment.**
   - *Who is your audience?*
   - *What can you assume your audience knows about the source text and rhetoric?*

2. **Establish the source text's rhetorical situation.**
   - *Who is the source text's author?*
   - *What is the source text's topic?*
   - *Who is the source text's audience?*
   - *What is the source text's purpose?*
   - *What was the occasion for writing the source text?*

3. **Determine the author's goal.**
   - *In a sentence or two, state clearly and specifically what you think the author is trying to accomplish in the source text.*

4. **Identify and evaluate the source text's rhetorical strategies.**
   - *strategies involving the text's content*
   - *use of arguments, evidence, and reasoning*
   - *use of logos, pathos, and ethos*
   - *strategies involving the text's structure*
   - *strategies involving the text's style*

5. **Determine your thesis.**
   - *State how successful the author is in achieving his or her rhetorical goal.*
   - *State which rhetorical strategies you will examine in your essay.*

SUMMARY CHART: HOW TO WRITE A RHETORICAL ANALYSIS ESSAY (CONTINUED)

6. **Write your rough draft.**
    - *Write the introductory section of your essay, indicating the topic of the source text, its title and author, and your thesis. Capture reader interest as well.*
    - *Summarize the source text and its rhetorical situation.*
    - *Draft the body of your essay, examining one rhetorical strategy at a time and supporting your judgment with specific examples from the source text. Explain how each example you cite supports your claim.*
    - *Write the concluding section of your essay, reminding readers of your thesis and maintaining reader interest.*

7. **Revise your essay.**
    - *Make sure your writing is developed.*
    - *Make sure your essay thoroughly develops and explains your assertions.*
    - *Make sure your writing is organized.*
    - *Make sure the assertions in your essay are easy to follow.*
    - *Make sure the assertions in your essay are connected logically.*
    - *Make sure your essay accurately reflects your thesis.*
    - *Make sure your writing is clear.*
    - *Make sure you have provided your readers with the information they need to understand your essay.*
    - *Make sure you have checked to be sure all of your sentences are clear.*
    - *Make sure your essay accurately represents the source text.*
    - *Make sure all of the material in your essay that needs to be documented is documented.*
    - *Make sure readers can tell which information in your essay came from your source text and which information comes from you.*

RHETORICAL ANALYSIS OF WRITTEN TEXTS REVISION CHECKLIST

	Yes	No
1. Have you analyzed the assignment to determine who *your* audience is?	___	___
2. Have you established the source text's rhetorical situation?	___	___
3. Have you paraphrased the author's goal?	___	___
4. Have you evaluated the author's rhetorical strategies in light of his or her goal?	___	___
5. Have you determined which of the author's rhetorical strategies you will evaluate in your essay?	___	___
6. Check the introductory section of your essay. Do you:		
• introduce the topic of your source text?	___	___
• introduce your source text?	___	___
• capture reader interest?	___	___
7. Examine the wording of your thesis. Do you:		
• state whether the author successfully achieves his or her goal?	___	___
• indicate which rhetorical strategies you will examine in your essay?	___	___
8. Do you summarize the source text and describe its rhetorical situation?	___	___
9. Check each section in the body of your essay. Do you:		
• examine one rhetorical strategy at a time?	___	___
• support your judgments with specific examples from the source text?	___	___
• explain the link between your assertions and their supporting evidence?	___	___
10. Have your revised your essay for:		
• accuracy?	___	___
• development?	___	___
• organization?	___	___
• clarity?	___	___
• documentation?	___	___

Chapter 8

RHETORICAL ANALYSIS OF VISUAL TEXTS

DEFINITION AND PURPOSE

Consider for a moment the power of images—how photographs, drawings, or graphics affect the way you experience texts. Images can add emotional punch to a reading, illustrate an assertion, or make a text more entertaining. Images can even make an argument, either alone or in combination with written text. In our daily lives, we are constantly surrounded by visual images. Which ones grab your attention? How do writers manipulate the visual aspects of a text to achieve their desired effects? By analyzing these images, what lessons can you learn about effectively using visual images in your own texts?

The ability to critically read and rhetorically analyze visual texts is becoming an increasingly important skill. Although visual texts have long been a part of human communication (think about the prehistoric cave drawings found throughout the world), they have become more central to communication over the last century. Since the advent of television, our culture has become more centered on visual images, and advances in computer technology have made it increasingly possible for students to incorporate visual images in their own texts. In fact, at some schools, visual presentations—films, streaming video, PowerPoint presentations, and posters—have replaced traditional print-based assignments like term papers and reports. In many majors, students are expected to develop the same kind of fluency in manipulating visual images as they are in manipulating the written word.

This chapter offers advice and instruction on how to read, interpret, and rhetorically analyze the types of visual texts. While you may not have much experience thinking about visual texts the way you will be instructed to do in this chapter, remember that the processes you will employ and the types of questions you will ask closely resemble those you commonly use to read, analyze, and interpret written texts.

READING VISUAL TEXTS CRITICALLY

You might find it odd to consider how you "read" visual texts like photographs, drawings, cartoons, or advertisements. People often draw a distinction between written and visual texts: they "read" words, not pictures. However, as discussed in Chapter 1, reading a text—any text—involves understanding, analyzing, and interpreting it. Similar processes apply to both written and visual texts.

Following are a series of questions you can consider to help you read visual texts critically. Answering them will give you a clearer sense of a visual text's content, creator, purpose, and audience as well as your response to the image.

QUESTIONS CONCERNING THE VISUAL TEXT ITSELF

- What image does the visual represent?
- What are the various parts of the visual?
- What written text, if any, accompanies the visual?

As with written texts, start your reading of a visual text by forming a clear understanding of its literal meaning—what is it in and of itself, what are its parts, and what is its relationship to any accompanying written text? Although this first step may sound easy, it can actually be difficult to examine a visual text objectively, to identify its constituent parts, and to find language that accurately describes what you see. Your first step is to summarize and paraphrase the visual text: state in your own words what you think the visual is depicting. At this point, you are not concerned with the visual's intention or purpose, only with its literal meaning. Pay particular attention to the details of the image. Your eye may immediately be drawn to only one or two aspects of the visual text, but don't stop your analysis there. Examine every aspect of the image—note what's in the background and in the foreground, in light and in shadow, in color and in black and white.

Next, identify the various parts of the visual text. When analyzing a written text, you may discuss its thesis, claims, examples, explanations, structure, and so forth. When analyzing a visual text, you will focus your attention on elements such as these:

Images: What images are contained in the visual? How many are there in the text? Which ones seem to command the most attention? Are there images of people in the text?

If so, who? What are they doing? Are particular objects included in the text? Which ones? What type of setting is depicted in the text: interior or exterior, urban or natural, realistic or fantastic?

Layout: How are the images arranged in the visual? How are they grouped? What aspects of the images are emphasized due to the layout? Which aspects are deemphasized? If there are people in the image, where do they appear in relation to the other images in the text? What appears in the foreground, and what appears in the background? What appears in light and what appears in shadows?

Color: How is color used in the visual text? What colors are used? What is highlighted by the text's use of color, and what is not? If you are examining a black-and-white image, how is shading used to highlight or emphasize particular elements? If there is written text, what color is it? How does color influence the way you respond to the writing?

Appeals: What elements of the visual text are intended to appeal to the reader's emotions, values, or needs? How does the author of the text manipulate its content and/or layout to elicit a particular emotional response from readers? What elements of the text are included to appeal to the reader's intellect or reason? Which elements, if any, are intended to establish the author's credibility or authority?

Note: Carefully examine any written text included in the visual. What does the text say? What is the relationship between the written and visual elements of the text? For example, does the text comment on the images or draw the reader's attention to particular visual elements of the text? How is the writing placed in the text, and where does it appear? Is the placement of the written text significant? Does it impact how you read the visual text?

QUESTIONS CONCERNING THE VISUAL TEXT'S CREATOR OR SOURCE

- Who created the visual text?
- What is the source of the visual text?
- In what publication or website does the visual appear?
- Toward what readership is the publication or website aimed?
- What, generally, is the editorial stance of that publication or website?

Although finding answers to these questions might prove difficult, you should try. As with written texts, identifying the authorship of a visual text is central to understanding and evaluating it. Authorial bias can affect visual texts just as it can written texts. If possible, identify who created the visual text. Who was the artist or photographer? What can you learn about that person's previous work and his or her credentials or affiliations? Approach visual texts as skeptically as you would written texts. We tend to trust visual texts more readily than we do written texts. After all, who hasn't heard the saying, "Pictures don't lie"? Of course, we know that pictures can lie—visual texts can be manipulated as easily as written texts. Visual texts can communicate truths, untruths, or half-truths. Understanding who created a visual text can help you establish its credibility.

Also consider the visual text's source. In what periodical did it appear? On what website? On what television show? In what film? In what advertisement? You need to understand the agenda of the visual text's source. What is the publication or website attempting to accomplish through its use of this particular visual text? Is its intention to inform, persuade, or entertain readers? What biases or agendas might influence the types of visuals a source employs or how it uses those sources? As noted in the chapter on critical reading (Chapter 1), if you are investigating the topic of abortion rights, it would be important to note whether a visual text you are examining was published by the National Abortion Rights Action League or by Operation Life. Each group has its own agenda on this issue, which may well influence how each designs and employs visual texts in its publications or on its website. Again, the possible bias does not disqualify or discredit a visual text. You simply need to take that bias into account when you read, analyze, or evaluate the text.

To better understand a publication's or website's general editorial stance, read some of the articles it publishes or posts and examine other visual texts it provides. While you may not be able to conclude definitively that the particular visual text you are examining reflects the publication's or website's general editorial stance, you will be in a better position to read that material in context. You will be able to conclude whether the particular visual text you are examining is typical of that publication or website.

QUESTIONS CONCERNING THE VISUAL TEXT'S PURPOSE

- What is the intended purpose of the visual?
- How does the creator attempt to achieve that purpose?

Purpose can be difficult to determine when analyzing a text—visual or written—because any text may be serving multiple purposes. Broadly speaking, a visual text may be attempting to inform, persuade, or entertain readers. Although it may be difficult to determine a visual text's exact intent, making an effort to do so is important. You can misread a visual text if you fail to understand its intended purpose.

For example, imagine an advertisement placed in a news magazine by the Sierra Club, one of the nation's largest environmental groups. The full-page ad consists of a black-and-white picture of a mountainside recently cleared of trees by a logging company. All that's left is a seemingly endless string of stumps, charred tree limbs, and muddy pits. In the lower left-hand corner of the page is a single message, printed in white type against the gray background: "The Sierra Club: *www.sierraclub.org.*" What is the purpose of this advertisement? Is it informative, persuasive, or both? Is it trying to inform readers about the Sierra Club's work, encourage them to find out more about the organization, or persuade them to join? While the picture itself may be striking, is the intention of the advertisement to entertain? How do you know? What if the text were different, that is, what if it read: "Help Us Fight Homelessness, *www. sierraclub.org*"? How would this new text change your interpretation of the advertisement's purpose?

Students sometimes run into problems when they read persuasive visual texts as if the texts were merely informative. We tend to read informative texts as if they were objective and factual; after all, that's what makes them different from persuasive texts. From experience, we know we need to read persuasive texts more skeptically than we do informative texts, because the author is actively attempting to sway our opinion about something or move us to act in a particular way. Our defenses are up when we read texts that we believe are persuasive in ways they are not when we read texts we think are primarily informative. In other words, our interpretation of a text's purpose influences how we read that text, how open we are to its message, and how critical we are as readers. Clarifying the purpose of the visual texts you read can help you read them more effectively and accurately.

QUESTIONS CONCERNING THE VISUAL TEXT'S AUDIENCE

- What audience is the visual text's creator trying to reach?
- How has the creator manipulated the visual text to successfully reach that audience?
- How does your understanding of the visual text's intended audience influence the way you read that text?

When you read a visual text, consider the type of reader its author or creator is attempting to reach. Sometimes you can base your conclusion on the publication in which the visual text appears: certain publications cater to certain types of readers. The general readership of *Inside Wrestling* magazine is likely different from the general readership of *Opera Aficionado* (although there may well be people who subscribe to both). Consider the interests and backgrounds of the people who would likely read the periodical or visit the website in which the visual text appeared. How might the author's interest in appealing to that type of reader influence the visual text he or she creates?

Another approach to analyzing audience is to consider the elements of the visual text itself: how did the author's view of his or her audience influence the way he or she constructed the visual text? Put another way, if you did not know the publication or website in which the visual text appeared, how could you determine the writer's or creator's sense of audience by carefully analyzing various elements of the text itself? Consider these questions:

- What types of images are included in the text? Would they appeal to a wide range of readers or to just certain types of readers?
- What examples are included in the text? Would they appeal to a popular or to a specialized audience?
- If there are human models in the text, who are they? What types of people are they? Who might identify with these models? Who might not?
- If there is written text, how formal is it? What cultural references does the written text include? What types of figurative language does it employ? Which readers would likely understand and appreciate this use of language?

Forming an understanding of the visual text's intended audience is important because it will guide the way you analyze that text. Central to analysis is a deceivingly simple question: Why did the author/creator construct the text this way? Assuming a rhetorical intent for all texts—that they are produced to have a particular effect on a particular audience—identifying the intended audience can guide the way you analyze the text itself. In other words, your analysis of the text will be based on your understanding of its intended audience.

QUESTIONS CONCERNING YOUR RESPONSE TO THE VISUAL TEXT

- What is my response to the visual text?
- Which aspects of the visual text elicit that response?
- What are the sources of my response?
- How does my response influence my understanding of the text?

Authors often incorporate visuals into their texts because they know readers are likely to respond to them in ways they will not respond to words alone. Visuals can stir our imagination, move us to anger or sympathy, attract us or alienate us, and cause us to laugh or to cringe. However, we often don't stop to consider our responses to visual texts: we are so wrapped up in responding to them that we don't consider the nature or cause of the response itself. The first step, then, is to recognize and articulate your reaction to a visual text. How does it make you feel? What is your response? Although it might prove difficult, find language that captures your reaction.

Next, identify which elements of the text evoke those responses. People looking at the same visual text may have very different emotional reactions to it, even if they are focusing on the exact same elements. Likewise, two people may have the same emotional response to a text even if they are focusing on different elements: one may be responding to a particular image included in the text and another to the text's layout. As you consider your response to a visual text, try to identify the specific elements that give rise to it. Encountering that text, you felt a particular way—what was in the text, exactly, that gave rise to your response?

Finally, consider why you respond to particular elements of the text the way you do. What knowledge, experience, or values do you have that cause you to react that way? Examining this link can be difficult, but doing so is extremely important, especially if you are going to discuss your response with someone else. For example, you and a classmate may have similar reactions to the same elements of a visual, but why you respond to those elements in a certain way may be very different. Articulating the link between the elements of the text and your responses can help you more fully understand your reactions and how they differ from others'.

READING A VISUAL TEXT—AN EXAMPLE

The following example of a visual text (see the next page) is an advertisement produced by the National Center for Family Literacy and published in the April 2008 edition of *Black Enterprise* magazine. Take a few minutes to carefully study the advertisement, then answer the following questions to get a better sense of how you are reading the visuals and text.

QUESTIONS CONCERNING THE VISUAL TEXT

- What images does the advertisement contain? How would you describe them?
- What do you assume is the relationship between the two people photographed in the advertisement? Why do you assume that? How does the photograph lead you to that conclusion?
- What else does the advertisement contain besides a photograph of the two people? For example, there's copy, but what else is there?
- What does the copy say? What words or ideas stand out in the copy? Why?
- Notice the National Center for Family Literacy name and logo at the bottom of the advertisement. Why are they included? What copy appears below the logo?
- Examine how the images and words on the page are arranged. What purpose might their arrangement serve?
- Notice how the copy employs two shades of gray. What purpose does that alternation serve?
- Which words stand out because they are flush with the margin? Which stand out because they are in dark type?
- What emotional appeals is the advertisement making? Examine how the people are posed for the picture. What appeal is the photographer making? Read the copy carefully. Point out instances in which particular words or phases are included to appeal to readers in specific ways.

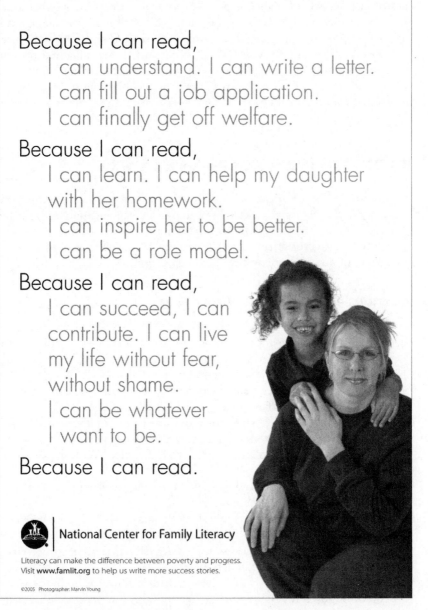

Because I can read,
 I can understand. I can write a letter.
 I can fill out a job application.
 I can finally get off welfare.

Because I can read,
 I can learn. I can help my daughter
 with her homework.
 I can inspire her to be better.
 I can be a role model.

Because I can read,
 I can succeed, I can
 contribute. I can live
 my life without fear,
 without shame.
 I can be whatever
 I want to be.

Because I can read.

National Center for Family Literacy

Literacy can make the difference between poverty and progress.
Visit **www.famlit.org** to help us write more success stories.

©2005   Photographer: Marvin Young

Source: National Center for Family Literacy

QUESTIONS CONCERNING THE VISUAL TEXT'S CREATOR OR SOURCE

- This advertisement appeared in *Black Enterprise* magazine. What do you assume or know about this publication?
- The advertisement was placed by the National Center for Family Literacy. What do you assume or know about this organization?
- Which types of people are likely to read *Black Enterprise*? What can you assume about their backgrounds and interests?
- How has the National Center for Family Literacy used images and copy to appeal to this type of reader?
- Why does the advertisement include copy like the following:
  - "Because I can read, I can understand. I can write a letter. I can fill out a job application. I can finally get off welfare."
  - "Because I can read, I can succeed, I can contribute."
  - "Literacy can make the difference between poverty and progress."

QUESTIONS CONCERNING THE VISUAL TEXT'S PURPOSE

- What is the advertisement's intended purpose? How do you know?
- Is the advertisement primarily a call to action ("Visit *www.famlit.org* to help us write more success stories."), or does it serve other purposes as well? If it serves other purposes, what are they?
- How has the National Center for Family Literacy attempted to achieve their purpose with this advertisement? How are their efforts related to the publication in which the advertisement appears?
- If the goal of the advertisement is primarily to inform readers, what do its creators intend for them to learn? How does the advertisement attempt to do this?
- If the advertisement is primarily a call to action, what is the action its creators want readers to take? How do they attempt to convince or move readers to act in this way?

QUESTIONS CONCERNING THE VISUAL TEXT'S AUDIENCE

- What audience is this advertisement attempting to reach?
- If the advertisement is a call to action, who is supposed to act? How do you know?
- How has the National Center for Family Literacy attempted to reach its intended audience? How has it manipulated the elements of the advertisement—for example, images, copy, layout, color—to reach its audience?

- Who do you assume is the speaker in the advertisement? Who is the first-person narrator? How do you know this? Why might the advertisement be written this way?
- What are the race, gender, and age of the people shown in the advertisement? Why do you think they were chosen as models for this advertisement? How might that choice be related to the intended audience?

QUESTIONS CONCERNING YOUR RESPONSE TO THE VISUAL TEXT

- How do you respond to the advertisement?
- Do you find it interesting? If so, why? If not, why not?
- Are you moved to take any action as a result of reading the advertisement? If so, what action and why? If not, why not?
- Do you respond one way to the photograph of the people and another way to the copy? Why?
- What personal experience or knowledge might influence the way you respond to this advertisement? What is the link between that experience or knowledge and your response?

WRITING A RHETORICAL ANALYSIS OF A VISUAL TEXT

Although on occasion you may be asked to write essays in which you just describe visual texts, you will more commonly be required to analyze and evaluate them rhetorically as well. When you write this type of essay, you will identify how the text's author attempts to achieve a particular rhetorical goal and assess his or her success.

STEP 1—CAREFULLY READ THE ASSIGNMENT

As always, be sure you understand the assignment's intent and requirements. The words *analysis* or *evaluation* may never appear in the assignment. Instead, you might be asked to "assess" or "critique" the text, to decide "how effective" it is, or to argue "how well" it achieves its goal. If you have any questions regarding the goals of the essay you are being asked to write, talk to your teacher.

Also be sure you understand whether you will be evaluating a visual text you locate on your own or if you will be working with an assigned text. If you are free to choose your own visual text for rhetorical analysis, clarify whether there are any restrictions on your choice. For example, does your teacher want you to work with a particular type of visual text (i.e., an advertisement, a political cartoon, a photograph, a sign, or a painting)? Are particular types of visual texts excluded from the analysis? Finally, if the choice of source texts is up to you, have your teacher approve your selection before you begin to write your essay.

STEP 2—ANALYZE AND DESCRIBE THE TEXT

Although this step sounds simple, in some ways it is the most difficult. You need to carefully and objectively examine the text, finding language to describe exactly what you see and read. In several chapters, this textbook discusses the issue of bias when it comes to writing and reading texts—readers need to understand and take into account possible authorial bias when they read texts and acknowledge the biases they themselves bring to the texts they read and write. The same concerns hold true for visual texts as well.

While you need to consider the biases that may have influenced the visual text's creation, you also need to be aware of any biases that could cloud or color your reading of it. Bias can lead you to misinterpret a visual image or actually fail to "see" what is on the page or computer screen because you are not looking for it. Therefore, when you analyze and describe a visual text, try to put aside as best you can any prejudices or assumptions you have concerning the text's content, message, creator, or source. Just as when you write a summary of a print text, your goal here is to be as objective as possible. Try to describe the visual text as objectively and accurately as you can, using language that is neutral and clear.

STEP 3—ESTABLISH THE TEXT'S RHETORICAL SITUATION

To establish the visual text's rhetorical situation, consider your answers to the following questions. Be sure to draw on the insights you gained through your earlier critical reading of the text:

- Who is the text's author or creator?
- Where was the text published, or where does it appear?
- What is the text's message? If there is more than one message, what are they? Does one message dominate?
- Who is the text's intended audience?
- How does the text want to affect that audience? What is the text's purpose?

If you have a hard time answering any of these questions, consider asking someone else—a classmate, roommate, parent, or friend—to examine the text and discuss it with them. Sometimes talking about a visual text with someone is the best way of determining its rhetorical situation.

STEP 4—DETERMINE HOW THE TEXT ATTEMPTS TO ACHIEVE ITS RHETORICAL GOALS

Once you have determined the text's rhetorical goals, identify how its creator manipulates its images and/or text to achieve those ends. Here you would examine how the various elements of the text you identified earlier work separately and together to achieve the text's purpose. Your goal is to find language to describe how the visual text "works," how it communicates its message, and how it accomplishes its goals. The various elements of the text you focus on at this stage in the writing process are the ones you will likely write about in your essay.

STEP 5—DETERMINE YOUR THESIS

Your thesis statement can be either open or closed. An open thesis statement would indicate how successfully you believe the visual text achieved its rhetorical goal. Using the National Center for Family Literacy ad found on page 156, an open thesis statement may read something like this:

> The National Center for Family Literacy produced an advertisement that successfully encourages readers to support their organization.

This thesis identifies what the writer believes to be the advertisement's goal or purpose (to encourage readers to support the sponsoring organization) and asserts a judgment concerning its success.

A closed thesis statement would indicate both your judgment of how well the visual text achieved its goals and the elements of the text you will examine to support your conclusion. Again, using the ad presented on page 156, a closed thesis statement could resemble this:

> Through its copy and its depiction of a mother and her daughter, the National Center for Family Literacy advertisement successfully encourages readers to support their organization.

This thesis still indicates the writer's judgment concerning how successfully the advertisement achieves its goal but also indicates how she will support her claim (by examining the advertisement's use of copy and its portrayal of a mother and her daughter).

STEP 6—WRITE A ROUGH DRAFT

Although the content and structure of the essays you write will vary by the type of visual text you are analyzing and evaluating, the following guidelines will help you write an effective rough draft.

Introductory Section

- Introduce the topic of your essay.
- Introduce the source text you will be working with.
- State your thesis.
- Capture reader interest.

You might consider opening your essay by introducing the topic the visual text addresses, discussing the specific genre of visual text you will be working with (for example, an advertisement or a web page), or paraphrasing the assignment you've been given. Next, introduce the specific visual text you will be working with in your essay, indicating its authorship, source, and perhaps its date of publication. You should also include your thesis statement, typically placed toward the end of your introduction.

Description of the Visual Text and Overview of the Rhetorical Situation

- Describe the visual text.
- Explain the text's rhetorical situation.

In this section of your essay, describe and summarize the visual text you will be working with. Students sometimes understandably question why this section of the paper is needed, especially if the visual text is going to accompany the essay they write: Why describe the text when readers will have access to it? Keep in mind that your description is preparing your readers for the argument you are going to make concerning the text's effectiveness. Through your description, you will bring to your readers' attention the aspects and elements of the text you will discuss in the body of your essay. You will introduce those aspects and elements in this section of your essay and evaluate them later.

The same advice holds true for explaining the visual text's rhetorical situation. You need to tell your reader where and in what context the visual text appeared, who created it, when it was created, and why it was produced. Identify what you believe to be the text's intended audience and purpose. If you believe your readers might interpret the text's purpose differently than you do in your essay, address those concerns here, acknowledging them and defending your own interpretation. The more clearly you explain the text's rhetorical situation in this part of your essay, the easier it will be to write a convincing argument in the body of your paper.

Body Paragraphs

- Develop your thesis one criterion or one example at a time.
- Cite specific examples from the visual text to support your assertions.
- Explain how those examples support the assertions you are making.
- Address possible objections or alternatives to your interpretations, as needed.

As you explain and develop the assertion(s) you put forward in your thesis, examine one evaluative criterion or example from the visual text at a time. For example, if you are basing your evaluation of a text on its use of color, examine one use of color in the text at a time, explaining how it supports the assertion you are making. Afterward, move on to your next example. If you are basing your evaluation on the text's use of color and layout, don't jump back and forth between the two—develop one criterion at a time.

Also, do not assume that the examples you cite speak for themselves or that your readers will understand on their own how the examples you draw from the visual text support the assertion you are making. Instead, carefully explain the link as you see it, and explain how each example lends credibility to your assertion.

Finally, be aware that any conclusions you have reached regarding the visual text are based on your interpretation of that text. Your judgments reflect the way you have interpreted and responded to the images and/or writing. Other readers could legitimately interpret the text differently. As you develop and explain your particular interpretation, note likely objections to your assertions or viable alternative interpretations, when necessary. Acknowledging and addressing these objections or alternatives increases your credibility as a writer and strengthens your assertions.

Conclusion

- Wrap up your essay in an interesting way.
- Remind readers of your thesis.

As with other types of source-based essays, you want to wrap up your analysis/evaluation of a visual text in a way that reminds readers of the primary assertions you've made and that maintains interest. One way to reassert your primary claims is to simply restate your thesis; however, this approach does little to sustain reader interest. Instead, consider closing your essay with an interesting question or provocative assertion, to either challenge other readers' interpretations of the visual text or to predict the future, perhaps speculating on how successful the visual text will be in achieving its desired goals.

STEP 7—REVISE YOUR ESSAY

When revising your analysis/evaluation of a visual text, make sure your writing is clear, developed, and well organized.

- *Clear*—your readers understand the assertions you are making and the link between your evaluations and the source text.
- *Developed*—you have thoroughly explained your assertions and have examined alternative interpretations when needed.
- *Organized*—your assertions are logically connected, and your evaluation is guided by an overarching thesis.

Check for Clarity

When you revise your essay, at some point try to switch roles: you are no longer the author of your paper but someone reading it for the first time. Are there any assertions a reader might have a difficult time understanding? Are there any terms that need to be more clearly defined? Is the connection between your analysis/evaluation and the source text itself always clear?

In other words, would readers understand exactly what aspects or elements of the source text you are analyzing, evaluating, or responding to? Have you explained your assertions thoroughly? Revise your essay as necessary to improve clarity.

Check the Development of Your Essay

Have you supported each of your assertions with references to the source text? Have you explained the connection between your assertions and the source text? The examples you cite from the source text cannot speak for themselves; do not expect your readers to understand the link between your assertions and the evidence you cite. Instead, clearly explain your reasoning.

Check the Organization

First, check your thesis statement. Does it accurately reflect and predict your essay's content and structure? If not, revise it. Second, check your topic sentences. Does each one introduce a new idea, provide a transition from the previous section of your essay, and, in some way, echo your thesis statement? Check the quality of the opening and closing sections of your essay—do they accomplish their intended goals? Finally, add transitions within paragraphs where needed to help guide your readers through your essay.

SAMPLE RHETORICAL ANALYSIS OF A VISUAL TEXT

The following sample essay analyzes and evaluates the National Center for Family Literacy advertisement found on page 156.

AN EFFECTIVE ADVERTISEMENT FOR LITERACY SUPPORT

The idea of an organization devoted to the promotion of literacy paying for a magazine advertisement may seem odd. After all, if people can read the ad, they are already literate and have no need of the organization's services. If they are illiterate, they cannot read the ad at all. So what would be the purpose of such an advertisement? Judging by the ad placed by the National Center for Family Literacy in the April 2008 edition of *Black Enterprise* magazine, the purpose would be to garner support for the organization's programs and services. Through its use of copy, layout, and models, the National Center for Family Literacy demonstrates just how effective such an ad can be.

Unlike many other advertisements in *Black Enterprise*, the one sponsored by the National Center for Family Literacy is simple—using shades of black and white rather than color. Most of the ad consists of copy printed on a white background with two models—seemingly a mother and her daughter—appearing in the bottom right-hand corner. The bottom left-hand corner contains the National Center for Family Literacy name and logo, the message "Literacy can make the difference between poverty and progress," and an appeal to "Visit *www.famlit.org* to help us write more success stories."

The copy consists of the phrase "Because I can read" repeated four times in boldface print. Below three of these phrases—which serve as headings—are first-person statements (presumably from the mother in the ad) printed in a lighter typeface to finish the sentence. Under the first heading, the copy explains how becoming literate helped her find a job and get off welfare. Under the second heading, the copy focuses on how becoming literate helped her become a better mother and role model for her daughter. Under the third, the copy explains how being able to read has enabled the mother to live without fear and shame, allowing her to achieve economic success.

One reason this advertisement works well is that its copy appeals to the type of person likely to read *Black Enterprise* magazine. *Black Enterprise* is aimed primarily at African-American businesspeople, entrepreneurs, and philanthropists, people who have established or work for successful companies, who are looking for business opportunities, or who seek charitable opportunities. Those who read this magazine are aware of how important it is to have a trained, literate workforce and may have a greater understanding of and sympathy for people who must overcome obstacles to succeed.

Consequently, the copy under the first heading reads, "Because I can read, I can understand. I can write a letter. I can fill out a job application. I can finally get off welfare." Many readers of *Black Enterprise* would want to support an organization that helps potential workers learn how to fill out a job application, join the workforce, and move off of welfare. The copy under the second heading appeals to the readers' emotions. Supporting the work of the National Center for Family Literacy will improve the life of the family pictured in the ad—thanks to the organization, the mother can now "help my daughter with her homework," "inspire her to be better," and be a better "role model." Supporting the National Center for Family Literacy is not just in the economic interest of those who read *Black Enterprise*, it is also a humanitarian act.

The copy under the third heading combines elements of the first two. It opens with an echo of the first: "Because I can read, I can succeed. I can contribute." The copy indicates that the National Center for Family Literacy can help women like the one in the advertisement enter the workforce and achieve economic success. The next two statements, however, return to emotional appeals: "I can live my life without fear, without shame. I can be whatever I want to be." The copy is designed to build a bridge between the readers' experiences and the National Center's mission by stressing the need to help people overcome fears and obstacles and by working hard, to succeed.

Also making the National Center for Family Literacy's ad effective is its use of layout—how the copy and visuals are arranged on the page. The phrase "Because I can read," is repeated four times, printed in boldface along the left-hand margin of the page. Due to their placement and appearance, these words catch the reader's eye first. This repeated phrase dominates the ad, leading the reader's eye down the page to the National Center for Family Literacy's logo. The lighter-colored text underneath each heading catches the reader's eye because of its appearance and the repetition of "I": nine of the thirteen lines under the headings begin with "I." The use of first person in these lines makes the advertisement's copy personal, encouraging readers to identify with the mother and daughter pictured in the lower right-hand corner. People are more likely to support a charitable organization if they can identify and empathize with those who will be receiving the aid.

In fact, the depiction of the people in the advertisement also makes it effective. The copy surrounds and frames the two people, a mother and her child. Reading the headings left to right leads the reader's eye directly toward them. The mother is squatting down and her daughter is standing behind her, leaning in, a hand on each of her mother's shoulders. The mother's right hand is on her knee; her left hand rests on top of her daughter's right hand. The mother has a slight, proud grin on her face, while the daughter shows a full-toothed smile. These are average people—the mother appears to be wearing a sweatsuit of some sort and the daughter a polo shirt. The mother and her daughter are quite ordinary people, people whom the readers of *Black Enterprise* might know or see every day on the street. The message of the ad is clear: the National Center for Family Literacy helps average families like this one.

Finally, the facial expressions and race of the mother and daughter are crucial elements of the advertisement. The daughter seems overjoyed with the fact that her mother can now read, while the mother is brimming with confidence. Who wouldn't want to support an organization that would improve the life of such a cute little girl? Significant, too, is the fact that the mother is white while her daughter is biracial. While *Black Enterprise* magazine primarily attracts African-American readers, the advertisement makes clear that the National Center for Family Literacy works to improve the lives of all people, regardless of race.

The National Center for Family Literacy advertisement that appeared in *Black Enterprise* magazine is not aimed at recruiting people who need the center's services. Instead, it is intended to attract possible donors and supporters. Beneath the center's logo at the bottom of the ad is copy that reads, "Literacy can make the difference between poverty and progress," and an appeal to "Visit *www.famlit.org* to help us write more success stories." Readers with a charitable heart may well consider supporting the organization after reading this successful ad.

Summary Chart

HOW TO WRITE A RHETORICAL ANALYSIS OF A VISUAL TEXT

1. **Carefully read the assignment.**
   - *Clarify your purpose.*
   - *Clarify the degree of freedom you have to select a visual text to evaluate.*

2. **Analyze and describe the text.**
   - *Examine every aspect of the text.*
   - *Attempt to put aside any biases you bring to the text.*

3. **Establish the text's rhetorical situation.**
   - *Who is the text's author or creator?*
   - *Where was the text published or where does it appear?*
   - *What is the text's message?*
   - *Who is the text's intended audience?*
   - *What is the text's purpose?*

4. **Determine how the text attempts to achieve its rhetorical goals.**
   - *How do the various elements of the text work separately and together to achieve the text's purpose or goal?*

5. **Determine your thesis.**
   - *Identify what you think the text's goal is and assert a judgment concerning how well it succeeds in achieving that goal.*
   - *Decide if you will use an open or closed thesis.*
   - *If you use a closed thesis, indicate which elements of the text you will examine in your essay.*

SUMMARY CHART: HOW TO WRITE A RHETORICAL ANALYSIS
OF A VISUAL TEXT (CONTINUED)

6. **Write a rough draft.**
   - *Write the introductory section of your essay, indicating the topic of your essay, identifying the source text you will be working with, stating your thesis, and capturing reader interest.*
   - *Provide a brief but thorough description of the text and explain its rhetorical situation.*
   - *Draft the body of your evaluation in a manner that is consistent with your thesis, examining one element at a time of the visual text, citing specific examples from the text to support any assertions you make, explaining how those examples support your claims, and addressing possible objections to or questions concerning your interpretation.*
   - *Write the concluding section of your essay, writing up your evaluation, reminding readers of your thesis, and maintaining reader interest.*

7. **Revise your essay.**
   - *Make sure your writing is clear.*
   - *Make sure your writing is well developed.*
   - *Make sure your writing is organized.*

RHETORICAL ANALYSIS OF A VISUAL TEXT REVISION CHECKLIST

	Yes	No
1. Have you carefully analyzed the assignment to determine whether you are supposed to describe, analyze, and/or evaluate the text?	_____	_____
2. Have you carefully examined every aspect of the source text?	_____	_____
3. Have you established the visual text's rhetorical situation?	_____	_____
4. Have you established how the creators of the visual text attempt to achieve their rhetorical goal?	_____	_____
5. Have you determined how well they achieve their goal?	_____	_____
6. Have you expressed your findings in a clear thesis statement that can guide the development of your essay?	_____	_____
7. In the introductory section of your essay, do you:		
• introduce the topic?	_____	_____
• introduce the source text?	_____	_____
• state your thesis?	_____	_____
• attempt to capture reader interest?	_____	_____
8. In the body of your essay, do you:		
• provide an overview or description of the visual text?	_____	_____
• develop your essay one criterion at a time?	_____	_____
• cite specific examples from the text to support your claims?	_____	_____
• explain how those examples support your assertions?	_____	_____
• address possible objections to your interpretation?	_____	_____
9. In the concluding section of your essay, do you:		
• wrap up your essay in an interesting way?	_____	_____
• remind readers of your thesis?	_____	_____
10. Have you revised your essay for:		
• clarity?	_____	_____
• development?	_____	_____
• organization?	_____	_____
11. Have you proofread your essay?	_____	_____

Chapter 9

INFORMATIVE SYNTHESIS

DEFINITION AND PURPOSE

In a synthesis, you combine information from two or more readings to support a position of your own. Your aim in the paper can be expository (to convey information) or argumentative (to convince readers that your thesis concerning the readings is correct). In either case, when writing a synthesis, you combine material from two or more readings with your own knowledge and reasoning to explain or support your thesis.

College writing assignments often require you to synthesize material. In some courses the assignment will be direct and clear: "Compare what Author A and Author B have to say about topic X. How are their views alike and how are they different?" Other times the assignment might be more subtle: "Authors A, B, and C all address topic X. Which do you find most convincing?" Completing either assignment would require you to form and defend a thesis by drawing information from two or more readings.

To write a synthesis, you first need to sort through the readings to find information you can use in your paper. Being able to annotate readings thoroughly is essential. Second, you need to find the best way to organize this material around your own thesis and the demands of the assignment. Third, you need to find a place in the essay for your own ideas, findings, or arguments. Composing a synthesis usually involves more than just stringing together quoted and paraphrased material from other writers. Fourth, as you write your paper, you need to keep straight who receives credit for which ideas. Through proper documentation, you need to clarify for your readers when you are drawing on the work of a particular author and when you are developing material yourself. Finally, as you revise your work, you need to keep clearly in mind the rhetorical situation of the assignment. In your efforts to work with other people's ideas, you cannot afford to lose sight of your readers' needs and the purpose of the assignment.

TYPES OF SYNTHESIS ESSAYS

Synthesis essays can assume many different forms in college, some rather specialized and sophisticated. One way to begin sorting through all this variety is to recognize that for the most part the assignments you receive will ask you to compose either an **informative** or an **argumentative** synthesis (see Chapter 10).

The goal of an informative synthesis is to clearly and efficiently communicate the information you have gathered from two or more readings. You do not defend a position of your own or critique the source texts in this type of paper. Your primary aim is to summarize the material in the readings and convey the information to your readers in a clear, concise, organized fashion, often comparing and contrasting the texts. In contrast, the goal of an argumentative synthesis is to convince your reader to accept an argument you are presenting on either the quality of the readings or the topic they address. You use the material in the source texts to support your thesis, sometimes summarizing the readings and sometimes critiquing them.

Either type of synthesis can be organized in a variety of ways. Often writers will choose to employ either a **block** or an **alternating** format. When you use a block format to structure your synthesis, you discuss only one source text at a time. With an alternating format, you switch back and forth between readings as you develop your thesis point by point.

Before examining each type of synthesis in more detail, read the following arguments concerning the relationship between television viewing and childhood violence. What is each author's stance on the topic? What aspects of the topic most capture the author's interest? How convincing is each author's argument?

Media Violence and Children's Emotions: Beyond the "Smoking Gun"

Joanne Cantor

Dr. Joanne Cantor is Director of the Center for Communication Research at the University of Wisconsin—Madison.

Research on media violence is often misunderstood by the general public. There are two important reasons why. One is a methodological issue: It is impossible to do the type of "smoking gun" research that would please the ardent skeptics. The other is that most public discussions of media violence don't adequately address the emotional consequences of viewing. I will briefly discuss the methodological issues and then focus on the important role of emotional reactions both in the risks of media violence and in potential remedies.

As for the methodological problems: We can't randomly assign children early in their lives to watch different doses of violence on television and then 20 years later see which children committed violent crimes. But the same type of limitation also exists for medical research: We can't randomly assign groups of people to smoke differing amounts of cigarettes for 20 years, and then count the number of people who developed cancer.

Tobacco researchers conduct correlational studies in which they look at the amount people smoked during their lives and then see the rate at which they have succumbed to cancer. They control statistically for other factors, of course—other healthy and unhealthy behaviors that either reduce or promote the tendency to develop cancer. Then they can find out whether smoking contributed to cancer, over and above these other influences. And since they can't do cancer experiments on people, they use animal studies. These are artificial, but they tell us something about the short-term effects of tobacco that can't be found from correlational studies. Putting the two types of research together, we now have powerful data about the effects of smoking on the development of cancer.

Similarly, media violence researchers do longitudinal studies of children's media exposure and look at the types of behaviors they engage in over time. We also control for other factors, such as previous aggressiveness, family problems, and the like. We don't look at media violence in a vacuum; we examine whether there is a correlation between television viewing and violent behavior, even controlling for other influences. We also do experiments. Like the animal experiments for cancer, these are not natural situations, but such experiments fill the gaps we cannot fill otherwise. They are meant to show short-term effects, like increases in hostility or more accepting attitudes toward violence—changes that we know increase the likelihood of violent actions, both in the short term and in the long run.

As with tobacco, the two types of media research form a powerful picture. Even though there are many studies that can be criticized, there are many more others that are valid. A recent meta-analysis[1] putting all the studies together, makes a compelling case that media violence does contribute to anti-social behaviors, including violence. It's also misguided to say the effects of media violence on violent behavior are trivial. To give an example, a recent national survey of Israeli middle-schools[2] showed that when World Wrestling Federation was introduced to Israeli TV in 1994, the widespread imitation of the wrestlers' behavior produced an epidemic of serious playground injuries. The mayhem continued until the frequency with which the program aired was reduced and educators offered extensive counseling to counteract the show's impact.

The second reason for misunderstanding media violence—the failure to address emotional consequences—is an area I have been investigating for more than 25 years. Two important areas of emotional effects are hostility and desensitization on the one hand, and fears and anxieties on the other.

Desensitization and Hostility

Desensitization is a psychological process by which an emotional response is repeatedly evoked in situations in which the action tendency that arises out of the emotion proves irrelevant. Desensitization is sometimes used to treat phobias, by gradually and repeatedly presenting a frightening stimulus under nonthreatening conditions. Over time, when desensitization works, the phobic response becomes less and less intense. In a somewhat analogous fashion, exposure to media violence, particularly that which entails bitter hostilities or the graphic display of injuries, initially induces an intense emotional reaction in viewers. Over time and with repeated exposure, however, many viewers exhibit decreasing emotional responses to the depiction of violence and injury. Desensitization to violence has been documented in a variety of outcomes. For example, it has been observed as reduced arousal and emotional disturbance while witnessing violence;[3] as greater hesitancy to call an adult to intervene in a witnessed physical altercation;[4] and as less sympathy for the victims of domestic abuse.[5] Few people would argue that any of these are healthy outcomes.

There is also ample evidence that viewing violence increases viewers' hostile feelings. Some people argue that the well-substantiated correlation between chronic hostility and violence viewing simply shows that people who are already hostile are more likely to choose violence. Well, it's true that violent, hostile people are more attracted to media violence,[6] but research shows that the relationship is bi-directional. A 1992 field investigation[7] is a good illustration of this fact. Researchers went to a theater and asked moviegoers to fill out the Buss-Durkee hostility inventory either before or after they viewed a film that they themselves had selected. The findings showed that both the male and female viewers who had chosen a violent movie were initially more hostile than the viewers who had selected a nonviolent movie. Moreover, viewers' levels of hostility became even higher after viewing the violent movie, but remained at the same low level after viewing the nonviolent movie.

This study once again disproves the sometimes-popular notion of "catharsis," that violence viewing helps purge people of their hostile inclinations. To the contrary. And this increase in hostility is not necessarily short-lived. A 1999 experiment[8] looked at the emotional and interpersonal consequences of repeated exposure to gratuitous violence. Researchers randomly assigned both male and female college students to view either intensely violent or nonviolent feature films for four days in a row. On the fifth day, in a purportedly unrelated study, the participants were put in a position to help or hinder another person's chances of future employment. The surprising results indicated that both the men and the women who had received the recent daily dose of film violence were more harmful to that person's job prospects, whether she had treated them well or had behaved in an insulting fashion. The repeated violence viewing apparently provided an enduring hostile mental framework that damaged interactions that were affectively neutral as well as those that involved provocation.

The research I've presented on the impact of media violence on desensitization and hostility demonstrates that we should not limit ourselves to considering the most obvious, final outcomes of viewing violence, that is, behaving violently, when attempting to understand its harmful consequences.

Fear and Anxieties

There is growing evidence that violence viewing also induces intense fears and anxieties in child viewers. A 1998 survey[9] of more than 2,000 third through eighth graders in Ohio revealed that as the number of hours of television viewing per day increased, so did the prevalence of symptoms of psychological trauma, such as anxiety, depression, and posttraumatic stress. Similarly, a 1999 survey[10] of the parents of almost 500 children in kindergarten through fourth grade in Rhode Island revealed that the amount of children's television viewing (especially television viewing at bedtime) and having a television in their own bedroom, were significantly related to the frequency of sleep disturbances. Indeed, 9% of the parents surveyed reported that their child experienced TV-induced nightmares *at least once a week*.

Finally a random national survey[11] conducted in 1999 reported that 62% of parents with children between the ages of two and seventeen said that their child had been frightened by something they saw in a TV program or movie.

Two recent studies of adults' retrospective reports[12,13] of memories of having been frightened by a television show or movie demonstrate that the presence of vivid, detailed memories of enduring media-induced fear is nearly universal. Of the students reporting fright reactions in the study we conducted at the Universities of Wisconsin and Michigan, 52% reported disturbances in eating or sleeping, 22% reported mental preoccupation with the disturbing material, and 35% reported subsequently avoiding or dreading the situation depicted in the program or movie. Moreover, more than one-fourth of the respondents said that the emotional impact of the program or movie (viewed an average of six years earlier) was still with them at the time of reporting!

Studies like these and many anecdotal reports reveal that it is not at all unusual to give up swimming in the ocean after seeing *Jaws*—in fact, a surprising number of people report giving up swimming altogether after seeing that movie. Many other people trace their long-term fears of specific animals, such as dogs, cats, or insects to childhood exposure to cartoon features like *Alice in Wonderland* or *Beauty and the Beast* or to horror movies.[14] I would like to note here that the impact of frightening media depictions are not *just* "psychological." As disturbing as unnecessary anxieties are by themselves, they can readily lead to physical ailments (especially when they disrupt sleep for long periods of time).

For the most part, what frightens children in the media involves violence or the perceived threat of violence or harm. It is important to note, however, that parents often find it hard to predict children's fright reactions to television and films because a child's level of cognitive development influences how he or she perceives and responds to media stimuli. My associates and I have conducted a program of research to explore developmental differences in media-induced fright reactions based on theories and findings in cognitive development. I have summarized this research and its implications for parents and others interested in children's mental health in my book *"Mommy, I'm Scared": How TV and Movies Frighten Children and What We Can Do to Protect Them.* This research shows that as children mature cognitively, some things become less likely to disturb them, whereas other things become potentially more upsetting.

As a first generalization, the importance of how things look decreases as a child's age increases. This finding is consistent with research showing that preschool children tend to sort and match stimuli based on perceptible characteristics, but as they mature through the elementary school years, this tendency becomes supplanted by the tendency to attend increasingly to the more conceptual aspects of stimuli. Both our experimental[15] and our survey[16] research supports the generalization that preschool children (approximately 3 to 5 years old) are more likely to be frightened by something that looks scary but is actually harmless than by something that looks attractive but is actually harmful; for older elementary school children (approximately 9 to 11 years), appearance carries much less weight, relative to the behavior or destructive potential of a character, animal, or object.

A second generalization from research is that as children mature, they become more responsive to realistic, and less responsive to fantastic dangers depicted in the media. This prediction is based on developmental trends in children's understanding of the fantasy-reality distinction. Our 1984 survey of parents[17] supported this trend. In general, parents' tendency to mention fantasy offerings, depicting events that could not possibly occur in the real world, as sources of their child's fear, decreased as the child's age increased, and the tendency to mention fictional offerings, depicting events that could possibly occur, increased. Further support for this generalization comes from our 1996 survey[18] of children's fright responses to television news. A random survey of parents of children in kindergarten through sixth grades showed that fear produced by fantasy programs decreased as the child's grade increased, while fear induced by news stories increased with age.

A third generalization is that as children mature, they become frightened by media depictions involving increasingly abstract concepts. Again, research in cognitive development shows that the ability to think abstractly increases throughout elementary school and continues to mature during the teenage years. Data supporting this generalization come from our 1986 survey[19] of children's responses to the made-for-television movie *The Day After*. Although many people were concerned about young children's reactions to this movie, which depicted the devastation of a Kansas community by a nuclear attack, the survey showed that the emotional impact of this movie increased as the viewer's age increased. Similarly, our survey[20] of children's reactions to television coverage of the war in the Persian Gulf showed that preschool and elementary school children were more likely to be frightened by the concrete, visual aspects of the coverage (such as the missiles exploding), whereas teenagers were more disturbed by the abstract components of the story (such as the possibility of the conflict spreading).

Coping with Media Violence Effects

An understanding of emotional reactions to media is also important in developing ways to prevent or reduce the harm produced by media violence. Research in cognitive development has helped us discover effective ways to reassure children who have been frightened by media threats. These are explained in *"Mommy, I'm Scared."* Strategies for coping with media-induced fears need to be tailored to the age of the child.[21] Up to the age of about seven, nonverbal coping strategies work the best.[22] These include removing children from the scary situation, distracting them, giving them attention and warmth, and desensitization.[23] Eight-year-olds and older can benefit from hearing logical explanations about why they are safe. If what they saw is fantasy, it helps children in this age group to be reminded that what they have seen could never happen.[24] If the program depicts frightening events that can possibly occur, however, it may help to give older children information about why what they have seen cannot happen to them[25] or to give them empowering instructions on how to prevent it from occurring.[26]

As for reducing the aggression-promoting effect of media violence, an understanding of emotional responses can be helpful in developing mediation strategies that can be used by parents or teachers. For example, as viewers become increasingly desensitized and more hostile, they become less and less likely to empathize with the victims of violence. One criticism of the way violence is usually portrayed on television is that it minimizes the apparent harmful consequences to the victim,[27] both promoting desensitization and increasing the likelihood of the adoption of aggressive attitudes and behaviors.

A genre of media violence that typically trivializes the consequences to the victim is the classic cartoon, Woody Woodpecker, for example. In a study just published[28] we showed not only that watching Woody could increase boys' endorsement of aggressive solutions to problems, but that empathy instructions could intervene in this effect. Second- through sixth-grade boys were randomly assigned one of three groups: (1) a no-mediation group, who watched the cartoon without instructions; (2) a mediation group who were asked, before viewing, to keep in mind the feelings of the man in the cartoon (this was the tree-medic who was the target of Woody's attacks); and (3) a control group, who didn't see a cartoon. As is frequently found in such studies, the kids who had just seen the violent cartoon without instructions scored higher on pro-violence attitudes than the kids in the control condition (showing stronger agreement with statements like, "sometimes fighting is a good way to get what you want"). However, the kids who were asked to think about the victim's feelings showed no such increase in pro-violence attitudes. As a side-effect, this empathy-promoting intervention reduced the degree to which the children found the cartoon funny. An empathy-promoting intervention may have a dual benefit therefore: intervening in the direct effect of viewing and perhaps reducing future choices of similar fare.

More research is needed to explore other ways to intervene in the negative effects of media violence. Given the fact that media violence is such a profitable business, it is not likely to go away in the near future. However, a greater understanding of the emotional consequences of viewing violence will help policymakers, teachers, parents, and children deal with the problem. To my mind, we need better public education for parents and teachers, including better information about media effects, more useful content labels, and additional mediation strategies based on research findings. We also need media literacy education for children, including helping them place what they see in perspective, and encouraging a critical analysis of their own media choices.

Endnotes

1. Paik, H., & Comstock, O. (1994). The effects of television violence on anti-social behavior: A meta-analysis. *Communication Research, 21,* 516–546.
2. Lemish, D. (1997). The school as a wrestling arena: The modeling of a television series. *Communication, 22*(4), 395–418.
3. Cline, V. B., Croft, R. O., & Courrier, S. (1973). Desensitization of children to television violence. *Journal of Personality and Social Psychology, 27,* 360–365.
4. Molitor, F., & Hirsch, K. W. (1994). Children's toleration of real-life aggression after exposure to media violence: A replication of the Drabman and Thomas studies. *Child Study Journal, 24,* 191–207.
5. Mullin, C. R., & Linz, D. (1995). Desensitization and resensitization to violence against women: Effects of exposure to sexually violent films on judgments of domestic violence victims. *Journal of Personality and Social Psychology, 69,* 449–459.
6. Goldstein, J., Ed. (1998). *Why we watch: The attractions of violent entertainment.* New York: Oxford University Press.
7. Black, S. L., & Bevan, S. (1992). At the movies with Buss and Durkee: A natural experiment on film violence. *Aggressive Behavior, 18,* 37–45.
8. Zillmann, D., & Weaver, J. B., III. (1999). Effects of prolonged exposure to gratuitous media violence on provoked and unprovoked hostile behavior. *Journal of Applied Social Psychology, 29,* 145–165.
9. Singer, M. I., Slovak, K., Frierson, T., & York, P. (1998). Viewing preferences, symptoms of psychological trauma and violent behaviors among children who watch television. *Journal of the American Academy of Child and Adolescent Psychiatry, 37,* 1041–1048.
10. Owens, J., Maxim, R., McGuinn, M., Nobile, C., Msall, M., & Alario, A. (1999). Television-viewing habits and sleep disturbance in school children. *Pediatrics, 104*(3), 552 (Abstract). Available at http://www.pediatrics.org/cgilcontent/ful/104/3/c27.
11. Gentile, D. A., & Walsh, D. A. (1999). MediaQuotient$^{(TM)}$: National survey of family media habits, knowledge, and attitudes. Minneapolis, MN: National Institute on Media and the Family.
12. Harrison, K., & Cantor, J. (1999). Tales from the screen: Enduring fright reactions to scary media. *Media Psychology, 1,* 97–116.
13. Hoekstra, S. J., Harris, R. J., & Helmick, A. L. (1999). Autobiographical memories about the experience of seeing frightening movies in childhood. *Media Psychology, 1,* 117–140.
14. Cantor, J. (1998). *"Mommy, I'm scared": How TV and movies frighten children and what we can do to protect them.* San Diego, CA: Harcourt Brace.
15. Hoffner, C ., & Cantor, J. (1985). Developmental differences in responses to a television character's appearance and behavior. *Developmental Psychology, 2,* 1065–1074.

16. Cantor, J., & Sparks, G. G. (1984). Children's fear responses to mass media: Testing some Piagetian predictions. *Journal of Communication, 34*(2), 90–103.

17. Cantor, J., & Sparks, G. G. (1984). Children's fear responses to mass media: Testing some Piagetian predictions. *Journal of Communication, 34*(2), 90–103.

18. Cantor, J., & Nathanson, A. (1996). Children's fright reactions to television news. *Journal of Communication, 46*(4), 139–152.

19. Cantor, J., Wilson, B. J., & Hoffner, C. (1986). Emotional responses to a televised nuclear holocaust film. *Communication Research, 13,* 257–277.

20. Cantor, J., Mares, M. L., & Oliver, M. B. (1993). Parents' and children's emotional reactions to televised coverage of the Gulf War. In B. Greenberg & W. Gantz (Eds.), *Desert Storm and the mass media* (pp. 325–340). Cresskill, NJ: Hampton Press.

21. Cantor, J. (1998). *"Mommy, I'm scared": How TV and movies frighten children and what we can do to protect them.* San Diego, CA: Harcourt Brace.

22. Wilson, B. J., Hoffner, C., & Cantor, J. (1987). Children's perceptions of the effectiveness of techniques to reduce fear from mass media. *Journal of Applied Developmental Psychology, 8,* 39–52.

23. Wilson, B. J. (1989). Desensitizing children's emotional reactions to the mass media. *Communication Research, 16,* 723–745.

24. Cantor, J., & Wilson, B. J. (1984). Modifying fear responses to mass media in preschool and elementary school children. *Journal of Broadcasting, 28,* 431–443.

25. Cantor, J., & Hoffner, C. (1990). Children's fear reactions to a televised film as a function of perceived immediacy of depicted threat. *Journal of Broadcasting & Electronic Media, 34,* 421–442.

26. Cantor, J., & Omdahl, B. (1999). Children's acceptance of safety guidelines after exposure to televised dramas depicting accidents. *Western Journal of Communication, 63*(1), 1–15.

27. *National Television Violence Study,* Volumes 1–3. (1996–1998). Thousand Oaks, CA: Sage Publications.

28. Nathanson, A. I., & Cantor, J. (2000). Reducing the aggression-promoting effect of violent cartoons by increasing children's fictional involvement with the victim. *Journal of Broadcasting & Electronic Media, 44,* 125–142.

Television Violence and Its Effects on Young Children

Betty Jo Simmons, Kelly Stalsworth, and Heather Wentzell

Betty Jo Simmons, Kelly Stalsworth, and **Heather Wentzell** *are faculty at Longwood College, Virginia.*

Introduction

After the introduction of television in 1939, E. B. White said it was "going to be the test of the modern world. We shall stand or fall by the television—of that I am quite sure" (Asamen & Berry, 1993, p. 10). These prophetic words are proving to be more accurate on a daily basis. With its ability to inform, entertain, teach, and persuade, television unquestionably has tremendous effects upon its viewers. Indeed, television has become the central activity in most homes today. Currently, in the United States, 98% of all households have at least one set. Even more astounding is the fact that it is watched an average of 7.5 hours per day (Asamen & Berry, 1993). Beckman (1997) concurs, saying that children watch more than 28 hours of television each week and in the process the average child, before the age of 12, has viewed over 8,000 murders.

Research on Television Violence

In order to clean up the airways for young audiences, the Federal Communications Commission (FCC) enacted The Children's Television Act in 1990. Many television stations show strictly positive programs, but the negative ones are also still being aired. This point is important because preschool children are curious and easily influenced. They tend to mimic and repeat what they hear and see on television without knowledge of right and wrong.

One of the main concerns with television programming is the violence viewed by children. Berk (1993) says that because young folks cannot fully understand what they see on television, they are very much under its influence. Davidson (1996) agrees that children are extremely vulnerable to television between the ages of 2 to 8 years because of their maturational inability to separate what they view from reality. Attention to violence on television became a matter of serious consideration in the 1950s, with the first congressional hearing taking place in 1952. From 1952 to 1967, many analyses were done of the content of television programs. In the late 1960s and early 1970s, the scrutiny shifted from content alone to specifically discerning the effects of violence on viewers. The resulting findings supported the idea that a causal relationship existed between television violence and aggressive behavior (National Institutes of Mental Health, 1983).

Imitating Violence

Levin and Carlsson-Paige (1996) lament the 1984 deregulation of broadcasting, noting that subsequently teachers began to observe an escalation of violence in their classrooms. They state that "Today, U.S. crime rates are increasing most rapidly among youth who were in their formative early years when children's TV was deregulated and violent programs and toys successfully deluged childhood culture" (p. 17). Governmental investigation led to several studies about the effects of violence. Two of the most well known were done by Bandura and Berkowitz. Bandura (1973), a social learning theorist, purported that children learn primarily through social modeling. From his studies, he concluded that children went through three stages—exposure, acquisition, and acceptance (Moody, 1980). He maintained that increased exposure to aggressive models led to reduced inhibitions toward violence. For example, when a television character acts violently and the consequences are positive, then the viewer is more likely to assume this behavior. Today, unfortunately even the "good" guys feel obligated to blow away their opponents (Munson, 1996).

Berkowitz (1962) examined the effects of television on aggressive drives. He concluded that exposure to televised violence does arouse aggressive behaviors, especially if viewers believe that aggression is justified. Noble (1975) maintains that aggressive behavior is harder to inhibit if viewers have a target which is associated with a television victim. Similarly, a study involving five different countries in which children were subjected to violence through television found evidence that even brief exposures caused them to be more accepting of other aggressive behavior. This research also concluded that the more children watched television, the more accepting they became of aggressive actions (Huesmann & Eron, 1986). Davidson (1996) reports that research done by Leonard Eron of the University of Michigan shows that violence children watched as eight-year-olds became a better predictor of adult aggression than socioeconomic and childrearing factors.

Cullingford (1984) reports on a study done by Shaw and Newell in which they interviewed families about their concerns over television. One of the major findings was that violence went almost unnoticed. Even when people were shown killings and then heavily prompted, most did not think of it as violent. The frightening truth was that "objectionable content" had become so acceptable that it was invisible. Later investigations by Drabman and Thomas (Geen, 1981) used observation to determine the effects of violent films on the way children resolved conflict. They, like Geen, who used blood pressure as the indicator, concluded that violence leads to desensitization (Molitor, 1994; Voojis & Voort, 1993). Thus, it is not hard to understand what Minnow, former chair of the Federal Communications Commission, meant when he said that in the 1960s, he worried that his children would not greatly benefit from television, but in the 1990s, he worries that his grandchildren may be harmed by it (Minnow, 1995).

Violence and Fear

In addition to theories that television can cause children to be more aggressive and less sensitive to the results of violence, there is also the theory that televised violence causes viewers to be afraid. According to this theory, the misconstrued world presented on television is seen as a mirror of reality and viewers become convinced they will fall victim to violence. It is reasoned that viewers absorb information without analyzing it and subsequently develop false beliefs about law enforcement and crime. Chen (1994), who found that crime during prime time is depicted 10 times greater than in reality, gives credence to the notion that television is distorted in its portrayal and resolution of crime and violence.

Levine (1996) says 3- to 5-year-old children live in a magical world that often leaves them terrified of things which completely surprise adults. On the other hand, there are those who disagree that television makes them afraid. According to Hamilton (1993), today's children are much more preoccupied with violence. Therefore, according to Dr. Daniel Koenigsberg, chief of child psychiatry at Saint Raphael Hospital, it is not so much that children are scared by it, as it is that they accept it and are intrigued by it. Thus, it is easy to see that not everyone agrees about the effects that violence has; however, it is generally agreed that it does play a significant role in the children's construction of social reality (Voojis & Voort, 1993).

Children's Programs Featuring Violence

According to Kaplan (1998), the National Coalition on Television Violence has classified the Mighty Morphin Power Rangers as the most violent program "ever studied, averaging more than 200 violent acts per hour" (p. 16). Furthermore, in an experimental study involving 5- to 11-year-olds (26 boys and 26 girls with ethnically diverse backgrounds), Kaplan (1998) reports that children who watched Power Rangers committed 7 times more aggressive acts than those who did not. Recognizing that children imitate what they see, several day care centers, nursery schools, and elementary schools have outlawed Power Rangers in play.

According to Evra and Kline (1990), "One of the dangers for preschoolers or early school-age children is their lack of ability to relate actions, motives, and consequences, and they may simply imitate the action they see" (p. 83). Levin and Carlsson-Paige (1996) purport that children cannot assimilate the Power Rangers into their own naturally limited experiences. Thus, unable to devise meaningful play from what they have seen, they act out "what they are unable to understand, primarily the kicking, fighting, and shooting" (p. 18). Teachers, according to Levin and Carlsson-Paige (1996), have observed that children become so fascinated by the Power Rangers that they excuse their own aggressiveness by saying they must do as the Power Rangers do.

Another show, similar in content, is the Teenage Mutant Ninja Turtles. Violence is also the main attraction in this program. The four heroes are pumped-up turtles named after four famous artists: Michelangelo, Donatello, Leonardo, and Raphael. Their mentor is a skilled ninja rat. Each has a distinctive personality and each fights best with specific weapons. The main "bad guy," Shredder, is so named because he has blades protruding from his clothes, which he does not hesitate to use when fighting. In one episode on the Cartoon Network, Shredder tried to use a robot to take over the world and the Turtles stopped him by fighting. At the end of the show, the characters discuss what is supposed to have been learned by the viewers. However, young children watching these shows would not necessarily learn from these messages because they can take in only so much information at a time. According to Evra and Kline (1990), the lack of understanding and well-developed behavioral control causes the main attraction to be primarily the action.

In what may be called the "Dynamic Duos" are found Bugs Bunny and Elmer Fudd, Tweety and Sylvester, the Road Runner and Wile E. Coyote, and Tom and Jerry. Each pair takes turns trying to outsmart and pummel one another. The goofy and colorful characters attract children and the only message that might be sent to children is how to solve problems through fighting.

Similarly, a new wave of cartoons, such as Beavis and Butthead, The Simpsons, King of the Hill, and Daria, are aimed at an adult audience; yet many children are intrigued by these animated cartoons. Most of the themes in these shows focus on adult life, things that young children would not understand. For example, those that focus on teenage life, such as Beavis and Butthead and Daria, show lazy characters concerned only with materialistic and selfish things. These programs also use adult language that is not appropriate for small children to hear. However, since children do watch these shows, they tend to repeat certain things that they see and hear.

For example, at the beginning to Beavis and Butthead, words come across the screen saying that the cartoon is not realistic and the acts in the show should not be repeated. However, such disclaimers do not register in the minds of children who are more intrigued by action than consequences.

For example, in the early 1960s, Schramm, Lyle, and Parker (1961) were pointing out the inherent danger involved in televised violence. They noted that a 6-year-old told his father he wanted real bullets because toy ones did not kill like Hopalong Cassidy's bullets. It appears that when children watch shows, they often do not remember the plot, but they do remember the actions of their favorite characters. Evra and Kline (1990) found that even 14-month-old children have a tendency toward some type of imitation of television.

Public Reaction

Even though there are shows on television that are designed for preschoolers, many American adults feel that there are still not enough programs for young children. In a press release on October 5, 1995, the Center for Media Education (CME) published the results of a national poll which showed strong public support of more educational programs. To quote from the poll:

> More than four in five American adults (82%) believe there is not enough educational children's programming on commercial broadcast television. Three in five adults surveyed (60%) support specific requirements that broadcasters air an hour of educational programming or more for children each day. More than a third of all parents (35%) would require two hours daily. 80% of Americans believe there are good reasons to regulate children's TV more strictly than programming intended for general or adult audiences. The two most frequently cited reasons for the lack of quality in children's broadcast programming are violent (43%) and insufficient educational programming (25%) (Poll on Children's Television, 1995, Center for Media Education).

These complaints are slowly being attended to with new educational programs and the revival of old ones, such as Schoolhouse Rock and Sesame Street. A rating system has recently been enacted. At the beginning of each show, letters and numbers, ranging from "G" to "Adult" appear at the top left-hand corner of the television screen, stating the appropriateness of the television show.

In 1997, in response to the public's demand for improvement in the quality of children's television, the Federal Communications Commission (FCC) issued stronger rules to regulate the Children's Television Act of 1990. According to the new expectations, broadcasters must produce 3 hours weekly of educational programming. These programs must make education the major focus with clearly articulated objectives, and a designated target age group. Fortunately, more stations are appearing and many of them do show programs that are, for the most part, appropriate for all audiences. Channels such as PBS, Animal Planet, The Family Channel, and the Disney channel are examples. However, there is still the question of violence on television. Especially so, since the Children's Television Act is not definitive about the meaning of educational programming. The act simply says that programs must contribute to the well-being of children "in any respect." The "in any respect" seems to be a loophole that dilutes the original intent (*U.S. News and World Report*, 1997).

Even when educational programs are produced, problems remain. One of them lies with the competition. With the availability of cable, violence continues to be prevalent. Children can and do quickly switch the channel to the Cartoon Network (*New York Times*, 1997). Furthermore, since educational programs are not big moneymakers, producers tend to schedule many of them early in the morning or in spots which are not the most normal viewing times. Another major consideration is what Zoglin contended in 1993, namely, that children are not much attracted to educational shows. He says, "The very notion of educational TV often seems to reflect narrow, schoolmarmish notions" (p. 64). Five years later, Mifflin (1997) pointed out that broadcasters agree because they have a hard time finding educational programs that children will watch (*New York Times*, 1997).

Recommendations

Naturally, children are easily confused when they watch the superhero beat up other characters. Therefore, recognizing and taking a proactive position against televised violence becomes a prime responsibility for all those involved in the care and nurturance of young children. With this premise in mind, the following recommendations are offered:

1. Parents, teachers, and communities must work together to combat the violence that is permeating society. They must work to build community programs to prevent violence and diffuse aggressive behavior. They must work on an individual level to teach acceptable and unacceptable standards.
2. Children must have their television viewing supervised and regulated which means that adults have to show responsible behavior themselves by refusing to watch programs that are violent in nature. If they are unwilling to abolish violent programs in their homes, they must take the time to ask questions of their children, explain the seriousness of violence to them, and help them to evaluate what they witness.
3. Parents must not let television become the dominant part of their family's life. It is imperative that drastic steps be taken to curtail the kind of socially unacceptable behavior, which is routinely and daily invited into the average home.
4. Parents and teachers must help young children develop appropriate behavior for social interactions. Children need guidance in learning to settle disagreements with verbal rather than physical skill.

5. Schools need to take television violence seriously, especially so, since it transfers to inappropriate behavior in the classroom. Thus, school personnel should take immediate steps to involve parents and the community in open dialog through newspaper articles, PTA meetings, and public forums.
6. The curriculum must be based upon the developmental needs of young children. Consideration must be given to fantasy, animism, and the inability of children to separate real from the pretend. Young children should be taught how to make decisions and how to work through problems by finding acceptable alternatives to violent acts.

References

Asamen, J., & Berry, G. (1993). *Children and television: Images in a changing sociocultural world.* London: Sage Publications.

Bandura, A. (1973). *Aggression: A social learning analysis.* Englewood Cliffs, NJ: Prentice Hall.

Beckman, J. (1997). *Television violence: What the research says about its effect on young children.* Winnetka, IL: Winnetka Alliance for Early Childhood.

Berk, L. (1993). *Infants, children, and adolescents.* Boston: Allyn and Bacon.

Berkowitz, L. (1962). *Aggression: A social psychological analysis.* New York: McGraw-Hill.

Center for Media Education (1995). Poll on children's television. Press release, October 1995 (also available online).

Chen, M. (1994). *The smart parent's guide to kid's TV.* San Francisco, CA: KQED Books.

Cullingford, C. (1984). *Children and television.* New York: St. Martin's Press.

Davidson, J. (February 2, 1996). *Menace to society.* Rolling Stone, pp. 38–39.

Defining the "educational" in educational TV for children (September 12, 1994) *U.S. News and World Report,* p. 90.

Evra, J., & Kline, W. (1990). *Television and child development.* Hillsdale, NJ: Lawrence Erlbaum Associates.

Geen, R. (1981). Behavioral and physiological reactions to observed violence: Effects of prior exposure to aggressive stimuli. *Journal of Personality and Social Psychology, 40,* 868–875.

Hamilton, R. (May/June, 1993). TV violence—What influence on young minds? *St. Raphael's Better Health*, 7–11.

Huesmann, R., & Eron, L. (1986). *Television and the aggressive child: A cross national comparison.* Hillsdale, NJ: Lawrence Erlbaum Associates.

Kaplan, P. (1998). *The human odyssey.* Pacific Grove, CA: Brooks and Cole.

Levin, D., & Carlsson-Paige, N. (l996). Disempowering the "Power Rangers." *The Education Digest, 61*, 17–21.

Levine, M. (1996). Handling the "boob tube." *Parents Magazine, 71*, 55–57.

Mifflin, L. (September 11, 1997). Can you spell "compliance," boys and girls? *New York Times*, p. C13.

Minnow, N., & LaMay, C. (August 6, 1995). Abandoned in the wasteland. *Detroit Free Press*, Magazine Section, pp. 12–16.

Molitor, F., & Hirsch, K. (1994). Children's toleration of real life aggression after exposure to media violence: A replication of the Drabman and Thomas studies. *Child Study Journal, 24*, 191–203.

Moody, K. (1980). *Growing up on television.* New York: Times Books.

Munson, M. (1995). Media mayhem. *Prevention, 47*, 86–89.

Noble, G. (1975). *Children in front of the small screen.* Thousand Oaks, CA: Sage Publications.

Schramn, W., Lyle, J., & Parker, E. (1961). *Television in the lives of our children.* Stanford, CA: Stanford University Press.

Television and behavior: Ten years of scientific progress and implications for the eighties (1983). Washington, DC: National Institutes of Mental Health.

Voojis, M., & Voort, T. (1993). Learning about television violence: The impact of critical viewing curriculum on children's attitudinal judgment of crime series. *Journal of Research and Development in Education, 26*, 133–141.

Zoglin, R. (1993). If not the Jetsons, what? *Time*, March 22, p. 64.

Does Cartoon Violence Beget Aggressive Behavior in Real Life? An Opposing View

Fran C. Blumberg, Kristen P. Bierwirth, and Allison J. Schwartz

Fran C. Blumberg is professor at Fordham University's Graduate School of Education; **Kristen P. Bierwirth** teaches in Linden Public Schools, Linden, New Jersey; and **Allison J. Schwartz** is a professor at Georgia State University's College of Education.

Nate and Amanda are in the family room playing *Diner Dash*, a computer game in which the goal is to quickly serve restaurant patrons their food before they become angry. Like many of their elementary school-age peers who involve themselves with multiple forms of media simultaneously, they are also watching the Cartoon Network television show *Squirrel Boy* that chronicles the adventures of a young boy whose best friend is a gangly talking squirrel. Their younger sibling, 2-year-old Kenny, also is multi-tasking as he looks up at the television screen to see Rodney J. Squirrel being forced into a catapult by a bully. Nate and Amanda agree that being launched to the moon in a catapult is not as funny as when Rodney was burned in his go-cart while racing down a steep slope. Meanwhile, toddler Kenny's attention becomes diverted to Amanda's stuffed animals when he experiences difficulty following the cartoon story line.

    Squirrel Boy, like many cartoons on the popular Cartoon Network, includes comical acts of aggression and violence. This program is not dissimilar to cartoons that younger generations enjoyed, such as *Bugs Bunny* or *Road Runner*, who found the seemingly belligerent antics of cartoon protagonists as comical. Currently, the common wisdom is that cartoon violence is "bad" even when tinged with humor or at least difficult to understand for younger children, as shown in Kenny's experience. As researchers, educators, and practitioners, we know better than to accept common wisdom. We know to look to science for answers, even if some of those answers are ones we do not like nor agree with.

Why Is Cartoon Violence Considered to Be "Bad"?

Violence can be generally defined as any intentional or accidental action that causes physical or psychological harm (as in the case of verbal abuse) to oneself, another person, animal, or at times, an inanimate object (see National Television Violence Study (NTVS) 1997). Cartoon violence is similar in that harm may be inflicted upon characters. However, the nature of cartoon harm may be fairly minor. For example, Potter and Warren's (1998) content analysis of prime time programming indicated that in comedy shows, violence was more likely to be verbal than physical. According to Kirsch (2006), cartoons show less serious acts of violence than adult-oriented dramas. Kirsch also noted that the comedic element of cartoons also may affect young viewers' beliefs about the applicability of violent acts they see in programs to real-world situations.

Among child and adult viewers, longstanding negative effects of exposure to media violence have included decreases in prosocial behaviors, increases in physiological arousal and enhanced aggressive thoughts, behaviors, and feelings (Ostrov et al. 2006). For example, Kremar and Hight (2007) found that preschoolers who watched an action cartoon or super-hero image, as opposed to young children who watched neutral video clips or animated characters, were more likely to create aggressive story endings. These findings supported the contention that a schema for aggression may be activated as a result of having viewed aggressive acts (Anderson and Carnagey 2004). Further, The Kaiser Family Foundation's 2006 report examining children and the electronic media indicated that 68% of parents of children 6 years of age and younger reported having seen their children imitate behaviors shown on television with 24% of these behaviors identified as aggressive (Rideout and Hamel 2006).

Children's understandings of what they view on television may affect how they are impacted by cartoon violence. According to Kendeou and colleagues (2005), the early comprehension skills of young children transfer across different media such as narratives and television. These skills enable them to make causal inferences and establish connections between events (van den Broek et al. 2005). Thus, because they understand the narrative, they should understand the context in which cartoon violence is shown.

However, while aspects of young children's comprehension of narratives may be relatively sophisticated, their understanding of narratives is best when the content is concrete, familiar, and provides structure allowing them to readily make inferences (Kendeou et al. 2007). Thus, young children tend to focus much of their attention on observable actions instead of internal causes such as characters' intentions (Kendeou et al. 2005). Van den Broek et al. (1996) found that 4-year-olds showed difficulty distinguishing central program content from peripheral or incidental content. This failure to selectively attend to relevant story or non-structural properties of events may, in turn, compromise their ability to incorporate the violent behaviors of cartoon characters into their behavioral repertoire (Kendeou et al. 2005).

Children's understandings of what they view on television also may be influenced by their ability to transfer knowledge from what they see in the media to what they do in daily life which, in turn, depends to some extent on their ability to differentiate between fantasy and reality. One cue that they use to make this distinction is animation (Condry 1989). Despite increased realism in animation over time (Fyfe 2006; Rutenberg 2001), most preschoolers still recognize cartoon programs as "make-believe" (e.g., McKenna and Ossoff 1998), and can differentiate cartoon characters engaged in life-like activities from those engaged in pretend activities (Rosen et al. 1997). Skolnick and Bloom (2006) reported that young children recognized that different fictional characters such as SpongeBob and Batman inhabited distinct fictional worlds. This ability has ramifications for their views of what actions are possible in these worlds as opposed to real life.

The character's motives and the consequences of violent actions also may help children interpret events shown on television. Adult intervention also may help children understand relationships between social acts portrayed on television and cues such as motives and consequences (Collins et al. 1981). For example, Pohan and Mathison (2007) note that teachers should recognize the general cultural messages imparted to children via television. These messages pertain to societal depictions of cultural diversity and appropriate modes of social interaction.

What Do Children Think When They See Cartoon Violence?

The impact of exposure to violence may remain regardless of whether children choose to imitate it. For example, Mathews et al. (2005) found neurological evidence of a link between exposure to violence on television and brain functioning. Specifically, non-aggressive children who had been exposed to high levels of media violence showed less activity in the frontal cortex, that area of the brain linked to attention and self-control. This pattern of neural activity was comparable to that of children diagnosed with disruptive behavior disorder (Mathews et al. 2005). Bear in mind that these measurements are made very shortly after exposure to the media violence. However, the crucial question concerns the duration of the impact of exposure to violence over time, particularly if children are able to perceive cartoon violence as fantastic and as immoral.

We do know that children view violent acts as moral transgressions: behaviors that infringe upon the rights and welfare of others (Wainryb and Turiel 1993). According to the domain-specific theory of moral development (see Smetana 2006; Turiel 1998), moral beliefs are influenced by the context in which an action is presented. For example, young children evaluate real life and hypothetical moral transgressions negatively and can provide rudimentary justifications as to why transgressions are impermissible and should receive punishment (Smetana et al. 1999; Smetana 2006).

Young children also differentiate between different types of transgressions, including realistic versus cartoon portrayals (Peters and Blumberg 2004; Smetana et al. 1993; Tisak and Turiel 1988; Turiel 1998) and can consider the degree of harm incurred when assessing the extent to which a transgression warrants punishment. Presumably, children's ability to make differentiated judgments about immoral acts may transfer to their ability to distinguish between the effects of cartoon and television violence and that found in real life situations.

We (Peters and Blumberg 2004) examined this issue in a study in which we showed 3- and 4-year-old children pictures of both realistic and cartoon-like moral transgressions (e.g., hitting, pushing, stealing, and failing to share). The children then were asked to indicate the extent to which the transgressions merited punishment and if so, how severe. They also were asked to justify this assessment. We found that preschoolers negatively evaluated all moral transgressions, both realistic and cartoon. When perceiving the magnitude of the transgression, children viewed physical harm as more egregious than that of psychological harm. Specifically, hitting was seen as more harmful to others and as deserving of greater punishment than failing to share. Additionally, preschoolers judged cartoon transgressions as more harmful than realistic transgressions. Because cartoons are characterized by exaggerated facial expressions and body actions, these characteristics may have influenced the children's perceptions of the cartoon transgressions as "bad."

Conclusion

Television continues to be the "most dominant medium even in those cultures where computers have reached a high diffusion rate" (Lemish 2007, p. 5) and the most significant source of leisure activity among children worldwide. Accordingly, questions concerning the impact of violent television content on vulnerable audiences, such as young children, will remain. We have directed our attention here to children's cartoons which are notably violent. Clearly, definitive conclusions about the potential ill effects of exposure to cartoon violence on young viewers are not easily made. However, scientific support can be found that the frequent comic contextualization of violence coupled with the young children's cognitive repertoire, notably, their abilities to distinguish right from wrong and fantasy from reality, may mitigate the likelihood that young viewers will perpetrate the violent acts shown in cartoons on others in real life. We suspect that this view is consistent most with the perspective of many children who are entertained by Saturday morning cartoons such as Amanda, who emphatically observed, "Everyone knows that cartoons aren't real!"

References

Anderson, C. A., & Carnagey, N. L. (2004). Violent evil and the general aggression model. In A. Miller (Ed.), *The social psychology of good and evil* (pp. 168–192). New York: Guilford Press.

Collins, W. A., Sobol, B. L., & Westby, S. (1981). Effects of adult commentary on children's comprehension and inferences about a televised aggressive portrayal. *Child Development, 52,* 158–163. doi: 10.2307/1129225.

Condry, J. (1989). *The psychology of television.* Hillsdale, NJ: Lawrence Erlbaum Associates.

Fyfe, K. (2006). Wolves in sheep's clothing: A content analysis of children's television. Parents Television Council. http://www.parentstv.org/PTC/publications/reports/childrensstudy/childrensstudy.pdf. Retrieved 20 July 2007.

Kendeou, P., Lynch, J. S., van den Broek, P., Espin, C. A., White, M. J., & Kremer, K. E. (2005). Developing successful readers: Building on early comprehension skills through television viewing and listening. *Early Childhood Education Journal, 33,* 91–98. doi: 10.1007/s10643-005-0030-6.

Kendeou, P., van den Broek, P., White, M. J., & Lynch, J. (2007). Comprehension in preschool and early elementary children: Skill development and strategy interventions. In D. S. McNamara (Ed.), *Reading comprehension strategies: Theories, interventions, and technologies.* Mahwah, NJ: Lawrence Erlbaum.

Kirsch, S. (2006). Cartoon violence and aggression in youth. *Aggression and Violent Behavior, 11,* 547–557. doi: 10.1016/j.avb.2005.10.002.

Kremar, M., & Hight, A. (2007). The development of aggressive mental models in young children. *Media Psychology, 10,* 250–269.

Lemish, D. (2007). *Children and television.* Malden, MA: Blackwell Publishing.

Mathews, V. P., Kronenberger, W. G., Wang, Y., Lurito, J. T., Lowe, M. J., & Dunn, D. W. (2005). Media violence linked to concentration, self-control. *Journal of Computer Assisted Tomography, 29,* 287–292. doi: 10.1097/01.rct.0000162822.46958.33.

McKenna, M. W., & Ossoff, E. P. (1998). Age differences in children's comprehension of a popular television program. *Child Study Journal, 28,* 53–68.

National Television Violence Study (NTVS). (1997). *Technical report 2.* Thousand Oaks, CA: Sage Publications Inc.

Ostrov, J. M., Gentile, D. A., & Crick, N. R. (2006). Media exposure, aggression and prosocial behavior during early childhood: A longitudinal study. *Social Development, 15*, 612–627.

Peters, K. M., & Blumberg, F. C. (2004). Preschoolers' moral judgments: Distinctions between realistic and cartoon-fantasy transgressions. *Proceedings of the 2004 Conference on Interaction Design and Children: Building a Community* (pp. 131–132). New York: ACM.

Pohan, C. A., & Mathison, C. (2007). Television: Providing powerful multicultural lessons inside and outside of school. *Multicultural Perspectives, 9*, 19–25.

Potter, W. J., & Warren, R. (1998). Humor as camouflage of televised violence. *Journal of Communication, 48*, 40–57. doi: 10.1111/j.1460-2466.1998. tb02747.x.

Rideout, V., & Hamel, E. (2006). *The media family: Electronic media in the lives of infants, toddlers, preschoolers and their parents.* http://www.kff.org/entmedia/upload/7500.pdf. Retrieved 20 July 2007 from The Henry J. Kaiser Family Foundation.

Rosen, C. S., Schwebel, D. C., & Singer, J. L. (1997). Preschoolers' attributions of mental states in pretense. *Child Development, 68*, 1133–1142. doi: 10.2307/1132296.

Rutenberg, J. (2001). Violence finds a niche in children's cartoons. *New York Times* (January 28), A1, A19.

Skolnick, D., & Bloom, P. (2006). What does Batman think about SpongeBob? Children's understanding of the fantasy/fantasy distinction. *Cognition, 101*, B9–B18. doi: 10.1016/j.cognition.2005.10.001.

Smetana, J. G. (2006). Social-cognitive domain theory: Consistencies and variations in children's moral and social judgments. In M. Killen & J. Smetana (Eds.), *Handbook of moral development* (pp. 119–153). Mahwah, NJ: Lawrence Erlbaum Associates.

Smetana, J. G., Schlagman, N., & Adams, P. W. (1993). Preschool children's judgments about hypothetical and actual transgressions. *Child Development, 64*, 202–214. doi: 10.2307/1131446.

Smetana, J. G., Toth, S. L., Cicchetti, D., Bruce, J., Kane, P., & Daddis, C. (1999). Maltreated and non-maltreated preschoolers' conceptions of hypothetical and actual moral transgressions. *Developmental Psychology, 35*, 269–281. doi: 10.1037/0012-1649.35.1.269.

Tisak, M. S., & Turiel, E. (1988). Variation in seriousness of transgressions and children's moral and conventional concepts. *Developmental Psychology, 24,* 352–357. doi: 10.1037/0012-1649.24.3.352.

Turiel, E. (1998). The development of morality. In W. Damon (Series Ed.) & N. Eisenberg (Vol. Ed.), *Handbook of child psychology: Vol. 3. Social, emotional, and personality development* (5th ed., pp. 863–932). New York: Wiley.

van den Broek, P., Kremer, K., Lynch, J., Butler, J., White, M. J., & Lorch, E. P. (2005). Assessment of comprehension abilities in young children. In S. G. Paris & S. A. Stahl (Eds.), *Children's reading comprehension and assessment.* Mahwah, NJ: Lawrence Erlbaum.

van den Broek, P., Lorch, E. P., & Thurlow, R. (1996). Children's and adults' memory for television stories: The role of causal factors, story-grammar categories, and hierarchical level. *Child Development, 67,* 3010–3028.

Wainryb, C., & Turiel, E. (1993). Conceptual and informational features in moral decision making. *Educational Psychologist, 28*(3), 205–218. doi: 10.1207/s15326985ep2803_2.

INFORMATIVE SYNTHESIS

DEFINITION

Your goal in writing an informative synthesis is to combine material on some topic you have gathered from two or more readings into a clear, organized essay. After finishing your essay, a reader should have a better understanding of the topic and should know the position of the various authors whose work you include. You are not trying to show how one author is correct in what she says and another is wrong. Neither are you trying to advocate a position of your own on the topic. Instead, you are trying to present other people's ideas or findings as clearly and concisely as you can, highlighting key similarities and differences. Teachers also commonly refer to these papers as "reports" or "comparison-contrast essays."

For example, if you were writing an informative synthesis of the essays included in this chapter, you would want to summarize what each writer had to say about the link between television viewing and childhood violence or at least certain aspects of the subject. In fact, a good way to write this paper would be to isolate for examination certain aspects of the topic that all of the writers address—that way you could draw direct comparisons among the pieces. As you point out for your reader important similarities or differences you see in the various essays, you would not argue that one author is correct in his or her position on the topic and that the others are misguided, nor would you comment on the quality of the writing or argument in any particular essay

To compose an informative synthesis, you employ many of the same skills needed to write summaries. As with writing summaries, you may encounter a number of problems when composing an informative synthesis:

1. Because of their content, language, or structure, the source texts themselves might be hard for you to understand. Because you need to form a clear understanding of the readings before you write about them, you need strong critical reading skills to write a successful synthesis.

2. You will often be looking for subtle differences among readings—not just different arguments or findings authors put forward, but slightly different interpretations of data, slightly different uses of terminology, slightly different emphases. Because a synthesis involves multiple source texts, when you examine a reading you plan to use in your paper, you also have to keep in mind the material contained in the readings you have already read. The more readings you are working with, the harder it is to keep track of the material contained in each and the easier it is to overlook the subtle differences between them.

3. You need to stay as objective as possible when examining the source texts and writing your essay. You do not editorialize in an informative synthesis: your goal is *not* to comment on the topic of the readings or on the quality of their writing. Instead, you need to be open-minded when reading them, to pull out from them material relevant to your thesis, and to present that material as clearly, concisely, and fairly as possible. As when you are writing a summary, remaining neutral can be difficult, especially when you feel strongly about a topic and must include in your informative synthesis ideas that disturb or anger you.

4. Organizing an informative synthesis can also be challenging. You need to decide how to construct your thesis so it adequately guides your reader through your work, how to order the information you include in your paper, and how to employ transitions within the body of your essay.

5. Supplying proper documentation in an informative synthesis can be problematic. One paragraph of your paper may contain information you have drawn from several different authors. Learning how to document such passages properly can be trying; remembering to do it is crucial. Improper documentation can lead to problems with clarity and plagiarism.

WRITING AN INFORMATIVE SYNTHESIS

Because writing an informative synthesis can be challenging, it is best to break the process down into a series of more manageable steps:

1. Analyze the assignment.
2. Review and annotate the readings.
3. Formulate a thesis and organizational plan.
4. Write your rough draft.
5. Revise your draft.

Remember that this method of writing a synthesis will not work for everybody. We all have our preferred way of writing papers, which can vary according to the type of essay we are composing and the time we have to complete the assignment. For example, some writers like to complete a rough draft before they write their thesis, while others must have a thesis in hand before they begin to write; some will rewrite a paper several times before they turn it in for a grade, while others revise very little. Use these directions as a rough guide for writing an informative synthesis. The important principle to keep in mind is to complete your paper in a series of steps, no matter the nature or order of those steps.

Step I—Analyze the Assignment

Read the assignment carefully to make sure your instructor is asking you to write an informative rather than an argumentative synthesis. If you have any doubt, ask your teacher to clarify the assignment. Make sure you understand how many sources you are required to consult when researching the topic or to include when writing your paper. Also, check on the type of source texts your teacher expects you to use if you are required to collect the readings yourself. Some instructors will want you to use only "academic" sources—material written by experts in the field.

Step 2—Review and Annotate the Readings

Once you have assembled the readings that will serve as the basis of your synthesis, read through them several times with your assignment in mind. In most cases, you will look for specific information in each reading, passages that address the topic of your paper. Thoroughly annotate the reading and then summarize it. As you work with the material, remember to be fair and open-minded. Consider how the author's perspective on the topic is similar to or different from what other authors have written and decide whether you think it should be included in your essay.

Step 3—Formulate a Thesis and an Organizational Plan

Your thesis in an informative synthesis serves an important function. More likely than not, it will indicate the topic of your essay and indicate how you will structure your synthesis: what you will discuss and in what order you will discuss it. Always keep in mind the rhetorical function of your thesis statement. When people read your paper, they need to know early on what you will be discussing and will look to your thesis as a guide.

Your thesis for an informative synthesis can be either open or closed. In an open thesis you indicate the topic and general structure of your paper:

> Cantor; Simmons, Stalsworth, and Wentzell; and Blumberg, Bierwirth, and Schwartz offer a range of appraisals concerning the effect of violent television on young viewers.

or

> While both Cantor and Simmons, Stalsworth, and Wentzell assert that violent television shows negatively impact children, Blumberg, Bierwirth, and Schwartz disagree.

With a closed thesis you list the specific issues you will address in your essay. However, you have to be careful not to put too much information in your thesis—doing so will only lead to cluttered prose. A possible closed thesis statement for the paper described above might read something like this:

> Cantor; Simmons, Stalsworth, and Wentzell; and Blumberg, Bierwirth, and Schwartz offer a range of appraisals concerning the effect of violent television on young viewers based on their examination of children's ability to differentiate reality from fantasy and draw distinctions among different genres of television shows.

Either type of thesis can be effective, but in general, the longer your paper will be, the more likely you are to use an open thesis.

When writing an informative synthesis, you can employ either a block or alternating format to organize your essay. With a **block format**, you discuss what one source says about the topic in relation to your thesis before moving on to what the next source says. However, instead of just summarizing each source text, you also compare and contrast them, pointing out their key similarities and differences. Suppose, for example, that you are writing an essay with the thesis, "Cantor; Simmons, Stalsworth, and Wentzell; and Blumberg, Bierwirth, and Schwartz offer a range of appraisals concerning the effect of violent television on young viewers." In outline form, your paper might look something like this:

Opening Section

Introduce the topic of your essay

Give your thesis

Section on Cantor Essay

Summarize Cantor's position on the topic

Discuss its relationship to the other two readings

Section on Simmons, Stalsworth, and Wentzell Essay

Summarize Simmons, Stalsworth, and Wentzell's position on the topic

Discuss its relationship to the other two readings

Section on Blumberg, Bierwirth, and Schwartz Essay

Summarize Blumberg, Bierwirth, and Schwartz's position on the topic

Discuss its relationship to the other two readings

Conclusion

You might, though, choose to use an **alternating format** to organize your essay, especially if you use a closed thesis. Remember that with a closed thesis, you list the specific issues you will address in your essay. Using an alternating format allows you to discuss what each source says about these specific issues in order. For example, suppose you are writing an essay with this thesis: "Cantor; Simmons, Stalsworth, and Wentzell; and Blumberg, Bierwirth, and Schwartz offer a range of appraisals concerning the effect of violent television on young viewers based on their examination of children's ability to differentiate reality from fantasy and draw distinctions among different genres of television shows." Using an alternating format, your paper might be organized like this:

Opening Section

Introduce the topic of your essay

Give your thesis

Effect of Violent Television and Children's Ability to Differentiate Reality from Fantasy

Cantor's views and their relation to the other authors' views

Simmons, Stalsworth, and Wentzell's views and their relation to the other authors' views

Blumberg, Bierwirth, and Schwartz's views and their relation to the other authors' views

Effect of Violent Television and Children's Ability to Draw Distinctions among Different Genres of Television Shows

Cantor's views and their relation to the other authors' views

Simmons, Stalsworth, and Wentzell's views and their relation to the other authors' views

Blumberg, Bierwirth, and Schwartz's views and their relation to the other authors' views

Conclusion

Of course, you could write the same paper using a block format. If you did, it might be organized like this:

Opening Section

Introduce the topic of your essay

Give your thesis

Cantor Essay

Her views on the relationship between violent television shows and children's ability to differentiate reality from fantasy and how they are similar to and/or different from the views of the other authors on the topic

Her views on the relationship between violent television shows and children's ability to draw distinctions among different genres of television shows and how they are similar to and/or different from the views of the other authors

Simmons, Stalsworth, and Wentzell Essay

Their views on the relationship between violent television shows and children's ability to differentiate reality from fantasy and how they are similar to and/or different from the views of the other authors on the topic

Their views on the relationship between violent television shows and children's ability to draw distinctions among different genres of television shows and how they are similar to and/or different from the views of the other authors

Blumberg, Bierwirth, and Schwartz Essay

Their views on the relationship between violent television shows and children's ability to differentiate reality from fantasy and how they are similar to and/or different from the views of the other authors on the topic

Their views on the relationship between violent television shows and children's ability to draw distinctions among different genres of television shows and how they are similar to and/or different from the views of the other authors

Conclusion

Alternating and block formats have their particular strengths and weaknesses. The alternating format allows you to compare and contrast the views of different writers fairly easily. In this paper, for example, you would be able to present each author's position on the relationship between television violence and children's conceptions of reality and fantasy in its own section of your own essay before moving on to discuss television violence and children's ability to recognize various genres of TV shows. If you were using a block format, you might discuss Cantor's views on page one of your paper and might not get to Blumberg, Bierwirth, and Schwartz's views until page six or seven. Your reader might have a hard time remembering Cantor's views by the time you reached Blumberg and her co-authors. Using a block format, however, allows you to give your readers a good sense of the general argument presented by each author in sequential order. Yet the block format often results in repetitive prose and frequently discourages students from discussing similarities and differences among the readings, simply summarizing each author's views instead.

Regardless of the structure you employ, your job in writing an informative synthesis involves more than summarizing what each critic has to say. In writing this paper, you would not be arguing a position of your own concerning the effect of television violence on children. Instead, you would point out for your readers important similarities and differences among the views advanced by the source texts' authors.

Once you have designed your thesis, you need to go back through the readings, consult your annotations, and locate material you want to include in your essay. Preparing an informal outline can be quite helpful at this point. In your outline, indicate the focus for each part of your paper, the material you will draw from the readings to develop that section of the essay, and the ideas you will contribute.

Step 4—Write Your Rough Draft

The introductory section of an informative thesis should, first, capture your readers' interest. You might consider opening your paper with an interesting anecdote, a case history, an important statistic, or a telling quotation from one of the readings. Writing an effective opening gives you the chance to be imaginative and creative. A second goal of the opening section of your synthesis is to introduce the topic of your essay. The title of the synthesis should give your readers some indication of your essay's topic, but you want to be sure to clarify the topic in your opening section. Finally, the introduction to your essay should contain your thesis statement. Whether your thesis is open or closed, you need to include it in your introduction to serve as a guide to the rest of your synthesis.

In the body of your essay, you will follow the structure supplied by your thesis, explaining ideas one author or issue at a time. If you were writing an informative synthesis using the three articles on television violence as your source texts, in the body of your paper you would summarize, paraphrase, and quote what each author has to say about the topic, including in your essay material that best captures each writer's views and illustrates your thesis. However, not all the material in your informative synthesis will come from the readings. You have significant contributions to make, too. Besides quoting, paraphrasing, and summarizing what various authors have to say, you will contribute transitions, elaborations, clarifications, and connections.

For example, in one paragraph of your essay, you may introduce the issue to be discussed, introduce a reading by giving the author's name and qualifications as well as the title of the article, quote a relevant passage from the piece, restate the author's ideas in your own words to clarify them, point out how the author's stance differs from the author you discussed in the previous paragraph, and provide a transition to your next paragraph. If you devote a sentence to each of these tasks, your paragraph will be six sentences long, with only one sentence coming directly from the reading. The rest of the material in the paragraph comes from you.

When concluding your informative synthesis, you want to reiterate the main issues or findings you have covered in the body of your essay and give your work a sense of closure. You might want to look back at your opening strategy and reemploy it in your conclusion, if possible. For example, if you opened your paper with a quotation, consider ending it with a quotation. If you began with a question, conclude with the same question, perhaps answering it this time. If you began with a story, come back to the story in your conclusion.

Step 5—Revise Your Draft

Revising a synthesis takes time. In fact, it is probably best to revise your paper in several stages. Initially, you might check the **content** of your essay. Here you have two concerns. First, reread what you have written to make sure you are being true to your own intentions. You might ask the following questions of your manuscript:

- Does my thesis accurately reflect my understanding of the readings?
- Have I said in my paper what I wanted to say?
- Have I covered all of the material I hoped to cover when annotating the readings?
- Have I covered the ideas I discovered as I wrote the essay, ideas I did not plan on addressing but developed as I wrote?

A related goal is to review the content of your essay in light of the assignment. Here the questions you ask might include:

- Have I met the demands of the assignment?
- Have I adequately covered the ideas contained in the reading?

- Have I avoided editorializing or arguing a particular position?
- Have I kept my reader in mind? Would this essay make sense to someone who knows little or nothing about the readings? Do any ideas need more development or explanation?

Next, you might review the **organization** of your essay. Here you are concerned with the quality of your thesis statement, topic sentences, and transitions. These are some of the questions you should be asking:

- Does my thesis guide the development of the essay? Put another way, does my essay follow the format suggested or outlined by my thesis?
- Do I have clearly stated topic sentences introducing the major sections of my essay? Are these topic sentences tied to the thesis?
- Have I supplied enough transitional devices to guide my reader through my synthesis, especially when I move from discussing one author to discussing another?

Finally, revise with an eye toward **accuracy** and **clarity**. Here your concerns are word choice, sentence structure, and documentation. Again, you need to ask yourself a series of questions as you review your work, making needed changes when any of your answers are no:

- In choosing words, have I remained as fair and objective as possible?
- Have I successfully avoided jargon and highly technical terms when such language would not be appropriate for my audience?
- Are my sentences easy to read?
- Have I varied the type and length of my sentences?
- Have I quoted material accurately and properly?
- Have I paraphrased material accurately, properly, and fairly?
- Have I documented material thoroughly and properly?

You may need to revise your informative synthesis several times to address all of these concerns adequately.

Check Quotations and Documentation

Before you turn in your final draft for a grade, be sure to check the accuracy of your quotations and documentation. Take the time to check any material you quoted against the source text to be sure you have accurately transcribed the information. Pay special attention to any passages where you have added language to or taken language out of a quotation: these changes should not alter the meaning of the source text. Also, check to be sure that you have documented all of the material in your paper that needs to be documented and that you have employed the proper form of documentation in each instance. Remember that all paraphrased and quoted material in your paper should be documented. Because you are combining information from two or more sources in your synthesis, be sure it is always clear to your reader which source text you are referring to in your documentation.

SAMPLE INFORMATIVE SYNTHESIS

Following is a sample informative synthesis of the three articles on television violence provided earlier in this chapter. Notice how the writer structures the essay and employs material from the readings.

Does Television Violence Pose a Danger to Young Viewers?

Research shows that at least one television set can be found in 98% of American homes and that the people living there watch TV around 7.5 hours a day. Children in those homes watch television about 28 hours a week, and before they are 12 years old have watched more than 8,000 murders on the screen (Simmons, Stalsworth, and Wentzell 181). Does television violence pose a danger to young viewers? Does it make them more violent and promote other anti-social behavior? Though many researchers believe watching violent television has a detrimental effect on children, not everyone agrees. Key differences of opinion center around children's ability to distinguish fantasy from reality and the long-term impact of watching violent cartoons.

In their article "Television Violence and Its Effects on Young Children," Simmons, Stalsworth, and Wentzell argue that children's lives are negatively impacted by television viewing. Their research focuses on two issues: (1) the ability of children to differentiate reality from fantasy when watching TV and (2) the short- and long-term effects of viewing violent shows. Simmons, Stalsworth, and Wentzell maintain "that children are extremely vulnerable to television between the ages of 2 to 8 years because of their maturational inability to separate what they view from reality" (182). They base this assertion on studies by the National Institutes of Mental Health that suggest "a causal relationship existed between television violence and aggressive behavior" (182).

According to the authors, in 1984, the United States government deregulated television which resulted in a greater number of violent television shows being aired. As children watched these shows, they began to imitate what they saw and became more violent, not drawing a distinction between reality and the fantasy world of television. Over time, these violence-prone children have grown up and contributed to today's crime rates. Simmons, Stalsworth, and Wentzell cite the results of a government study which suggests a three-stage process linking television viewing and violence: exposure, acquisition, and acceptance. As children are exposed to increasing amounts of violence on television, they begin to acquire anti-social beliefs and to accept violence as a norm in their lives (182). In fact, the amount of violent television that eight-year-olds watched is a better "predictor of adult aggression than socioeconomic and childrearing factors" (182).

Simmons, Stalsworth, and Wentzell believe that watching violent cartoons is especially damaging to children. They maintain that shows like "Mighty Morphin Power Rangers" are among the most violent on television. In fact, children who watched this particular show were 7 times more aggressive afterwards than children who did not watch the show (183). Watching the confrontations between Bugs Bunny and Elmer Fudd or Tweety and Sylvester teach children that violence is an acceptable way to solve problems. Studies show that "when children watch these shows, they often do not remember the plot, but they do remember the actions of their favorite characters" (185) and imitate them.

Joanne Cantor, Director of the Center for Communication Research at the University of Wisconsin, largely agrees with Simmons, Stalsworth, and Wentzell. In her article, "Media Violence and Children's Emotions: Beyond the 'Smoking Gun,'" Cantor cites a meta-analysis of studies that make a "compelling case" for the argument that watching violent television as children leads to more anti-social, violent behavior as adults (174). However, Cantor offers a more detailed analysis of this link than Simmons, Stalsworth, and Wentzell provide. For example, Cantor also maintains that children's inability to distinguish between reality and fantasy contributes to the negative impact of watching television, but she explains how this phenomenon changes as children mature. Younger children (ages 3–5) are more strongly impacted by fantasy violence; older children (ages 9–11) are more strongly impacted by realistic violence (176–7). In a study of children's reactions to television news, Cantor found that "children in kindergarten through sixth grades showed that fear produced by fantasy programs decreased as the child's age increased, while fear induced by news stories increased with age" (177).

According to Cantor, one reason young children are so influenced by television violence is that it often minimizes how that violence harms the victim. As a result, children become desensitized to the effects of violence on others and are then more likely to act violently themselves—a finding which matches the "exposure, acquisition, and acceptance" process cited by Simmons, Stalsworth, and Wentzell. Cantor mentions cartoons as especially being responsible for children's desensitization to violence. As evidence, Cantor cites a study she conducted in which one group of children watched violent cartoons after they were asked to consider how the victims in those shows might be harmed by the actions inflicted on them, another group watched the cartoons without these instructions, and a third group did not watch any cartoons. She found that "the kids who had just seen the violent cartoon without instructions scored higher on pro-violence attitudes than the kids in the control condition (showing stronger agreement with statements like, 'sometimes fighting is a good way to get what you want')" (178). Cantor warns that these violent attitudes formed in childhood can have long-term consequences, including increased violence in adulthood (174).

An opposing view on the relationship between television viewing and violence among children is offered in "Does Cartoon Violence Beget Aggressive Behavior in Real Life? An Opposing View" by Fran Blumberg, Kristen Bierwirth, and Allison Schwartz. In this article, the authors focus exclusively on the impact that violent cartoons have on children, an issue discussed by both Cantor and Simmons, Stalsworth, and Wentzell. When comparing the nature of violence in prime-time shows and cartoons, Blumberg, Bierwirth, and Schwartz cite studies which demonstrate that "cartoons show less serious acts of violence than adult-oriented dramas" and that the comic nature of cartoons reduces the likelihood that children will believe that the violent acts they see on TV can be applied in real-world situations (190).

Blumberg, Bierwith, and Schwartz agree that children may exhibit negative, aggressive behavior after watching violent TV shows, acknowledging that "a schema for aggression may be activated as a result of having viewed aggressive acts" (190). However, they believe that effects of watching violent cartoons is mitigated by the children's ability to draw a distinction between fantasy and reality: the authors cite several studies which show that when viewing animation, "most preschoolers still recognize cartoon programs as 'make-believe'" and "can differentiate cartoon characters engaged in life-like activities from those engaged in pretend activities" (191).

In addition, Blumberg, Bierwith, and Schwartz contend that most researchers who link cartoon viewing and childhood violence study children shortly after they have watched the violent shows. They question the long-term impact of watching violent cartoons. According to Blumberg, Bierwirth, and Schwartz, children do see violent acts in cartoons as wrong and "immoral," believe the violent acts deserve punishment, believe that perpetuators of cartoon violence are "bad," and can differentiate between realistic and cartoon depictions of violence (192). In short, the authors argue that children's abilities to draw distinctions between reality and fantasy and to apply moral judgments to what they watch on TV make it less likely that they will repeat the aggressive acts they see on television in their daily lives.

The authors of all three articles agree that children are exposed to more violent television shows than ever before and all agree that viewing these shows impacts them in some way. Both Simmons, Stalsworth, and Wentzell and Cantor believe watching these shows has an extremely detrimental effect on children, leading them to commit more violent acts in real life and perhaps increasing the chances that they will grow up to a life of crime. Blumberg, Bierwith, and Schwartz question the connections between television and childhood violence, arguing that children are able to distinguish between fantasy and reality well enough to avoid any long-term consequences associated with viewing violent shows. One point all the authors agree on, though, is that children are best served by watching television shows with their parents who can explain the programs and answer their children's questions.

Summary Chart

HOW TO WRITE AN INFORMATIVE SYNTHESIS

1. **Analyze the assignment.**
   - *Determine whether you are being asked to write an informative or argumentative synthesis.*
   - *Determine the number and types of readings you are expected to use in your paper.*

2. **Review and annotate the readings.**
   - *Review the readings with your assignment in mind, looking for and marking information related to the topic of your paper.*
   - *Briefly summarize each reading.*

3. **Formulate a thesis.**
   - *Determine what stance you will assume in your essay.*
   - *Determine whether you will use an open or closed thesis statement.*

4. **Choose an organizational plan.**
   - *Decide how you will order the ideas you will develop in your essay.*
   - *Decide whether you will present your ideas using a block or alternating format.*

5. **Write your rough draft.**
   - *Follow the organization plan implied or stated by your thesis.*
   - *Summarize and combine (synthesize) material from the source texts to support your thesis.*
   - *Both paraphrase and quote material as necessary.*
   - *Add transitions, elaborations, clarifications, and connections where needed.*
   - *Include a concluding paragraph.*

6. **Revise your draft.**

    Revise to improve the content of your essay.

    - *Does your thesis accurately reflect your position and intention?*
    - *Have you communicated in your paper what you want to communicate?*
    - *Will your paper give your reader a thorough understanding of the source texts and your thesis?*
    - *Have you avoided editorializing in your paper?*
    - *Would your essay make sense to someone who has not read the source texts?*

    Revise to improve the organization of your essay.
    - *Does your thesis guide the development of your essay?*
    - *Do you provide topic sentences to introduce major sections of your essay?*
    - *Have you provided transitions that help lead your reader through your paper?*

    Revise to improve the accuracy and clarity of your essay.
    - *Have you used language that is as fair and impartial as possible?*
    - *Have you avoided jargon and overly technical language when they would not be appropriate?*
    - *Have you checked for sentence variety and clarity?*
    - *Have you proofread for spelling, punctuation, and usage errors?*

7. **Check your quotations and documentation.**
    - *Have you quoted and paraphrased material properly, accurately, and fairly?*
    - *Have you documented all the material that needs to be documented?*
    - *Have you documented material employing the proper format?*

INFORMATIVE SYNTHESIS REVISION CHECKLIST

	Yes	No
1. Have you checked your assignment to be sure you have written the proper kind of synthesis essay: informative or argumentative?	——	——
2. In your introduction do you:		
• introduce the topic of the paper?	——	——
• offer your thesis?	——	——
• capture your readers' interest?	——	——
3. Examine the wording of your thesis. Does it clearly indicate what stance you will assume in your essay?	——	——
4. Examine the structure of your essay. Does it follow the organizational plan indicated by your thesis?	——	——
5. Check each section in the body of your essay. Do you:		
• examine just one issue at a time?	——	——
• combine information from your source texts?	——	——
• explain the link between the examples you cite and the assertion you are making?	——	——
• make clear the relationship you see among your source texts?	——	——
6. Examine your transitions. Have you provided adequate signals to help guide your readers through your work?	——	——
7. The first time you introduce a source text, do you give the full title of the piece and the author's full name?	——	——
8. Have you properly documented all quoted, summarized, and paraphrased material?	——	——
9. Have you reviewed your quotations for accuracy and variety?	——	——
10. Is your works cited or reference list correct?	——	——

	Yes	No
11. Have you reviewed your essay to be sure the content accurately communicates your position and intention?	____	____
12. Have you reviewed your word choice for clarity and accuracy?	____	____

Chapter 10

....

ARGUMENTATIVE SYNTHESIS

DEFINITION AND PURPOSE

In an argumentative synthesis, you use material from various readings to support and illustrate an argument of your own, usually concerning the quality of writing in the source texts or an issue they address. If your argument centers on the quality of the readings, you might argue that one text is better written or more convincing than the others. If, however, your teacher asks you to present an argument on the issue the readings address, you will draw on the material in the readings to support your thesis.

For a number of reasons, writing an argumentative synthesis can be challenging:

1. As with the informative synthesis, the sources you consult when gathering information for this type of essay can be difficult to read. They will often present complex arguments themselves or employ terminology or research methodologies new to you. Being able to read this material critically is essential if you hope to write a successful argumentative synthesis.
2. As you read these source texts, you will need to critique them. For example, if you are arguing that one is better written than another, you will have to critique both to determine the relative strengths and weaknesses of each. If you are using the readings to develop an argument of your own

on the topic they address, again you will have to critique the source texts to determine the quality of the arguments and information in each. You want to base your argument on the best available material.

3. When you compose your argumentative synthesis, you have to be concerned, first, with the content and quality of *your* argument. You need to decide if the material you are including in your paper will achieve the desired effect on your reader—will your audience be convinced by your argument? At the same time, since you are working with source texts, you have to pay close attention to the way you are using other people's findings or arguments to be sure you are fairly representing their work.

4. Part of composing an argumentative synthesis is deciding how best to order the claims, evidence, findings, or arguments you present. You need to decide which ideas or arguments you will present in which order and to provide effective transitions between and within the major sections of your argument.

5. In supporting your argument with source material, you will need to be quoting, summarizing, and paraphrasing other people's ideas, arguments, and findings. As a result, documentation becomes a challenge. You will need to be explicit and clear in acknowledging the source of the information you use to support your assertions.

THE ELEMENTS OF ARGUMENT

As you develop, draft, and revise your argumentative synthesis, pay particular attention to the three basic elements of any argument: **claims**, **grounds**, and **warrants**. According to British philosopher Stephen Toulmin in *The Uses of Argument* (Cambridge University Press, 1958), every argument involves an assertion (claim) that is supported by evidence (grounds) and rests upon a particular set of assumptions or line of reasoning (warrant). Effective arguments employ clear, limited claims; reliable, appropriate grounds; and fully developed, explicit warrants. Understanding each of these elements can help you compose more effective argumentative synthesis essays.

CLAIMS

A **claim** is an assertion you want your readers to accept. In an argumentative synthesis essay, your thesis statement is a claim, one you will develop and support with other claims in the body of your essay. Suppose, for example, you are writing an argumentative synthesis using the articles on television violence found in Chapter 9 and decide on the following thesis: "Due to her use of statistics, examples, and reasoning, Cantor's argument that viewing violent television shows harms young children is more persuasive than Blumberg, Bierwirth, and Schwartz's argument that children are not harmed by what they watch on TV." Your thesis is a claim: Cantor's argument is stronger than

Blumberg, Bierwirth, and Schwartz's argument. You will support this assertion with three other claims or "because" statements: Cantor's argument is stronger because she employs more effective statistics, better examples, and a clear line of reasoning. In the body of your essay you will develop these three claims with valid grounds and warrants if you want readers to accept your thesis.

When you compose an essay from source texts, most of your claims will be based on what you read and can include:

- claims concerning the source text's topic;
- claims concerning the source text's content, organization, or style;
- claims concerning the quality of the source text's writing; and
- claims concerning your response or reaction to the source texts.

Your teacher may give you several readings to study or require you to collect material on your own outside of class. In either case, you will be expected to critique the readings, form an argumentative thesis or claim, and explain or defend that assertion in your essay.

Well-written claims are **accurate, clear**, and **limited**. Any claim you make about a reading should be accurate: you should not misrepresent what an author writes. Claims should also be clear and unambiguous. "There are several good things about Cantor's argument" is not a clear claim. What does the writer mean by "good" or by "things"? When forming claims, be as specific as you can, using language that precisely captures the assertion you want to make. Also, avoid broad, unlimited claims because such assertions are usually inaccurate and difficult to support. Claims like "Cantor's essay is the best piece of writing ever produced" or "There is absolutely no value at all to Cantor's argument" are not sufficiently limited. In writing limited claims, you may find yourself using words like "most" instead of "all," "often" instead of "always," or "likely" instead of "certainly." Limited claims (including limited thesis statements) are easier to explain and defend than unlimited, sweeping claims.

GROUNDS

Grounds is another name for the evidence you use to support a claim. As with claims, when you compose a source-based argumentative synthesis essay, you will draw most of your grounds from readings, though many teachers will allow you to use relevant personal experience to support a claim as well. Source-based grounds can include facts, statistics, testimony, and opinions. Each type of evidence has its own strengths and limitations. When deciding how to employ each in support of a claim, consider the questions that follow. Remember: the quality of your essay often depends on the quality of the grounds you employ to support your claims. If you rely on weak, questionable, or irrelevant grounds to support your claims, your writing is unlikely to convince thoughtful readers.

Facts: information the author of the source text presents as verifiably true

- Is the information up to date?
- Does the information come from a reliable source?
- Is the information documented?
- Is the information clear and unambiguous in its meaning?
- Is the information relevant to the claim you are making?
- Is the information consistent with your understanding, knowledge, or experience?
- Is the information consistent with what other source texts contend?

Examples: illustrations drawn from the source text to support your claim

- Are the examples relevant to the claim you are making?
- How much background information do you need to provide so that your reader will understand the examples you incorporate from the source text?
- Are the examples true or fictional? Is either acceptable given your assignment?
- Do the examples come from a reliable source?
- Are the examples timely?
- Are the examples representative and typical or limited and unique?

Statistics: data the author of the source text employs to support his or her claims

- Do you understand the statistics, what they mean, and their limitations?
- Do the statistics come from a reliable, trustworthy source?
- What are the possible biases of the source text? How might those biases affect the statistics offered in the piece?
- How do the statistics compare with evidence found in other source texts?
- Does the author of the source text acknowledge the limitations of the statistics?
- Are the statistics relevant to the claim you are trying to support in your essay?
- Can you adequately explain the link between the statistics you cite and the claim you are supporting?

Testimony: personal experiences offered by the author of the source text in support of his or her claims

- Does the testimony come from a reliable, qualified source?
- Is the testimony firsthand or secondhand?
- How is the testimony relevant to the claim you are trying to support?
- What background information from the source text will you need to provide so that your reader will understand the meaning and nature of the testimony?
- Does the author of the source text acknowledge the limitations of the testimony?
- How does the testimony complement (or contradict) other grounds provided in the essay?

Opinions: what the author of a source text believes to be true

- Is this the opinion of the source text's author or is the author offering someone else's opinion?
- Is the person sufficiently qualified to offer an opinion worth citing in your essay?
- How will you make clear in the body of your essay that this opinion comes from a reliable source?
- Does the author sufficiently explain and clarify his or her opinion?
- Does the author support that opinion with evidence?
- Is the opinion sufficiently qualified?
- Is the opinion supported by other types of evidence in the source text or by evidence you have gathered from other sources?

Whatever grounds you employ in your essay, be sure they are **relevant**, **reliable**, and **appropriate**. As you defend or illustrate a claim, first be sure the evidence you use is relevant to the assertion you are making. Writing an argumentative synthesis can be confusing because you are working with multiple texts and multiple claims. As you select the grounds you will use to support a particular claim, be sure they clearly relate to that claim and not to some other assertion you are making in your essay. Also, be sure the grounds are reliable—examine the credentials and possible biases of the source text's author, the publication's or Web site's credibility, and the date of publication. Finally, be sure your grounds are appropriate for the assignment and audience. As you write papers in classes across the curriculum, you will discover that what counts as valid grounds in one class may not count as valid grounds in another. Learning what grounds are appropriate for arguments in a field of study is part of learning how to reason like a member of that discipline. Analyze the texts you read in class to determine the kinds of evidence successful authors in that field of study utilize in their arguments and ask your instructor for help if you have doubts about the appropriateness of evidence you plan to use in any essay.

One final note about grounds: Most writers know that they can support a claim in an argumentative synthesis essay by quoting, paraphrasing, or otherwise alluding to the work of authors who agree with the position they are advancing. Citing authorities who support the claims you make improves your work's credibility. However, there are other ways to use source material to support an argument. For example, consider citing authorities who *disagree* with the claim you are making. Incorporating counterexamples into your argumentative synthesis can be effective if you employ them correctly. First, acknowledging alternative positions increases your credibility as a writer. It demonstrates your knowledge of the subject matter, your fairness, and the confidence you have in your own position. However, citing counterexamples alone will not help you achieve these benefits; instead, you must integrate them into your essay by refuting them, conceding to them, or accommodating them.

When you **refute** counterexamples, you offer a fair summary of the opposing view, then demonstrate how that position is wrong, problematic, or otherwise flawed. You can then explain how your position is better. When you **concede** to an opposing view, you acknowledge how and when the opposition might be right in its assertions. However, you then demonstrate how that fact does not seriously damage your own position or thesis. Finally, when you **accommodate** an opposing view, you explain how that position and your own may be equally correct and how, by combining them, one might gain a better, more comprehensive understanding of the issue. In short, be imaginative in your use of source material as grounds in an argumentative synthesis. Just be sure the grounds you use are linked to your claims with strong warrants.

WARRANTS

Warrants are a little harder to understand than claims or grounds because they tend to be more abstract. Simply stated, though, a warrant is a line of reasoning, set of assumptions, or explanation that links a claim to its grounds. When writing an argumentative synthesis, remember that in most cases the grounds will not speak for themselves: you need to explain how they support the claim you are making. For instance, suppose you wrote the following passage, a claim supported by an example:

> Cantor's argument is stronger than Blumberg, Bierwirth, and Schwartz's, in part, due to her use of statistics to support and illustrate many of her claims. For example, she notes that in one study, even as adults, 52% of respondents who had been frightened by a television show when a child still had occasional problems sleeping and 35% reported "avoiding or dreading the situation depicted in the program or movie" (00).

Are you ready to move on to your next claim now? Have you sufficiently supported your claim by citing an example or two from the text? No. What's missing here is your warrant—before you move on to your next claim, you have to *explain how* the use of statistics you cite makes Cantor's argument more convincing than Blumberg, Bierwirth, and Schwartz's. What is it about citing statistics or citing *these* statistics that makes Cantor's argument more convincing? Why might readers be more convinced by Cantor's argument than by Blumberg, Bierwirth, and Schwartz's because Cantor includes these statistics in her essay? As you explain the link between your assertion and the evidence you provide for it, you are articulating your warrant.

As you draft and revise your argumentative synthesis, you need to ask yourself a series of questions concerning the nature and effectiveness of your warrants.

1. *Is my warrant stated or unstated? If unstated, will the link between my claims and my grounds be sufficiently clear for my readers?*
   In everyday conversation, many warrants go unstated: the link between a claim and its grounds is so clear or so readily accepted that no warrant is

needed. In academic writing, however, warrants usually need to be stated and explained. The aim of an academic argument is to let your reader know where you stand on an issue (your claim), to convince your reader to accept this position as reasonable or correct by supporting it with evidence (your grounds), and to explain how this evidence makes the case for the claim (your warrant). Two writers may make the same assertion in their papers and may even support those assertions with similar evidence, but how they explain the link they see between the evidence and the claim will likely differ. In academic writing, warrants can help make your essay distinctive. Therefore, examine your essay for any unstated warrants and decide whether they need to be made explicit. If you think there is any chance your readers may question the link between a claim and its grounds, state your warrant.

2. *Is my warrant logical and reasonable?*

How *do* the grounds you employ actually support your claim? What assumptions are you making about the link between your grounds and claims? Are you assuming that your readers will recognize and accept the connection you see between your claims and grounds? Is the connection you see between them logical and reasonable? Will your readers see the connection as logical and reasonable?

3. *Is my warrant clear, fully explained, and supported?*

Underdeveloped warrants are a common problem with argumentative synthesis essays: writers, understanding that they need to state their warrants, simply fail to explain them adequately. Clear, well-developed warrants are crucial to successful arguments, especially if you believe your audience will question the validity of your claim or grounds. In these cases, you may need to explain your warrant at length, perhaps even acknowledging alternative readings of your grounds as you clarify your own interpretation. Determining whether your warrants are sufficiently explained and supported can be difficult, which is why you should have other people read and critique drafts of your writing. Specifically ask them to read your essay skeptically; to question the validity of your claims, grounds, and warrants; and to indicate any weaknesses they note or questions they have. Sometimes the warrants themselves rest upon unstated assumptions that need to be explained and defended.

ARGUMENT AND PERSUASION

Rhetoricians often draw a distinction between argument and persuasion. Argument, they maintain, involves demonstrating the credibility of a position; persuasion involves moving readers to accept or act on that position. The most commonly acknowledged agents of persuasion are logos (logic), pathos (emotion), and ethos (character): writers can often persuade readers to accept or act on an argument by appealing to the readers' logic or emotions or by sufficiently establishing their own credibility or character (see Chapter 7 for a further discussion of logos, pathos, and ethos).

APPEALS BASED ON REASON

In an argumentative synthesis, successful appeals to **logos** largely depend on the quality of your claims, grounds, and warrants. Clear, qualified claims supported by valid grounds and clear, reasonable warrants will go a long way toward persuading a reader that your position is reasonable enough to accept and act on. Such writing, however, rarely happens by accident. It results from careful, critical drafting and revision. Here are a few steps you can take to improve the logical appeal of your argumentative synthesis essay:

1. **Make clear, limited claims.**
   Be sure all of your claims are clear, reasonable, and limited. Vague claims will not be convincing and neither will unreasonable assertions or sweeping generalizations. The claims you make—including your thesis—form the framework around which you will build your argumentative synthesis. If your claims are unclear, unreasonable, or unconnected to one another, the logical appeal of your essay will be diminished.
2. **Employ grounds that are relevant, credible, and timely.**
   As you decide what evidence or examples to offer in support of a claim, choose the material that is most relevant to your assertion. First, avoid using grounds that are only tangentially related to your claim. Second, be sure the grounds you employ come from credible sources. If you use reliable sources in your essay, readers are more likely to see your assertions as reasonable. Basing your paper on material drawn from questionable sources will bring into question the legitimacy of your own assertions. Finally, be sure the material you use in your paper is timely. As a rule, draw on the most recent research you can find when writing your paper—employing out-of-date source texts may hamper your efforts to sway readers' opinions.
3. **Explain your reasoning process.**
   One of the best ways to improve the logical appeal of your essay is to explain your reasoning process on the page. Lay bare for your readers the reasoning process that led you to your conclusions: elaborate on the meaning of your claims, explain connections among your assertions, explore alternative arguments, and discuss the links you see between your claims and their grounds. Most academic audiences will expect to find this type of discussion and explanation in your essay.

APPEALS BASED ON EMOTION

Successful persuasive appeals to **pathos** can be difficult to achieve but can also be very effective. Employing pathos to persuade readers is tricky because it can have the opposite effect if used incorrectly or clumsily. Pathos can quickly turn into bathos, or unintentionally comic appeals to emotion. However, when used sparingly and appropriately, emotionally charged grounds or language can prove very persuasive. Here are a few suggestions on how to employ pathos effectively in an argumentative synthesis essay.

1. **Include in your essay material that might appeal to your readers' interests.**

   While it is often difficult to know with any degree of certainty what material might appeal to your readers' interests, it may be possible to make some educated guesses. For example, what might interest them given their economic, political, educational, or religious backgrounds? What can you assume they know or may want to know about the topic of your essay? What aspects of the topic interest you? How similar are you to your audience—can you assume they might have similar interests? Though it is very difficult to make completely accurate assessments of what material might interest your readers, the closer you come to hitting the mark, the more likely you are to obtain a positive emotional response to your writing.

2. **Include in your essay material that might appeal to your readers' needs or fears.**

   As you consider what material to include in your argumentative synthesis, can you identify examples, arguments, testimonials, statistics, or other material that might appeal to your readers' needs or address their concerns? Your goal is not to play on your readers' emotions. Instead, you want to connect emotionally with readers, to construct a bridge between your essay and reader needs or concerns, thus helping them see the relevancy of your essay to their lives. Is there material, for example, that might appeal to your readers' concerns about their physical, psychological, or financial safety; need for self-affirmation; or desires for joy or happiness? Successfully employing this type of material in your argumentative synthesis greatly increases the chances that readers will find your essay persuasive.

3. **Employ language that is evocative or captivating.**

   Another way to improve the emotional appeal of your argumentative synthesis is to use especially evocative or captivating language. Words have both denotative (literal) and connotative (emotional) meanings. You will often face instances when you can choose among words that have roughly the same denotative meaning but vary widely in their connotative implications. In these cases, consider using language that more effectively appeals to your reader's emotions. Also consider your use of figurative language. While most academic writers employ extended metaphors sparingly, the use of analogies, allusions, and other figurative language is more common. Your goal is not to produce flowery prose. Instead, your aim is to employ language that persuades readers to accept or act on your arguments by developing in them an emotional understanding of your topic.

APPEALS BASED ON CHARACTER AND CREDIBILITY

In one sense, **ethos** is closely linked to logos because it has to do with the credibility of the claims, grounds, and warrants you employ in your essay. Ethos involves trust and character: do you demonstrate through the quality of the claims, grounds, and warrants you employ in your writing that you are a trustworthy, knowledgeable, fair-minded individual? If you do, then you may persuade some readers to accept your position through your own ethos as a writer. Ethos, though, also has to do with the quality of your own prose. Even if you compose a synthesis with strong claims, grounds, and warrants, you will lose credibility if your prose is marred by misspellings, grammatical problems, typos, or other surface errors. Readers may feel that they cannot trust authors who are careless with their writing; if an author is so sloppy with word choice, syntax, spelling, or punctuation, how sloppy has the author been with his or her research, reasoning, and documentation? Persuasion depends on trust, and you may lose the trust of your readers—and your credibility as a writer—if your writing is full of easily correctable errors. Here are a few steps you can take to improve ethos in your argumentative synthesis:

1. **Present informed, balanced arguments.**
   You will enhance your credibility as a writer if you present a balanced argument in your essay, examining the strengths and weaknesses of your assertions and exploring alternative points of view. Presenting a balanced argument requires you to research and consider a range of perspectives on your essay's topic. Examining this range of perspectives in your essay increases the likelihood of readers seeing you as a knowledgeable, fair-minded writer, and readers are more likely to consider and perhaps adopt arguments presented by writers they perceive as informed and fair.

2. **Demonstrate the credibility of your source texts.**
   Another way to enhance your ethos is by demonstrating the credibility of the source texts you use in your essay. Readers are more likely to accept or act on your arguments if they perceive that your claims are supported by authoritative sources. In-text documentation is one way to demonstrate that your arguments are supported by credible sources. You can also establish the authority of your source texts by including in your essay the full name of the person who wrote the text and a summary of his or her credentials when you first quote or paraphrase material from him or her.

3. **Employ fair, balanced language.**
   Just as you want the content of your argumentative synthesis to be fair and balanced, you also want to avoid language that might make you appear narrow-minded or uninformed. While on occasion you will want to employ emotionally evocative language (see discussion of pathos above), consistently employing words that make you sound shrill, sarcastic, or hostile will usually hinder your efforts to persuade readers to consider or accept your arguments, especially if you are addressing a neutral or possibly antagonistic audience. In these cases, you might be better served using language that is more judicious and fair.

4. **Proofread your work carefully.**

Finally, remember that the quality of your own prose influences whether your readers perceive you as a credible authority. Argumentative synthesis essays that are full of surface-level errors are unlikely to persuade many readers. Rightly or wrongly, most readers will judge the quality of your argument by the quality of your prose: in their minds, error-laden writing is likely to reflect error-laden thinking. You can help ensure that your writing is persuasive simply by proofreading your essay thoroughly before you submit your final draft for review.

WRITING AN ARGUMENTATIVE SYNTHESIS

Because argumentative syntheses are so complex, writing them in a number of steps or stages is often helpful. Here are some of the steps you might consider following when writing an argumentative synthesis:

1. Analyze the assignment.
2. Annotate and critique the readings.
3. Formulate a thesis.
4. Choose an organizational plan.
5. Write your rough draft.
6. Revise your draft.
7. Check quotations and documentation.

STEP I—ANALYZE THE ASSIGNMENT

Some teachers will not specify the type of argument they want you to present in your synthesis. If this is the case, you will need to decide for yourself whether you want to focus on the quality of the writing in the readings or on the issue they address. However, if a teacher specifically asks you to focus your argument on the quality of the source texts, his assignment might include directions such as these:

> Review the readings in Chapter 6 of the textbook. Which author do you believe presents the most convincing case? Why?

> * * * * *

> Review the readings in Chapter 6 of the textbook. Which piece is better written? How so?

In the first assignment, the teacher wants you to analyze, evaluate, then compare the **arguments** presented by the various writers, arguing that one presents the best case. In the second assignment, the teacher wants you to analyze, evaluate, then compare the **styles** of the various writers, arguing that one produces the best-written text.

However, when a teacher wants you to take a stand on the topic the readings address, her directions may read something like this:

> Review the readings in Chapter 6 of the textbook. Where do you stand on the issue? Present an argument in favor of your position using the readings for support.

Here the teacher wants you to read the articles, think about the arguments presented by each author, reflect on your own knowledge and feelings concerning the topic, then present an argument in which you assume and defend a position of your own on the issue.

Once you have determined the type of argument the teacher wants you to write, check the assignment to determine the number and types of sources the teacher wants you to use in your paper. Sometimes instructors specify a certain number of readings you must use in your paper, asking you, for example, to base your paper on four to six sources. Other times teachers specify the types of readings you have to use: those provided in class, those you find on your own in the library, academic sources only, and so on. If you have any questions about the number or type of readings you need to use in your synthesis, be sure to check with your instructor.

STEP 2—ANNOTATE AND CRITIQUE THE READINGS

As you begin to collect the readings you plan to use when writing your argumentative synthesis, you need to annotate and critique them (see Chapter 6 for advice on critiquing readings). First, annotate each reading, identifying its thesis, primary assertions, and evidence. Next, analyze and critique the content and structure of each reading. If you base your argument on other authors' faulty writing or reasoning, your essay will likely reflect their weaknesses; likewise, if you base your argument on solid, well-written sources, your argument will likely be stronger. The questions you want to ask of a reading include:

- What, exactly, is the main point of this reading?
- How has the author supported his ideas, arguments, or findings?
- How well has the author explained or supported his ideas, arguments, or findings?
- Do I find the reading convincing? Why or why not?
- How have the structure and tone of the piece influenced my reaction?
- What is the quality of the writing?
- How do the author's ideas, arguments, or findings compare with those found in the other sources I have read?

Place your annotations in the margins of the reading, on sheets of paper, or on index cards. If you use paper or index cards, be sure you copy all the bibliographic information you will need to complete a reference list entry on the source, in case you use any of that material in your paper. In an argumentative synthesis, all quoted, paraphrased, or summarized material needs to be documented.

STEP 3—FORMULATE A THESIS

Formulating a clear thesis statement is an essential step in writing a successful argumentative synthesis. Your thesis statement tells your readers the position you plan on advancing in your paper and will likely indicate the structure of your essay. Put another way, your thesis statement establishes in your readers' minds certain expectations concerning the content and form of your paper. When you satisfy those expectations, your readers will have an easier time following your argument; if you do not, however, readers may feel your work is confusing and disorganized. So you need to spend some time forming and refining your thesis statement.

In an argumentative synthesis you advance a position of your own concerning the quality and/or topic of the readings. If you are focusing on the quality of the readings themselves, you can assume a number of different positions. For example, suppose you are writing an argumentative synthesis using the readings on television violence found in Chapter 9. You may argue that one essay is more convincing than another:

> While both Cantor and Simmons, Stalsworth, and Wentzell argue that watching violent television shows harms children, Cantor offers the more persuasive argument.

Or you may argue that one work is better written than another:

> While both Cantor and Simmons, Stalsworth, and Wentzell argue that watching violent television shows harms children, Cantor's essay is more clearly written.

In either case, the thesis sets out the position you will be developing in your paper.

As with other types of essays, thesis statements for argumentative syntheses can be either open or closed. While both of the examples above are open thesis statements, they could easily be modified to give the reader a better indication of what exactly will be covered in the paper:

> While both Cantor and Simmons, Stalsworth, and Wentzell argue that watching violent television shows harms children, Cantor offers the more persuasive argument through her use of statistics and compelling examples.

* * * * *

> While both Cantor and Simmons, Stalsworth, and Wentzell argue that watching violent television shows harms children, Cantor's essay is more clearly written because she avoids unnecessary jargon and employs a more casual style of writing.

If, however, your goal in composing an argumentative synthesis is to assert a position of your own on the topic of the readings, your thesis will read a little differently, something like this (employing an open thesis):

> Although researchers offer varying assessments and positions, watching violent television shows is harmful to children.

Or perhaps this (employing a closed thesis):

> Although researchers offer varying assessments and positions, watching violent television shows is harmful to children because they often imitate the violent acts they see, come to see violence as normative, and carry with them the effects long after they have grown up.

STEP 4—CHOOSE AN ORGANIZATIONAL PLAN

If you use a **block format** to organize your essay, you would critique in turn what each author has to say about the topic, then advance your own position. Suppose you were working with this thesis: "Although researchers offer varying assessments and positions, watching violent television shows is harmful to children because they often imitate the violent acts they see, come to see violence as normative, and carry with them the effects long after they have grown up." In outline form, your paper might look like this:

Argumentative Synthesis—Block Format

Opening Section

   Capture reader interest

   Introduce the topic

   Give your thesis

Discussion of Blumberg, Bierwirth, and Schwartz Article

   Introduce the article—title, author, publication information

   Summarize the article—Blumberg, Bierwirth, and Schwartz's argument

   Critique the article—strengths and weaknesses of their argument

      Tie criticisms to specific passages in the article

      Fully explain or defend your criticism

      Draw links with other source texts

Discussion of Simmons, Stalsworth, and Wentzell Article

   Introduce the article—title, author, publication information

   Summarize the article—Simmons, Stalsworth, and Wentzell's argument

   Critique the article—strengths and weaknesses of their argument

      Tie criticisms to specific passages in the article

      Fully explain or defend your criticism

      Draw links with other source texts

Discussion of Cantor Article

Introduce the article—title, author, publication information

Summarize the article—Cantor's argument

Critique the article—strengths and weaknesses of her argument

Tie criticisms to specific passages in the article

Fully explain or defend your criticism

Draw links with other source texts

Your Argument Concerning Harmful Effects of Violent Television Shows on Children

How watching violent television shows harms children because children imitate the violence they see

Tie arguments to specific examples from the articles

Fully explain and defend your assertions

Refer back to other authors' opinions to bolster your position

How watching violent television shows harms children because children come to see violence as normal or acceptable behavior

Tie arguments to specific examples from the articles

Fully explain and defend your assertions

Refer back to other authors' opinions to bolster your position

How watching violent television shows harms children because the effects the shows have on them stay with children for years

Tie arguments to specific examples from the articles

Fully explain and defend your assertions

Refer back to other authors' opinions to bolster your position

Conclusion

In the opening section of your paper, you would introduce the topic of your essay, capture reader interest, and offer your thesis. In the body of your paper, you would critique the arguments offered by each of your source texts, focusing your attention on what they have to say about why or how watching violent television shows harms children. Finally, you would present your own argument, supporting your position with specific references to the source texts to help support or explain your thesis.

If you prefer, you could organize the paper using an **alternating format**, structuring your essay around the aspects of the topic you have chosen as your focus rather than each source text. In this case, your paper might be organized like this:

Argumentative Synthesis—Alternating Format

Opening Section

Capture reader interest

Introduce the topic

Give your thesis

Discuss how watching violent television shows harms children because children imitate the violence they see

Explain your assertion

Support your argument with convincing grounds, including material from the source texts

Explain how your position differs from the positions presented in the source texts

Discuss how watching violent television shows harms children because children come to see violence as normal or acceptable behavior

Explain your assertion

Support your argument with convincing grounds, including material from the source texts

Explain how your position differs from the positions presented in the source texts

Discuss how watching violent television shows harms children because the effects the shows have on them stay with children for years

Explain your assertion

Support your argument with convincing grounds, including material from the source texts

Explain how your position differs from the positions presented in the source texts

Conclusion

In the opening of your paper, you would again introduce the topic of your essay, capture reader interest, and state your thesis. In the body of your essay, you would argue, in order, that watching violent television shows harms children because they imitate the acts they see, because they come to believe that violence is a normal, acceptable way to act, and because the effects remain for years. In developing your argument, you would explain your claims or assertions, support them with grounds (e.g., evidence, examples, reasons) and include material from the source texts when appropriate, and discuss how your position differs from the ones presented in those texts.

Once you have drafted at least a preliminary thesis for your paper and have some sense of the assertions that will serve as the focus of your synthesis, you will need to return to the readings to locate material to include in your essay. Remember that the focus of an argumentative synthesis should be the argument you are advancing, not the material from the readings. In other words, your first responsibility is to develop a sound argument; the source material serves to illustrate or support *your* assertions.

STEP 5—WRITE YOUR ROUGH DRAFT

When you feel you are ready to begin writing your rough draft, be sure you have in front of you all of your source texts and notes. Some students like to begin writing immediately—they need to see some of their ideas in writing before they can decide on a final thesis or organize their paper. Other students have to begin with a clear thesis and outline in hand. Follow the method of composing that is most comfortable and successful for you.

When writing your essay, you will support your argument with material from the readings. You can use source material to give your readers background information on the topic (quote or paraphrase material you think your reader needs to know to understand your argument), to support your assertions (quote or paraphrase material that substantiates or illustrates your claims), or to acknowledge opposing views (quote or paraphrase material that calls into question your assertions; you then must decide whether to refute, accommodate, or concede to these different perspectives).

STEP 6—REVISE YOUR DRAFT

Revising your argumentative synthesis to make it ready for others to read is a time-consuming process again best approached in a series of steps. First, revise to improve the **content** of your paper, focusing on the quality and clarity of the argument you are advancing. Here are some questions you might ask about your draft as you revise to improve its content:

- Have I clearly indicated the point I want to prove?
- Have I clearly indicated the reasons I believe others should accept my position?
- Have I supported each of those reasons with expert testimony, statistics, or some other means of support as well as with clear explanations?
- Have I acknowledged opposing views in my paper when necessary? Have I found ways of refuting, accommodating, or conceding to them?

Next, review the **organization** of your essay, asking these questions:

- Is the thesis statement clearly worded, and does it control the structure of the essay?

- Have I provided clear transitions between the major sections of my essay?
- Are there clear connections between the material I draw from the readings and my own elaborations and explanations?

Finally, when checking the **accuracy** and **clarity** of your work, ask yourself:

- Have I chosen words that are clear yet contribute to the effect I wanted to elicit from my readers?
- Are my sentences clearly structured with adequate variety?
- Have I quoted and paraphrased material accurately and properly?
- When incorporating quoted or paraphrased material in my synthesis, have I supplied enough background information on the source text so the material makes sense to my readers?
- Have I defined all the terms I need to define?
- Have I documented all the material that needs to be documented?

STEP 7—CHECK QUOTATIONS AND DOCUMENTATION

Before you turn in your final draft for a grade, set aside time to check the accuracy of your quotations and documentation. First, make sure that you have quoted material accurately by comparing your text against the source text. Second, be sure that you have documented all of the material in your paper that needs to be documented, including all paraphrased information. Because you are combining information from several source texts in your synthesis and presenting your own argument as well, be sure your readers can always tell through your documentation the source of the material you include in your paper.

SAMPLE ARGUMENTATIVE SYNTHESIS

Following is an argumentative synthesis essay drawing on the readings found in Chapter 9. As you read the essay, consider how it is structured, how it uses material from the source texts, and how the writer develops the paper's argument.

Lost Innocence: The Dangers of Television Violence for Young Viewers

Most American children have grown up watching violent television shows. Whether prime-time drama or Saturday morning cartoons, children are exposed to a wide range of violent television programs. In fact, according to researchers Betty Simmons, Kelly Stalsworth, and Heather Wentzell, before children are 12 years old they have witnessed over 8,000 murders on television. They also found that only 2% of American homes do not have a television (181). In effect, then, almost all American children are exposed to television violence, a fact that warrants concern. Television violence harms children because it causes them to confuse fantasy and reality, encourages them to imitate the violent acts they see, and results in psychological damage that may last a lifetime.

Cognitively, young children have a difficult time separating the fantasy of the television world from the reality of their lives. Whether they are watching cartoons or newscasts, movies or commercials, children often believe what they see on the set is real. Simmons, Stalsworth, and Wentzell cite one of many studies which show "that children are extremely vulnerable to television between the ages of 2 to 8 years because of their maturational inability to separate what they view from reality" (182). As a result, what children watch on television shapes their view of the world, a world which is a frightening place full of potential threats and violence. Almost all parents have had to comfort a frightened child at bedtime because something on television frightened him or her, whether it was a monster destroying a city, a maniac stealing a child, or images of soldiers being killed on the nightly news. At young ages, everything children see on television is equally real. According to Joanne Cantor, Director of the Center for Communication Research at the University of Wisconsin, "There is growing evidence that violence viewing . . . induces intense fears and anxieties in child viewers" (175):

> A 1998 survey of more than 2,000 third through eighth graders in Ohio revealed that as the number of hours of television viewing per day increased, so did the prevalence of symptoms of psychological trauma, such as anxiety, depression, and posttraumatic stress. . . . Indeed, 9% of parents surveyed reported that their child experienced TV-induced nightmares *at least once a week.* (175)

The children in these studies were frightened because they believed that the violence they saw on television was all real and posed a potential threat to their safety and security. As Simmons, Stalsworth, and Wentzell claim, young children "live in a magical world that often leaves them terrified of things which completely surprise adults" (183).

Educators Fran Blumberg, Kristen Bierwirth, and Allison Schwartz, however, believe that watching violent television shows, especially cartoons, is not detrimental to children's well-being. These researchers support their assertions by citing the results of several studies, but their own prose casts doubts on the validity of their claims. For example, they cite a 2006 study by Kirsch which asserts that cartoon violence is different than violence portrayed on other types of shows—it is more verbal than physical and therefore less harmful. However, they paraphrase Kirsch as concluding that "the comedic element of cartoons *also may* affect young viewers' beliefs about the applicability of violent acts they see in programs to real-world situations" (190, emphasis added).

Blumberg, Bierwirth, and Schwartz end up conceding that children may have a difficult time differentiating television, even cartoons, from real life, as other researchers have concluded. In fact, they even cite studies of brain activity which demonstrate "neurological evidence of a link between exposure to violence on television and brain functioning," activating the area of the brain associated with self-control and "disruptive behavior disorder" (192). Blumberg, Bierwirth, and Schwartz downplay these results by pointing out that the studies have nothing to say about the long-term effects of childhood exposure to violent television. Presumably, any neurological changes that result from children watching violent television shows are short-lived and therefore not harmful. Finally, Blumberg, Bierwirth, and Schwartz argue that children who view violent cartoons make moral judgments about what they see, agreeing that violent characters should be punished. However, they then leap to an unconvincing conclusion: "*Presumably*, children's ability to make differentiated judgments about immoral acts *may* transfer to their ability to distinguish between the effects of cartoon and television violence and that found in real life" (192, emphasis added). Blumberg, Bierwirth, and Schwartz's arguments do not adequately call into question the many other studies that demonstrate children's inability to differentiate between reality and fantasy on television.

This inability to distinguish between what is make-believe and what is real on television holds real consequences for children. Besides increasing children's fears, this confusion contributes to the fact that children often imitate what they see on TV. Simmons, Stalsworth, and Wentzell note that because children are "curious and easily influenced," they often "mimic and repeat what they hear and see on television" (181). Most everyone can testify to the truth of this statement. Most people have seen young children engage in light-saber fights after watching *Star Wars* or bop some kid on the head after watching some cartoon on Nickelodeon. Children may mean no harm by imitating what they see on television, but the consequences can be tragic, as when they imitate what they see the Rock, Randy Horton, or the Undertaker do on Worldwide Wrestling or play with firearms they find in the home because they have seen characters use guns on TV. The National Institutes of Mental Health affirms a causal link between "television violence and aggressive behavior" in children (Simmons, Stalsworth, and Wentzell 182). Researchers Evra and Kline agree, asserting that "One of the dangers for preschoolers or early school-age children is their lack of ability to relate actions, motives, and consequences, and they may simply imitate the action they see" (quoted in Simmons, Stalsworth, and Wentzell 184). In other words, young children likely do not understand the real-life consequences of imitating the violence they see on TV.

While asserting that "definitive conclusions about the potential ill effects of exposure to cartoon violence on young viewers are not easily made," Blumberg, Bierwirth, and Schwartz conclude that several factors reduce the chances that children will imitate the violence they see on television:

> . . . scientific support can be found that the frequent comic contextualization of violence coupled with young children's cognitive repertoire, notably, their abilities to distinguish right from wrong and fantasy from reality, may mitigate the likelihood that young viewers will perpetrate the violent acts shown in cartoons on others in real life. (193)

These researchers seem to believe that children possess the cognitive and moral maturity required to keep them from imitating violent acts they see on TV. Again, though, they hedge their conclusion with "may"; in the end, they have to acknowledge that children may, in fact, imitate the violence they see on television, as numerous other studies have found. According to Cantor, children lack the ability to understand the impact of their violent acts: "One criticism of the way violence is usually portrayed on television is that it minimizes the apparent harmful consequences to the victim, both promoting desensitization and increasing the likelihood of the adoption of aggressive attitudes and behaviors" (178). On many television shows, especially cartoons, violence is depicted as normal, harmless, and even funny. The more frequently children see violence depicted this way, the less likely they are to understand the harm violent acts can have on others:

> . . . a study involving five different countries in which children were subjected to violence through television found evidence that even brief exposures caused them to be more accepting of other aggressive behavior. This research also concluded that the more children watched television, the more accepting they became of aggressive actions. (Simmons, Stalsworth, and Wentzell 182)

Given that every week children watch over 28 hours of TV (181), they may come to see violence and aggression as normal and acceptable aspects of life.

Finally, the life-long impact of watching violent television shows as a child may warrant the most concern. Perhaps young children confuse reality and fantasy when they watch TV and maybe they do imitate some of the violent acts they see; however when they grow up, one would assume that children grow out of these beliefs. At a certain point in their lives, children do come to realize that TV is not "real" and that hurting others has real consequences. Unfortunately, however, watching violent television shows as children may have lasting effects. Many of the claimed links between watching violent television shows as children and later anti-social behavior are startling. For example, some researchers assert that current high crime rates may be attributed to what today's criminals watched on television: "U.S.

crime rates are increasing most rapidly among youth who were in their formative early years when children's TV was deregulated and violent programs and toys successfully deluged childhood culture" (Simmons, Stalsworth, and Wentzell 182). Other studies have shown that the amount of violent television shows criminals watched when they were eight years old is a better predictor of their adult aggression than other socioeconomic factors (182). Cantor cites a study conducted at the Universities of Wisconsin and Michigan which asked adults to reflect back on frightening television shows they watched as children:

> . . . 52% reported disturbances in eating or sleeping, 22% reported mental preoccupation with the disturbing material, and 35% reported subsequently avoiding or dreading the situation depicted in the program or movie. Moreover, more than one-fourth of the respondents said that the emotional impact of the program or movie (viewed an average of six years earlier) was still with them at the time of the reporting. (176)

These studies do not claim that watching violent television shows as children causes adults to be fearful or turn to a life of crime. Instead, they point out a correlation between exposure to television violence as a child and anti-social behavior among some adults. At a minimum, research shows that what people watch on television as children contributes to who they become as adults.

Given the overwhelming evidence that watching violent television can have both short- and long-term negative consequences for children, what action is needed to address the problem? It seems unlikely that violence will be eradicated from television shows any time soon; even trying to take such actions raises serious freedom of speech issues. Instead, the best course of action is for parents to monitor what their children watch, limit their exposure to violence on TV, and explain to them the harmful effects violence has on others. Joanne Cantor explains how such acts can mitigate the ill effects of television violence on children and concludes her article with one last suggestion: "We also need media literacy education for children, including helping them place what they see in perspective, and encouraging a critical analysis of their own media choices" (178).

Additional Readings

Four Legs Good, Two Legs Bad: The Anti-human Values of "Animal Rights"

Wesley J. Smith

Wesley J. Smith *is a senior fellow at the Discovery Institute and consultant to the Center for Bioethics and Culture.*

If you are reading these words, you are a human being. That used to matter morally. Indeed, it was once deemed a self-evident truth that being a *Homo sapien* created intrinsic moral value based simply and merely on being human—a principle sometimes called "human exceptionalism."

No more. Human exceptionalism is under unprecedented assault across a broad array of societal and intellectual fronts. Bioethics, as this journal has often described, is a primary example. The predominating view among mainstream bioethicists is that human life per se does not matter morally. Rather, to be considered a full member of the moral community, one must achieve the status of being a "person" by possessing sufficient cognitive attributes such as being self-aware over time or being able to value one's life.[1]

This approach creates a potentially disposable caste consisting of hundreds of millions of humans: all unborn life—early embryos may not have a brain, and fetuses are generally considered unconscious; infants—they have not yet developed sufficient capacities; and people like the late Terri Schiavo—who have lost requisite capacities through illness or injury. The point of personhood theory is insidious: It grants permission to kill human non-persons or use them as mere natural resources ripe for the harvest.

Bioethics is by no means the only existent threat to human exceptionalism and to its corollary, the sanctity/equality-of-human-life ethic. Materialistic Darwinism also denigrates the unique moral value of human life based on the philosophical belief that because human beings evolved out of the same primordial mud as the rest of earth's flora and fauna, we are consequently not special or unique. The fervent embrace of human unexceptionalism led one Darwinian materialist to assert, "We are all of us, dogs and barnacles, pigeons and crabgrass, the same in the eyes of nature, equally remarkable and equally dispensable."[2]

John Derbyshire, of *National Review* fame, has similarly written that a Darwinian understanding of biology leads to the conclusion that human beings are only "special in the way that an elephant is special by virtue of having that long trunk. . . . We are part of nature—an exceptionally advanced and interesting part, but . . . not *special*."[3] (Emphasis within the text.)

A third equally dangerous threat to the equality/sanctity-of-human-life ethic—the subject of the balance of this article—comes from the animal-rights/liberation movement. Indeed, animal liberation is particularly subversive to our perceived status as a unique and special species because it advocates the creation of an explicit human/animal equality. Moreover, of the three threats to human exceptionalism I have mentioned (and there are others), only animal-rights activists engage in significant violence and lawlessness to coerce society into accepting their values. Thus, not only is animal-rights/liberation a unique danger to human exceptionalism (particularly among the young), but it also presents a potent threat to the rule of law.

The Ideology of Animal Rights

Defenders of the sanctity/equality-of-human-life ethic need to combat animal rights as forcefully as they do personhood theory. To understand why, we need to look past the public image of animal-rights/liberation groups, such as the People for the Ethical Treatment of Animals (PETA), as committed animal lovers who engage in wacky advocacy tactics such as posing nude to protest fur. For beneath this relatively benign facade lurks an ideologically absolutist movement that explicitly espouses equal moral worth between humans and animals.

What's wrong with wanting to protect animals? Absolutely nothing. Indeed, advocating for animal welfare can be a noble cause. But this isn't the ultimate agenda of animal rights/liberation. Thus, to understand the profound threat the movement poses to human exceptionalism, it must be distinguished from the animal-welfare movement.

The first distinguishing factor between animal rights and animal welfare is that, unlike the former ideology, the latter approach accepts human exceptionalism. As a consequence, animal welfarists argue that while human beings may have a right to use animals for our betterment and enjoyment, we also have a fundamental duty to do so in a proper and humane manner. Welfarists also believe we have a human duty to prevent unnecessary animal suffering. Thus, they engage in activities such as neutering feral cats and campaigning on behalf of more humane methods of slaughtering food animals.

In contrast, animal rights/liberation—while often engaging in welfare-type actions—is actually a radical departure from animal welfare. Whereas welfarists urge steady improvement of our treatment of animals and take actions to reduce animal suffering, the goal of the liberationists is to completely end every human use of animals. Thus, Gary L. Francione, director of the Rutgers University Animal Rights Law Center, seeks the eradication "of the property status of animals."[4] In his view there should ultimately be no domesticated animals. Similarly, PETA asserts that "animals are not ours to use—for food, clothing, entertainment, experimentation, or any other reason."[5]

To truly understand the subversive nature of the animal-rights philosophy, we have to look deeply into the movement's ultimate beliefs. For example, is the life of a monkey as precious as that of a human being? Animal-rights believers say yes. Is butchering a cow morally equivalent to lynching a black man during the Jim Crow era? PETA's "Animal Liberation Project" explicitly stated that it is.[6] Is artificially inseminating turkeys the moral equivalent of rape? Yes, according to Gary Francione, who criticized Peter Singer (and a colleague) for participating in a turkey-insemination demonstration. "I suggest that there is no non-speciesist way to justify what Singer and Mason claim to have done," Francione raged, "without also justifying the rape of a woman, or the molestation of a child, in order to see what those acts of violence 'really involved.'"[7] Many animal-rights activists and academics assert that animals should be considered "persons" with legal rights including full standing in the courts. Legislation will soon be introduced in Spain to grant full personhood rights to great apes.[8]

We cannot fully comprehend why animal liberationists believe these things—and why the most radical among them act violently against those they consider animal abusers—without understanding that liberationists *fervently* reject any hierarchy of moral worth between humans and animals. And this raises an important question: If being human does not convey moral worth to the liberationist, what does?

Space doesn't permit a complete exposition of all aspects and every nuance of animal-rights ideology. For our purposes, it is sufficient to explore the two primary ideological approaches: one that focuses on sentience as the source of moral value, and another that focuses on what has been called "painience," that is, the ability to feel pain.

Rutgers's Gary Francione is the best-known animal-liberation theorist advocating sentience as the primary measurement of moral value. "I argue that all sentient beings should have one right: the right not to be treated as our property—the right not to be valued exclusively as means to human ends," Francione stated in an interview.[9] (For these purposes, sentience can be defined as "a state of elementary or undifferentiated consciousness.")[10] In this view, since animals are not unconscious, they have a "right" not to be used instrumentally. Hence, each and every human use of animals—no matter how seemingly benign—is as wrong as if the same use were made of a non-consenting human being. Thus, to the true liberationist, cattle ranching is as odious as slavery because cows and humans are both sentient beings.

The second primary approach to crafting moral equality between humans and animals takes a slightly different trail to arrive at the same anti-human destination. In this view, if a being is capable of feeling pain, that attribute alone creates "equality of the species." Richard Ryder, a former professor at Tulane University, has written that the ability to feel pain—a capacity he calls "painience"—is what confers moral worth. Since animals can feel pain, he writes, the goal should be to "gradually bring non-humans into the same moral and legal circle as ourselves," toward the end that we "will not be able to exploit them as our slaves."[11]

PETA adopts the same concept in a slightly broader fashion. The issue for PETA is not just pain per se, but existential as well as physical suffering. Since PETA asserts that any use of animals by humans causes suffering, the group opposes sheep raising and wool shearing, eating dairy products, zoos, medical research using animals—even seeing-eye dogs. Or as Ingrid Newkirk, the head of PETA, once infamously stated, "There is no rational basis for saying that a human being has special rights. A rat is a pig is a dog is a boy."[12] Illustrating the profound harm to human welfare that would result from society's acceptance of animal-rights/liberation ideology, when Newkirk was asked if she would sacrifice five thousand rats or chimpanzees if it would result in a cure for AIDS, she retorted, "Would you be opposed to experiments on your daughter if you knew it would save fifty million people?"[13]

At this point, we need to consider the beliefs of Peter Singer, who is often called the godfather of animal rights because his 1975 book *Animal Liberation* is widely seen as having jump-started the modern movement. But unlike the true animal liberationist, Singer is not explicitly opposed to all animal research, or even, necessarily, to the eating of meat. (For example, he recently approved of using monkeys in Parkinson's disease research.[14]) Instead, Singer is an "interest utilitarian," that is, he believes that actions are not right or wrong per se, but must be judged upon their anticipated or actual consequences. Under this view, those actions which best serve the interests of most (not necessarily human) beings are those that should be pursued.

Utilitarianism isn't new, of course. But Singer became notable by asserting in *Animal Liberation* that the interests of animals should be given "equal consideration" to the interests of people in making utilitarian analyses. To do otherwise, he declared, is "speciesism"—that is, discrimination against animals—a wrong as odious in his view as racism and sexism.[15] Thus, when Singer was told recently that experiments on 100 monkeys benefited 40,000 people, he decreed that the experiment was "justifiable."[16] But he would almost surely have said the same thing if the experiment had been with cognitively disabled human beings, since the interests of the many were served by using those with lesser capacities. Indeed Singer once suggested that cognitively disabled people, rather than chimps, should have been used in hepatitis-vaccine experiments—because the human beings have lower capacities than normal chimpanzees.[17]

A Campaign to Diminish the Intrinsic Value of Human Life

It is tempting to dismiss such assertions and beliefs as being so far into fringe territory that they are not worthy of serious concern. I believe the contrary is true. For many years the argument over animal rights has been generally one-sided: Supporters are vocal and energized, while those who oppose according animals "rights" are generally subdued. As a consequence, animal-rights values are seeping into public consciousness. For example, a 1995 Associated Press poll found that 67 percent of respondents agreed with the statement "an animal's right to live free of suffering is just as important as a person's right to live free of suffering."

More worrisome, animal-rights/liberation ideology seriously threatens to undermine human exceptionalism—especially with the young, among whom liberationists make their most intense conversion efforts. PETA is particularly active in this regard. As the largest international animal-rights advocacy group, with hundreds of thousands of dues-paying members and a big following among the Hollywood set, in 2004, PETA received contributions of $27.8 million. More than 30 million people viewed its websites and the organization sent out monthly e-news action alerts to more than 200,000 subscribers. Its media department booked more than 2,700 interviews for its representatives. And PETA is targeting the young: Its education department reached 235,000 teachers and *11 million* students with educational materials, also sending out 332,000 copies of *Grr!* magazine to kids and teens.[18]

PETA's advocacy can only be described as profoundly misanthropic in that it literally equates the worst evils perpetrated by the most notorious governments with normal practices of animal husbandry. PETA's infamous "Holocaust on Your Plate" pro-vegetarian campaign is a case in point. For more than two years, PETA representatives literally toured the world— focusing most heavily on college campuses and places where young people gather in large numbers—arguing that eating meat and wearing leather were morally akin to horrors of the Holocaust.

This reprehensible message wasn't presented between the lines or done subtly in the hope that the reader would infer the comparison. Rather, eating-meat-equals-killing-Jews was the explicit and unequivocal theme of the entire national campaign. First, there were the pictures. PETA juxtaposed pictures of emaciated concentration-camp inmates in their tight-packed wooden bunks with pictures of chickens being kept in cages. In another truly despicable comparison (on several levels), a picture of piled bodies of Jewish Holocaust victims was juxtaposed with images of the bodies of dead pigs. (If the KKK did that, it would be called hate speech.)

The text of the campaign was just as offensive. In a section titled "The Final Solution," PETA made this astonishing comparison: "Like the Jews murdered in concentration camps, animals are terrorized when they are housed in huge filthy warehouses and rounded up for shipment to slaughter. The leather sofa and handbag are the moral equivalent of the lampshades made from the skins of people killed in the death camps."

Forget for the moment that Hitler was sometimes a vegetarian and that the Nazi government passed some of the most far-reaching animal-protection laws of the era. That PETA can't distinguish between the unspeakable evil of the Shoah and animal husbandry reveals a perverted sense of moral values that is almost beyond comprehension. (PETA eventually apologized for "Holocaust on Your Plate," but not because they realized they were wrong factually and morally for making the odious comparison. Rather, in a typical non-apology apology—entitled "An Apology for a tasteless comparison," PETA's executive director Ingrid Newkirk sought to justify the entire approach: "The 'Holocaust on Your Plate' Campaign was designed to sensitize people to different forms of systematic degradation and exploitation, and the logic and methods employed in factory farms and slaughterhouses are analogous to those used in concentration camps. We understand both systems to be based on a moral equation indicating that 'might makes right' and premised on a concept of other cultures or other species as deficient and thus disposable.")[19]

A Movement Growing More Violent

The animal-rights/liberation threat goes far beyond the philosophical. Because animal rights/liberationists believe that slaughtering animals for food is akin to murder, and that medical research using them is morally equivalent to Mengele's experiments in the death camps, violence in the name of saving animals is a growing threat. Indeed, according to John E. Lewis, deputy assistant director of the FBI's Counterterrorism Division, animal-rights terrorism has become one of the FBI's most urgent concerns: "One of today's most serious domestic terrorism threats comes from special interest extremist movements such as the Animal Liberation Front (ALF), the Earth Liberation Front (ELF), and Stop Huntingdon Animal Cruelty (SHAC) campaign. Adherents to these movements aim to resolve specific issues by using criminal 'direct action' against individuals or companies believed to be abusing or exploiting animals or the environment."[20]

While no one has yet been murdered (with perhaps the exception of Dutch politician Pim Fortuyn, who was shot to death by an animal-rights fanatic), harassment, intimidation, vandalism, and threats of violence and death have become routine tactics employed by the most radical activists against those they deem abusers of animals. For example, in the United Kingdom, a farm family that raised guinea pigs for medical testing was subjected to years of personal threats and property vandalism by animal liberationists who demanded they get out of the guinea-pig-raising business. The family had courageously refused to be intimidated, but when the liberationists *robbed the grave* of a beloved relative and refused to give the body back, they had finally had enough. Seeing no relief in sight, and desperately wanting to be left alone, the family gave in.[21]

In the U.S., the often-criminal activities of Stop Huntingdon Animal Cruelty (SHAC) epitomize the lengths to which some liberationists will go to impose their will on society. SHAC was formed to literally put Huntingdon Life Sciences, a medical-testing laboratory, out of business. Toward this end, SHAC pioneered a particularly insidious terrorist tactic called "tertiary targeting." Here's how it works: SHAC militants seek to completely isolate Huntingdon from the wider business community and thereby drive it out of business. To accomplish their mission, SHAC not only targets executives and employees of Huntingdon, but the company's product and service providers, such as banks, insurance companies, auditors, etc. To force these companies to cease doing business with Huntingdon, SHAC websites identify targets, providing home addresses, phone numbers, and the names and ages of children and even where they attend school. Targeted people may receive anonymous death threats or mailed videotapes of family members taken by SHAC activists. Companies have been bombed. Homes have been invaded and vandalized.

The tactic is insidiously effective. SHAC and their allies have intimidated scores of businesses, including the auditing firm Deloitte & Touche, into cutting ties with Huntingdon Life Sciences. In the United Kingdom, so many banks have been intimidated from doing business with Huntingdon that the company has had to turn to the Bank of England for a commercial account. Even the New York Stock Exchange backed off on listing Huntingdon's parent company in October, 2005—on the very day it was to be placed on the Big Board—after Exchange executives' personal information was published on SHAC websites.[22] (The company was finally listed in December, 2006, a never-explained delay of more than a year.)

With the notable exception of Francione—who laudably and unequivocally condemns threats and violence in the name of animal rights—the silence from most mainstream leaders of the movement in the face of such tactics has been deafening. PETA, for example, refuses to condemn SHAC and a similar outfit called the Animal Liberation Front (ALF), and has even compared lawlessness in the name of animal rights to the Underground Railroad and the French Resistance.[23] Worse, Jerry Vlasak, an especially notorious animal-rights leader, told a U.S. Senate subcommittee hearing that the "murder" of those "who hurt animals and will not stop after being told to stop" is "morally justified."[24]

Conclusion

Most people, particularly those in the pro-life movement, take human exceptionalism for granted. They can no longer afford to do so. The great philosophical question of the 21st century is whether we will knock ourselves off of the pedestal of moral distinctiveness. The stakes of this debate over human exceptionalism, which includes but is not limited to the animal-rights issue, could not be more important. After all, it is our exalted moral status that both bestows special rights upon us and imposes unique and solemn moral responsibilities—including the human duty not to abuse animals.

Unfortunately, the liberationists are oblivious to this point. By denying our unique status as human beings they dilute the very concept of evil and reduce it to the banal. Slavery is evil: Raising sheep is not even wrong. The Rwandan and Cambodian genocides were evil: Humanely slaughtering millions of animals to provide the multitudes with nourishing food is not even wrong. Rape is evil: Inseminating mares and milk cows is not even wrong. Mengele's human experiments were pure evil: Testing new drugs or surgical procedures on animals to save children's lives is not even wrong.

Even more fundamentally, the way we act toward one another and the world is based substantially on the nature of the beings we perceive ourselves to be. In this sense, the entire planet will rue the day that liberationists succeed in convincing society that there is no justification for the reigning hierarchy of moral worth. After all, if we ever came to consider ourselves as just another animal in the forest, that would be precisely how we would act.

Notes

1. For example, see John Harris, "The Concept of the Person and the Value of Life," *Kennedy Institute of Ethics Journal,* December 1999, pp. 293–308, and Tom Beauchamp, "The Failure of Theories of Personhood," Ibid., pp. 309–323.

2. John Darnton, "Darwin Paid for the Fury He Unleashed: How a Believer Became an Iconoclast," *San Francisco Chronicle*, September 25, 2005.

3. John Derbyshire, "God and Me," *National Review Online*, October 30, 2006.

4. Gary L. Francione, "Animals as Property," 2 *Animal Law* i, 1996.

5. See PETA website, *www.peta.org*.

6. Maria Garriga, "Outrage on the Green," *New Haven Register*, August 9, 2005. See also, Wesley J. Smith, "Liberation Theology," *National Review Online*, August 4, 2005.

7. Gary L. Francione, "Abolition of Animal Exploitation," *The Abolitionist*, September 2006.

8. See Wesley J. Smith, "Let Great Apes Be Apes," *San Francisco Chronicle*, June 18, 2006.

9. "The Animal Spirit" website, "An Interview with Professor Gary L. Francione on the State of the U.S. Animal Rights Movement," found at: http://www.theanimalspirit.com/garyfrancione.html.

10. See Answers.com, http://www.answers.com/topic/sentience.

11. Richard Ryder, "All Beings That Feel Pain Deserve Human Rights," *Guardian*, August 6, 2005.

12. Interview in *Washingtonian*, August 1986.

13. Michael Specter, "The Extremist," *New Yorker*, April 14, 2003, p. 57.

14. Wesley J. Smith, "The Animal House Falls Apart," *National Review Online*, November 30, 2006.

15. Singer writes about speciesism ubiquitously. See, for example, the revised and updated Peter Singer, *Animal Liberation* (New York, Avon Books, 1990), Chapter 1, "All Animals Are Equal," pp. 1–23.
16. Gareth Walsh, "Father of Animal Rights Activism Backs Monkey Testing," *Sunday Times* (London), November 26, 2006.
17. Jill Neimark, "Living and Dying with Peter Singer," *Psychology Today*, January–February 1999, p. 58.
18. Source: "PETA Annual Review, 2004."
19. See, for example, Joseph J. Sabia, "PETA Cheapens the Holocaust," *Front-Page Magazine.com*, October 16, 2003. See also, Wesley J. Smith, "PETA to Cannibals: Don't Let Them Eat Steak," *San Francisco Chronicle*, December 21, 2003.
20. Statement of John E. Lewis before the Senate Committee on Environment and Public Works, May 18, 2005. See also, Catherine E. Smith, "Threats.com," *Intelligence Report*, Southern Poverty Law Center, Summer 2005.
21. Peter Richards, "Animal Rights Militants Admit Grave Robbing," *Guardian*, April 11, 2006.
22. See Wesley J. Smith, "Wall Street Goes Wobbly," *Weekly Standard*, October 17, 2005.
23. Source: PETA Website, "Ask Carla."
24. Transcript: United States Senate Committee on the Environment and Public Works hearing, October 26, 2005.

Building a Culture of Animal Welfare: Past, Present and Future

Leticia V. Medina

Leticia V. Medina serves as the Manager of Animal Welfare & Compliance at Abbott Laboratories and is a council member of the Institute for Laboratory Animal Research.

1. Introduction

In the past century, and especially over the past 50 years, a growing emphasis has been placed on animal welfare around the world. In the United States a very significant reason for this growing interest is a dramatic change in how individuals perceive animals. This shift is largely due to a change in demography. Much of the population has moved from rural environments where they would have been exposed to agricultural animals to more urban environments where their exposure is often limited to pet animals (G. Golab, AVMA, personal communication). The United States Department of Agriculture (USDA) commissioned the philosopher, Bernard Rollin, to expound the reasons why U.S. society's view of anticruelty had changed so drastically in the last half of the 20th century. He listed five social and conceptual reasons but then stated "they are not nearly as important as the precipitous and dramatic changes in animal use that occurred after World War II. These changes include huge conceptual changes in the nature of agriculture and a significant increase in animal research and testing (Rollin, 1995, 2004)."

Concurrently, there has been a significant increase in the number of animal welfare and animal rights organizations. Animal welfare organizations promote responsible, humane care for all animals and recognize that people have moral responsibilities to ensure animal welfare for animals that are used for human purposes (Blackwell & Rollin, 2008). Animal rights extremist organizations promote a philosophy that animals should be given equal rights to humans and they strongly oppose what they consider to be the exploitation of animals for human purposes, such as biomedical research. "Between 1960 and today, the number of active animal rights groups has grown from about 15 to more than 250 in the U.S. alone. The Foundation for Biomedical Research (FBR) estimates there are about 20 major national animal rights groups that focus exclusively or primarily on animal research (M. Stebbins, FBR, personal communication)." Globally, there are over 900 independent animal welfare and/or animal rights organizations in over 150 countries (WSPA-USA, 2008).

The past 50 years have also seen significant advances in science and medicine. Examples include the development of lifesaving vaccines (polio, rubella), cardiovascular bypass surgical procedures and treatments for many ailments such as diabetes and cancer. Many of the advances have been based on data from animal research. Although a majority of the public may not understand how research with mice can benefit humans and other animal species, there is plenty of scientific data to prove the importance and validity of animal research. FBR reports that "seven of the last ten Nobel Prizes in medicine have relied at least in part on animal research (FBR, 2008)." A majority of human medical advances are eventually adopted for veterinary use and thus result in enhanced animal welfare practices. For example, scientists have learned more about recognizing and responding to pain and distress in a wide variety of animal species.

Throughout this period of advancing scientific and medical knowledge, there has been a parallel increase in animal welfare regulatory oversight, development of training programs for laboratory animal care specialists and development of alternative research and testing methods (Quimby, 1994). These changes have all played a role in the biomedical research community's growing interest and commitment to enhanced laboratory animal welfare.

This paper provides a brief overview of how society has been moving towards adopting a stronger culture of animal welfare. Primary emphasis will be on the culture of animal welfare within biomedical research programs with a brief review of the past, where we are at present, and where we might be headed in the future.

2. Past

A review of animal protection history shows that a majority of cultures adhere to a code of ethical conduct with regards to animals. Even one of the earliest recorded laws, the Code of Hammurabi, 1780 BC, includes mention of animal protection: "not even a dog that entered the city could be put to death untried (Johns, 1910)." The rise of organized animal protection agencies in the U.S. began in the last half of the 19th century (Wolfle, 2003). It is clear that the vast majority of animal welfare laws exist in response to public concerns and perceptions about the care and treatment of animals. A review of the Animal Welfare Act (AWA) shows that the original law was passed in 1966 in direct response to public concerns about animals used in research (Schwindaman, 1999). Since then, public interest in animal welfare has continued to grow as evidenced by the following statement: "By the early 1990s, the U.S. Congress had been consistently receiving more letters, phone calls, faxes, e-mails, and personal contacts on animal-related issues than on any other topic (Rollin, 2004)."

Animal welfare concerns were also being recognized and addressed from within the biomedical research community. The Animal Care Panel (ACP) was founded in 1950 by five research veterinarians that recognized the need to develop expertise with laboratory animals to ensure optimal animal welfare and good science (Brewer, 1999). In 1967, the ACP was changed to the American Association for Laboratory Animal Science (AALAS) (Wolfle, 2003). AALAS members are dedicated to the humane care of laboratory animals and to quality research that benefit people and animals. Likewise, the American Board of Laboratory Animal Medicine (ABLAM) was founded in 1957 and renamed in 1961 to the American College of Laboratory Animal Medicine (ACLAM) to encourage education and research in laboratory animal medicine and to establish standards for laboratory animal veterinarians (Wolfle, 2003). In 1965, the American Association for Accreditation of Laboratory Animal Care (AAALAC) was founded by leading veterinarians and researchers to raise the standards for laboratory animal care through a voluntary assessment and accreditation program based on the Guide for the Care and Use of Laboratory Animals (NRC, 1996) or current revision. In 1996, AAALAC changed their name to the Association for the Assessment and Accreditation of Laboratory Animal Care, International to reflect their commitment to improve life sciences and animal care and use practices around the world (Wolfle, 2003). Currently, there are more than 770 animal care and use programs in 29 countries that have earned AAALAC International accreditation (AAALAC, 2008).

In 1985, the Improved Standards for Laboratory Animals amendment to the AWA was passed and established new concepts in the regulation of research facilities. This amendment mandated the formation of an Institutional Animal Care and Use Committee (IACUC), relief of pain and distress, limits on survival surgeries, exercise for dogs, psychological well being for nonhuman primates and the creation of the Animal Welfare Information Center (Kulpa-Eddy et al., 2005). These changes were promulgated to ensure more rigorous oversight of laboratory animal care and use practices and higher standards for animal welfare.

Animal welfare within biomedical research programs continues to improve. Although analgesics are given more consistently to larger species than to small rodents undergoing surgery, recent studies report behavioral changes indicative of pain in rats undergoing laparotomies without analgesics (Roughan & Flecknell, 2001). As scientific studies elucidate these pain reactions and the biomedical research community becomes more adept at recognizing subtle behavioral changes in rodents, analgesia practices will continue to improve.

Rollin defends the biomedical research community when he states, "Now it is clear that researchers are not intentionally cruel. Rather, they are motivated by plausible and decent intentions: to cure disease, advance knowledge, ensure product safety, develop advanced surgical techniques for use in human health (Rollin, 2004)." He acknowledges that despite this lack of intention they may still inflict suffering on the animals they use (Rollin, 2004). The biomedical research community must acknowledge that at times laboratory animals feel pain or distress. In fact, a majority of animal research is quite innocuous but some research does cause animal pain or distress because of the diseases or biological processes that are studied. In those instances, the ethical obligation is to use nonanimal alternatives if available, but if not available, ensure the fewest animals are used and minimize animal pain and distress by using supportive care and the rigorous application of humane endpoints.

3. Present

The current generation of animal care, veterinary and research staff has never worked in a program where laboratory animal welfare wasn't emphasized. Individuals in the animal research field understand that animal welfare is a priority not only because ethical science demands it but also because loss of public support could be devastating to future scientific and medical progress. As science has taught us more about how to improve animal welfare, public concern has brought a greater focus to animal welfare issues globally. A 2007 opinion survey in Britain revealed that 76% of the general public accepts animal experimentation as long as there is no unnecessary suffering caused to the animals (MORI, 2007).

In research programs across the world, minimum animal welfare standards are no longer viewed as best practices. Rather, programs are going above and beyond these minimum legal requirements and guidelines to establish unique ways to enhance animal welfare. One way they accomplish this is by adopting alternatives, also known as the 3Rs of refinement, reduction and replacement, as first described by Russell and Burch (1992). Many institutions have created special positions or committees to focus on environmental enrichment, alternatives and animal welfare initiatives that go above and beyond the mandatory IACUC oversight. Examples of the "above and beyond" approach include Merck's Animal Alternatives Committee (James et al., 1995), and Abbott's Caring for Animals in the Research Environment (CARE) Committee (L. Medina, unpublished data). These institutions and many more have recognized that it is no longer good enough to adhere to the laws and guidelines; instead they are contributing to furthering animal protection practices in biomedical research. Thus, many institutions are funding alternatives research and developing animal welfare award programs to reward staff that initiate and promote alternatives.

There are more organizations globally that focus on promoting alternatives such as the Center for Alternatives to Animal Testing (CAAT), the National Centre for the Replacement, Refinement and Reduction of Animals in Research (NC3Rs) and the United Federation of Animal Welfare (UFAW). These organizations vary in their missions, but most fund research projects to advance the knowledge or application of one or more of the 3Rs. Other organizations have been created as part of a government's commitment to examining how to validate alternative methods for drug safety testing (Laroche et al., 2007).

An important area of progress today is pain management for laboratory animals. The increase in biomedical research has contributed to veterinary and human medical knowledge and enabled significant enhancements to animal welfare. For example, as recently as the early 1990's, veterinarians did not routinely provide analgesia for cats undergoing spays. Less than 20 years later, it would be unacceptable to forgo analgesics.

A growing number of scientists agree that unrelieved pain induces secondary negative affects, such as fear and anxiety in animals (Phillips, 2007). Research investigators hesitate to adopt alternative practices without scientific evidence to prove that these changes will not negatively impact their study data. The Australian Code states, "The underlying presumption in the selection and use of a pain management protocol is that, while pain and distress cannot easily be evaluated in animals, investigators and teachers must assume that animals experience these in a manner similar to humans unless there is evidence to the contrary (see section 1.20 of the Code) (NHMRC, 2008)." The question about whether analgesics add an unacceptable variable to certain types of animal research is systematically being answered by scientists who run side-by-side studies to show if analgesics affect animal study data. ACLAM's position statement on pain and distress in laboratory animals clarifies, "Pain is an undesirable variable in most research projects and, if not relieved, can lead to unacceptable levels of stress and distress in animals (ACLAM, 2008)." Each scientific scenario must be carefully analyzed as some animal models could be invalidated by analgesics that induce changes in pain receptors. Whereas analgesic use for laboratory rodents was rare in the late 1990s, it is a much more common practice today, but it's not as widespread as it should be. A recent report indicates that, "although the use of analgesics has increased over the past ten years, the overall level of post-operative pain relief for laboratory rodents is still low (Richardson & Flecknell, 2005)." This is an animal welfare issue that needs more attention. IACUC and animal welfare committees must not continue to accept the response, "we think that analgesics might affect our data." The animal research community must take responsibility to ensure the most current knowledge about rodent pain control is used and studies must be performed to validate rodent analgesic use in research to promote animal welfare.

The creation of advanced technologies such as automatic blood sampling has led to less pain and distress in laboratory animals and thus more consistent data. Instead of restraining animals for each blood sample collection, the animals are surgically implanted with vascular catheters, provided analgesics and allowed time for recovery. Then the vascular catheter from the animal is attached to tubing which runs through a computer-run blood-sampling machine. Animals may move in their home cages and often sleep through the majority of the blood samples, thus avoiding the acute stress from restraint. Studies with rats have shown that automated blood sampling plus oral analgesics results in reduced corticosterone, which is often elevated with acute pain or distress (Goldkuhl et al., 2008). These refined methods may also reduce animal use because crossover pharmacokinetic studies can be conducted in rats that previously would have required separate sets of animals.

Replacement methods are also being embraced as they become available and are validated to provide data that was formerly produced in animal studies. There are a growing number of examples of alternatives such as the in vitro Limulus Amoebocyte Lysate (LAL) assay as an alternative for the rabbit pyrogen test (Ding & Ho, 2001). There are a growing number of high-throughput in vitro assays used to screen compounds for cardiovascular safety, such as the hERG assay. This assay replaces some, although not all, animal studies required by the Food and Drug Administration as part of an integrated cardiovascular risk assessment for new compounds (Porsolt et al., 2005).

Each year, more animal research programs are going above and beyond the minimum standards to seek voluntary accreditation by AAALAC. In addition, companies that use contract laboratories for animal studies are routinely performing audits to ensure that these suppliers are adhering to animal care laws and guidelines. All of these measures have contributed to building a culture of animal welfare in animal research programs internationally.

4. Future

As the world becomes smaller and smaller through increased technology and travel, globalized standards for animal welfare will become more prevalent. One of the more significant indications of global concern about animal welfare was the 2005 addition of animal welfare guidelines to the international Animal Health Code (Kahn, 2007) by the World Organization for Animal Health (OIE). OIE is comprised of more than 170 member countries and its primary focus is to prevent the spread of epizootic animal diseases through increased transparency and collaboration among members. There are eight guiding principles for animal welfare outlined in the Animal Health Code with a majority of these principles being applicable to laboratory animal research programs worldwide. The OIE animal welfare principles include the internationally recognized "five freedoms" and "3Rs" as well as the statement "that the use of animals carries with it an ethical responsibility to ensure their welfare to the greatest extent practicable (OIE, 2008)."

Advances in laboratory animal welfare will continue with increased resources and attention being devoted to this important issue. Alternatives that have been developed will continue to gain widespread acceptance by countries that are in close communication and collaboration to ensure harmonization of scientific and regulatory practices. For example, the European, U.S. and Japanese centers for the validation of alternative methods have worked together to accept alternative skin irritation/corrosion toxicity tests through rigorous review and scientific validation (ICCVAM, 2008). Future enhancements of high throughput screening will allow even greater screening of compounds without animals to select a few for further development in animal studies. Potentially, bioreactors, bacteria, insects and worms will play larger roles in early drug discovery work as we learn how to gain the most knowledge out of simple living systems and extrapolate them to data that is applicable to human and nonhuman mammals.

Additionally, non-animal surgical or technical training tools will become more common in veterinary, medical and undergraduate coursework. Highly complex, anatomically similar models of human and animal body parts are being created and used for various types of training ranging from endotracheal intubation to cardiovascular stent placement. Teachers should embrace these changes as long as they meet the needs of students but insist on retaining certain animal training practices if there is evidence to show that some training is optimized when performed with animals. One compromise is when animal shelters invite veterinary students to perform spay and neuter surgeries. Student surgical training is achieved while animal welfare is advanced.

Computers will play an increasing role as our advances in intelligent design allow us to build increasingly complex systems. To date, there is no computer that mimics the enormously complex and numerous cell-cell interactions and biochemical communications that exist within a living person or animal. However, there has been great progress in our understanding of molecular biology, genetics and in developing human subsystems for use in research. These advances provide powerful tools for research that avoids unnecessary use of animals. It cannot be emphasized enough that despite this progress animal research will remain a vital part of an integrated research program to help further clarify the complex scientific and medical questions that remain to be answered (Williams, 2006). Thus, the research community must remain ever vigilant and committed to making science more humane and less dependent on animals, whose involvement in this noble endeavor is nonetheless not voluntary.

5. Concluding Remarks

Innovation in research methods will result in refined techniques that reduce animal use, reduce pain and distress and replace animal models. Humane science is the goal. Establishing clear lines of responsibility, humane endpoints, and a thorough plan for monitoring and intervention strategies helps to prevent, minimize and alleviate pain and distress in laboratory animals (NIH, 2008). There are still opportunities to improve but overall the international biomedical research community has made tremendous strides in adopting practices that promote a culture of animal welfare. Animal welfare is not only an ethical imperative but also important for good science and for the continued support of the public. Biomedical research continues to unravel many of life's mysteries and assist with the discovery and development of lifesaving healthcare products for both people and animals. The challenge remains for individuals and institutions involved with animal research to invest more into animal welfare research so that additional alternatives can be discovered and humane science will continuously advance.

References

AAALAC, 2008. Data for this paper were retrieved from the Association for Assessment and Accreditation of Laboratory Animal Care International, Frederick, Maryland. 2008. World Wide Web (URL: http://www.aaalac.org). (September, 2008).

ACLAM, 2008. Data for this paper were retrieved from the Guidelines—Position Statements, Pain and Distress in Laboratory Animals, American College of Laboratory Animal Medicine (ACLAM), Chester, New Hampshire, 2008. World Wide Web (URL: http://www.aclam.org/education/guidelines/position_pain-distress.html). (September, 2008).

Blackwell TE, Rollin BE. Leading discussions on animal rights. J Am Vet Med Assoc 2008;233(6):868–71.

Brewer NR. The Architectonics of Laboratory Animal Science. In: Mcpherson C, Mattingly S (editors). 50 Years of Laboratory Animal Science. Memphis: American Association for Laboratory Animal Science; 1999.

Ding JL, Ho B. A New Era in Pyrogen Testing. Trends in Biotech 2001;19(8):277–81.

FBR, 2008. Data for this paper were retrieved from Education, Nobel Prizes, Foundation for Biomedical Research (FBR), Washington, DC. World Wide Web (URL: http://www.fbresearch.org/Education/NobelPrizes/tabid/427/Default.aspx). (October, 2008).

Goldkuhl R, Carlsson HE, Hau J, Abelson KSP. Effect of subcutaneous injection and oral voluntary ingestion of buprenorphine on post-operative serum corticosterone levels in male rats. Eur Surg Res 2008;41:272–78.

ICCVAM, 2008. Data for this paper were retrieved from the ICCVAM Evaluation of EPISKIN™, EpiDerm™ (EPI-200), and the Rat Skin Transcutaneous Electrical Resistance (TER) Assay: In Vitro Test Methods for Assessing Dermal Corrosivity Potential of Chemicals. Interagency Coordinating Committee on the Validation of Alternative Methods (ICCVAM), Research Triangle Park, NC, 2008. World Wide Web (URL: http://iccvam.niehs.nih.gov/). (October, 2008).

James ML, Mininni LA, Anderson LC. Establishment of an animal alternatives committee. Contemp Topics in Lab Anim Sci 1995;34(3):61–4.

Johns CHW. Babylonian Law—The Code of Hammurabi, the 11th Edition of the Encyclopedia Britannica, Cambridge: Cambridge University Press; 1910.

Kahn S. The role of the World Organisation for Animal Health (OIE) in the development of international standards for laboratory animal welfare. Proc. of 6th World Congress on Alternatives & Animal Use in the Life Sciences, Alt Anim Test and Exper 2007 (Special issue);14:727–30. Available on Center for Alternatives to Animal Testing (CAAT), 2008. World Wide Web (URL: http://altweb.jhsph.edu/wc6/paper727.pdf). (November, 2008).

Kulpa-Eddy JA, Taylor S, Adams KM. USDA perspective on environmental enrichment for animals. ILAR Jour 2005;46(2):83-94.

Laroche C, Lalis G, Brekelmans C. The European partnership for alternative approaches to animal testing. Proc. of 6th World Congress on Alternatives & Animal Use in the Life Sciences, Alt Anim Testing and Exper 2007 (Special issue);14:769-73. Available on Center for Alternatives to Animal Testing (CAAT), 2008. World Wide Web (URL: http://altweb.jhsph.edu/wc6/paper769.pdf). (November, 2008).

MORI, 2007. Data for this paper were retrieved from Views on Animal Experimentation, a research study conducted by the Ipsos MORI research group: World Wide Web. (URL: http://www.ipsosmori.com/_assets/ publications/pdf/views-on-animal-experimentation-report.pdf) (September, 2008).

NHMRC, 2008. Data for this publication were retrieved from The Assessment and Alleviation of Pain and Distress in Research Animals, Guidelines to promote the wellbeing of animals used for scientific purposes, National Health and Medical Research Council (NHMRC), Australian Government. 2008. World Wide Web (URL: http://www.nhmrc.gov.au/ PUBLICATIONS/ synopses/_files/ea18.pdf) (November, 2008).

NIH, 2008. Data for this publication were retrieved from the Guidelines for Pain and Distress in Laboratory Animals: Responsibilities, Recognition and Alleviation, Office of Animal Care and Use, Animal Research Advisory Committee (ARAC) Guidelines, National Institutes of Health (NIH) 2008. World Wide Web (URL: http://oacu.od.nih.gov/ARAC/Pain_Distress.pdf) (September, 2008).

NRC (National Research Council). Guide for the Care and Use of Laboratory Animals. Washington: National Academy Press, 1996.

OIE, 2008. Data for this paper were retrieved from the Introduction to the Recommendations for Animal Welfare, World Organization for Animal Health (OIE), Paris, France, 2008. World Wide Web (URL: http://www.oie. int/eng/normes/mcode/en_chapitre_1.7.1.htm). (September, 2008).

Phillips P, 2007. How does pain rank as an animal welfare issue? Australian Animal Welfare Strategy Science Summit on Pain and Pain Management Proceedings. World Wide Web (URL: http://www.daff.gov.au/__data/ assets/pdf_file/0003/299082/clive-phillips.pdf). (September, 2008).

Porsolt RD, Picard S, Lacroix P. International Safety Pharmacology Guidelines (ICH S7A and S7B): Where Do We Go from Here? Drug Dev Res 2005;64:83–9.

Quimby FW. Twenty-five years of progress in laboratory animal science. Lab Anim 994;28:158–71.

Richardson CA, Flecknell P. Anesthesia and post-operative analgesia following experimental surgery in laboratory rodents: are we making progress? Altern Lab Anim 2005;33(2): 119–27.

Rollin BE. Farm Animal Welfare: Social, bioethical and research issues. Ames: Iowa State University Press, 1995.

Rollin BE. Annual Meeting Keynote Address: Animal agriculture and emerging social ethics for animals. J Anim Sci 2004;82:955–64.

Roughan JV, Flecknell PA. Behavioural effects of laparotomy and analgesic effects of ketoprofen and carprofen in rats. Pain 2001;90:65–74

Russell WM, Burch RL. The Principles of Humane Experimental Technique (Reprinted by Universities Federation for Animal Welfare 1992). Available at Center for Alternatives to Animal Testing (CAAT), Baltimore, Maryland. 2008. World Wide Web (URL: http://altweb.jhsph.edu/publications/humane_exp/het-toc.htm). (September, 1998).

Schwindaman DF. The History of the Animal Welfare Act. In: Mcpherson C, Mattingly S (editors). 50 Years of Laboratory Animal Science. Memphis: American Association for Laboratory Animal Science; 1999.

Williams RW. Animal Models in Biomedical Research: ethics, challenges and opportunities. In: Runge MS, Patterson C (editors). Principles of Molecular Medicine, Second edition. Totowa: Humana Press; 2006.

Wolfle T. 50 Years of the Institute for Laboratory Animal Research (ILAR): 1953-2003. ILAR Journal 2003; 44(4):324–37.

WSPA-USA, 2008. Data for this paper were retrieved from the About Us, World Society for the Protection of Animals (WSPA), Boston, Massachusetts. 2008. World Wide Web. (URL: http://www.wspa-usa.org/pages/12_about_us.cfm). (September, 2008).

Animal Suffering: Learning Not to Care and Not to Know

William Crain

William Crain *edits the publication* ENCOUNTER Education for Meaning and Social Justice.

At a recent New Jersey public hearing, the topic was a proposed black bear hunt. A small boy walked up to the microphone, said his name was Bobby, and told the officials that shooting bears was terrible. "How would you like it if someone shot at you? You wouldn't like it, would you?" Then Bobby threw up his arms and said, "But you won't care what I say because I'm only 7 years old," and walked back to his seat in a dejected manner.

Many parents and teachers have observed that young children have a strong affinity to animals. Preschool teachers often keep gerbils, hamsters, and other small animals in their classrooms to make the settings attractive to the children. Cartoons and children's books also appeal to children by featuring animals as their central characters. Donald Duck, Mickey Mouse, and the Three Little Pigs are children's staples.

In fact, animals are so important to young children that they routinely dream about them. Psychologist David Foulkes (1999) found that 3- to 5-year-olds dream about animals more than about people or any other topic, and animal dreams are nearly as common among 5- to 7-year-olds. Other researchers also have found that animals take center stage in children's dreams (Crain 2003, 50).

But as children grow up in the Western world, they find that their deep feelings for animals aren't shared by their dominant culture. Like Bobby, they are often dismayed by adult indifference to our fellow creatures.

The Rude Awakening

For most children, the first and most upsetting confrontation with adult views seems to occur when children discover the source of the meat they eat. In a preliminary study of 28 urban, middle class children, one of my undergraduate students, Alina Pavlakos, found that most 5-year-olds didn't know where meat comes from. They all knew they ate meat, but when asked, "Do you eat animals?," most said, "Nooo!," as if the idea were outrageous.

Pavlakos found that children soon learn otherwise, most by the age of six or so. As several writers (Goodall 2005, 142; Singer 2002, 215) have informally observed, some children become so distraught when they learn the facts that they want to become vegetarians, but their parents rarely permit it. Even the developmental psychologist Lawrence Kohlberg (1981, 15), who usually championed children's independent thinking, spent six months persuading his young son to abandon vegetarianism.

From Caring Child to Detached Adult

We need much more research on how children respond to adult practices and views with respect to animals and food. It seems that in the process of socialization children undergo a considerable transformation—from a caring child to a detached adult. Most U.S. adults eat meat, tolerate hunting, and don't lose sleep over the treatment of animals in zoos, rodeos, circuses, or research labs. In fact, when it comes to today's most widespread and horrible animal suffering—that on factory farms—most adults know little about it. This, at least, is what another undergraduate student, Srushti Vanjari, and I have found.

From December, 2005, to the present, Vanjari and I have distributed brief questionnaires in two colleges (The City College of New York and the

University of Miami), in two hotel lobbies, and at a senior citizen center in the New York metropolitan area. Our sample totals 213 respondents. We selected one hotel that was expensive and another that was inexpensive to tap into different social classes. In these samples, 73 to 90% of the respondents rated their knowledge of factory farms as either slight or nonexistent (with a large majority of these respondents rating their knowledge as nonexistent).

Admittedly, our surveys are informal, and several of my colleagues have questioned our results. They believe that the current decade has witnessed a dramatic rise in vegetarianism as people have become aware of the mistreatment of animals. This also is the impression of some major writers. For example, Michael Pollan wrote in 2006 that "vegetarianism is more popular than it has ever been, and animal rights, the fringiest of fringe movements until just a few years ago, is rapidly finding its way into the cultural mainstream" (p. 305). Actually, a 2008 Harris poll found that only 3.2% of U.S. adults followed a vegetarian diet, and only half of these did so out of a concern for animal welfare (Vegetarianism in America 2008).

It is possible of course that a dramatic rise in animal consciousness is now beginning for real. But we need data—not impressions—to know. It's quite possible that a large majority of adult Americans continue to view animal suffering with detachment, if they know about it at all.

How, then, might our society produce this detachment? The following are some mechanisms at work (see also Joy 2006).

Detachment Mechanisms

Media Screening

Factory farms and slaughter houses are usually in relatively isolated, rural parts of the country, so most people aren't exposed to them. Still, the media might bring the factory farms into our homes, but it does not. Except for an occasional late-night cable documentary, it's rare to see footage of animals on factory farms on television or in motion pictures (Singer 2002, 216).

Language

Sometimes our language hides the identity of animals as food. We eat pork, not pigs; veal, not calves; meat, not flesh. The killing of wildlife, too, is disguised. Wildlife managers and hunters say a person "takes" or "harvests" deer. They almost never say a person actually "kills" an animal.

The 19th century philosopher Arthur Schopenhauer (1995, 177) pointed out that the English language more subtly distances us from animals by referring to them with the impersonal pronoun it, as if animals were mere objects. The personal pronoun who is incorrect. Our language also replaces who with the impersonal pronouns that and which. So just as it's ungrammatical to speak of "the shovel who is by the door," it's also improper to speak of "the bird who is by the door." Our language requires us to use the words that or which, as if the bird were a thing—not a living being.

Denial

It's not just the media and our language that hide the suffering of animals from us; we also hide it from ourselves. Many of us would rather not learn about the treatment of animals, especially when it might spoil our meals (Robbins 1987, 143; Singer 2002, 217).

John Robbins refers to our wish to look away as "repression" (1987, 143–144) and "denial" (1987, 144–145). These are defense mechanisms in psychoanalytic theory, and of the two, denial more accurately describes what occurs in the case of animal suffering. Most of the time, people try to keep from looking at the facts. However, in psychoanalytic theory, defense mechanisms work unconsciously, beneath awareness. When people consciously defend themselves against knowledge, then, it's not pure denial, but a kind of "conscious denial."

Statistics and Abstractions

As Jonathan Balcombe (2006) points out, our society also distances us from animals by considering them as population statistics rather than individuals. Population statistics are more general and abstract, and it's easier to think about reducing the size of a population than to imagine a particular animal being killed.

Thus documents such as New Jersey's *Comprehensive Black Bear Management Policy* talk about "population control" and "desired densities" (New Jersey Fish and Game Council 2007, 36). Even some defenders of animals focus on populations. The Blue Ocean Institute (2009) asks us to avoid eating fish such as groupers and Atlantic bluefin tuna because their numbers are in peril. The Institute recommends that we eat fish such as Atlantic herring and chub mackerel because these fish stocks are at healthy levels.

But what about the individual fish? Each fish pulled from the sea writhes and gasps for oxygen. Each wants to live.

Humans can think of animals as population statistics because of our mental capacity for abstraction and generalization. The developmental psychologist Heinz Werner (1948, 271–272) described how this capacity develops as the child grows. Children under the age of 10 years or so tend to think in specific pictorial images. For example, young children don't consider "space" in general but think of particular spaces, such as their bedroom, the pond down the street, or the space under the stairs where they like to hide. Only later, as children move toward adolescence, can they think about space more abstractly and generally, as when they understand that the rule "area = height x width" applies to *any* area.

Western scientific culture places a high value on such equations because they use quantitative measurement. As a measurable quantity, space doesn't depend on personal preferences, opinions, or emotions. It is purely objective. Using the same abstract approach, wildlife managers speak of target deer densities such as 20 deer per square mile. Phrasing the goal in this way has considerable appeal in our science-admiring society. The danger is that it distances us from what we are actually doing—killing individual deer.

It is especially easy to think of herd animals as population statistics, rather than individuals, because they strike us as so similar. But the more researchers learn about a species, the more they discover that each animal has an individual personality. This is true with respect to deer, black bears, wolves, and many mammals (Inglis 2005; Balcombe 2006). Even fish, including sharks and octopuses, have individual temperaments (Balcombe 2006, 54-57, 210). It seems that whenever scientists look beyond statistics and get to know the members of a species, individuality comes to the fore.

Abstract reasoning detaches us from animals in many ways. Sometimes we keep discussions on a theoretical plane. A case in point is Richard Louv's immensely popular book, *Last Child in the Woods* (2005). This book has done more than any other to raise public awareness about children's alienation from nature. Louv wants children to have direct experience with nature and develop reverence for it. But Louv defends hunting and fishing, and it's difficult to see how killing an animal for sport shows reverence for the animal. To defend his position, Louv moves to the abstract intellectual level. When it comes to fishing, Louv says the central question is whether fish feel pain, and the answer "depends on your definition of pain and suffering" (pp. 192–193). Louv chooses not to delve into the matter, but says that the answer "is not so clear as it may seem. Certainly, the definition is not settled" (pp. 192–193). So what appears straightforward to us when we watch a fish gasping for oxygen becomes a matter of abstract definition—and therefore removed from our emotional responsiveness (Crain 2006).

Motives for Maintaining Detachment

Will people become more sensitive to animal suffering? Perhaps, but it won't happen automatically. Detachment serves emotional purposes, making life more comfortable for us.

Avoiding Empathic Pain

As Robbins suggests, if we open ourselves to animal suffering, we cannot help from sharing some of their pain. Because of our natural empathy, we hurt too. Robbins (1987, 145) adds that we suffer because we are not apart from animals; "our pain arises from our kinship with life." To avoid the pain, we look the other way.

The Need for Cultural Belonging

If we do open ourselves to animal suffering, we are likely to want to do something about it. In particular, we are likely to try a vegetarian diet. But this opens us to another kind of distress—that which comes from being separate from our culture.

In his book, *The Omnivore's Dilemma* (2006), Michael Pollan discovered how a vegetarian diet can frustrate the need for cultural belonging. As part of his investigation of meat-eating in our society, Pollan decided to try out vegetarianism himself. During this time, Pollan wrote, "Healthy and virtuous as I may feel these days, I also feel alienated from traditions I value: cultural traditions like the Thanksgiving turkey, or even franks at the ballpark, and family traditions like my mother's beef brisket at Passover. These ritual meals link us to our history along multiple lines: family, religion, landscape, [and] nation" (Pollan 2006, 315).

As students of anthropology know, Pollan has a point. In every society one might consider, food is central to the social fabric. Food is tied to rituals, taboos, gender roles, forms of indebtedness, land rights, and feasts of social solidarity (Haviland 1990, 396–397).

Thus, to deviate from a society's customary way of eating is to alienate oneself from the dominant culture. Since humans have a strong need to belong, departure from social norms is emotionally difficult. In fact, the child psychologist Susan Isaacs implied that a young child's wish to adopt a vegetarian diet can cause mental disturbances. A vegetarian diet, she said, would cut the child off "in the most unhealthy way from the common ethos of his time" (1966, 164). When I have asked my vegetarian students about Isaacs's statement, they generally have said it's an exaggeration, but they do acknowledge that their vegetarianism has caused tensions within their families and has made them feel isolated, odd, or different.

Conclusion

Opening ourselves to animal suffering, then, isn't easy. Applying "detachment mechanisms" blocks us from emotional pain and satisfies the strong need to belong to the mainstream culture. However, personal growth sometimes means confronting negative feelings and departing from the mainstream. We develop strength and maturity by attending to our own sense of what is right.

References

Balcombe, J. 2006. Pleasurable kingdom. London: Macmillan.

Blue Ocean Institute. 2009. Seafood. Full list. Available online at <www.blueocean.org/seafood/seafood-search-result?type=all>

Crain, W. 2003. Reclaiming childhood: Letting children be children in our achievement-oriented society. New York: Holt.

Crain, W. 2006, Spring. Review of Last Child in the Woods by Richard Louv. Encounter: Education for Meaning and Social Justice 19 (1): 47–48.

Foulkes, D. 1999. Children's dreaming and the development of consciousness. Cambridge, MA: Harvard University Press.

Goodall, J., with G. McAvoy and G. Hudson. 2005. Harvest of hope. New York: Warner Books.

Haviland, W. A. 1990. Anthropology (6th ed.). Fort Worth, TX: Holt, Rinehart and Winston.

Inglis, J. 2005. The science behind Algonquin's animals-Researchers-Jeremy Inglis. Available online at <www.sbaa.ca/researchers.asp?cn=289>.

Isaacs, S. 1966. Intellectual growth in young children. New York: Shocken Books. (Originally published in 1930).

Joy, M. 2006. Food for thought. Carnism and the psychology of eating meat. VegFamily. Available online at <www.vegfamily.com/articles/carnism.htm>.

Kohlberg, L. 1981. The philosophy of moral development: Essays on moral development, Vol. 1. New York: Harper & Row.

Louv, R. 2005. Last child in the woods: Saving our children from nature-deficit disorder. Chapel Hill, NC: Algonquin Books.

New Jersey Fish and Game Council. 2007, July 24. Draft Comprehensive Black Bear (Ursus americanus) Management Policy, Part I. Available online at <www.state.nj.us/dep/ fgw/pdf/2007/CouncilDraftBearPolicy.pdf>.

Pollan, M. 2006. The omnivore's dilemma. New York: Penguin.

Robbins, J. 1987. Diet for a new America. Novato, CA: Kramer.

Schopenhauer, A. 1995. On the basis of morality. Translated by E. F. J. Payne. Providence, RI: Berghahn. (Originally published in 1839.)

Singer, P. Animal liberation. 2002. New York: HarperCollins.

Vegetarianism in America. 2008. Vegetarian Times. Available online at <www.vegetariantimes.com/features/archive_of_editorial/667>.

Werner, H. 1948. Comparative psychology of mental development. New York: Science Editions.

Summary Chart

HOW TO WRITE AN ARGUMENTATIVE SYNTHESIS

1. **Analyze the assignment.**
   - *Determine whether you are being asked to write an informative or argumentative synthesis.*
   - *Determine the number and types of readings you are expected to use in your paper.*

2. **Review and annotate the readings.**
   - *Review the readings with your assignment in mind, looking for and marking information related to the topic of your paper.*
   - *Briefly summarize and critique each reading.*

3. **Formulate a thesis.**
   - *Determine what stance you will assume in your essay.*
   - *Determine whether you will use an open or closed thesis statement.*

4. **Choose an organizational plan.**
   - *Decide how you will order the ideas you will develop in your essay.*
   - *Decide whether you will present your ideas using a block or alternating format.*

5. **Write your rough draft.**
   - *Follow the organization plan implied or stated by your thesis.*
   - *Combine your insights, ideas, arguments, and findings with material in the source texts to develop and support your thesis.*
   - *Both paraphrase and quote material as necessary.*
   - *Add transitions, elaborations, clarifications, and connections where needed.*
   - *Include a concluding paragraph.*

6. **Revise your draft.**

Revise to improve the content of your essay.
- *Have you clearly indicated the point you want to prove?*
- *Have you clearly indicated the reasons you believe others should accept your position?*
- *Have you supported each of those reasons with expert testimony, statistics, or some other means of support as well as with clear explanations?*
- *Have you acknowledged opposing views in your paper when necessary? Have you found ways of refuting, accommodating, or conceding to them?*

Revise to improve the organization of your essay.
- *Is the thesis statement clearly worded, and does it control the structure of the essay?*
- *Have you provided clear transitions between the major sections of your essay?*
- *Are there clear connections between the material drawn from the readings and your own elaborations and explanations?*

Revise to improve the accuracy and clarity of your essay.
- *Have you chosen words that are clear and contribute to the effect you want to elicit from your readers?*
- *Are your sentences clearly structured with adequate variety?*
- *Have you defined all the terms you need to define?*
- *Have you proofread for spelling, punctuation, or usage errors?*

7. **Check your quotations and documentation.**
- *Have you quoted and paraphrased material properly, accurately, and fairly?*
- *When incorporating quoted or paraphrased material in your synthesis, have you supplied enough background information on the source text so that the material makes sense to your readers?*
- *Have you documented all the material that needs to be documented?*
- *Have you documented material employing the proper format?*

ARGUMENTATIVE SYNTHESIS REVISION CHECKLIST

	Yes	No
1. Have you checked your assignment to be sure you have written the proper kind of synthesis essay: informative or argumentative?	____	____
2. Have you carefully read, annotated, and critiqued all of the source texts you will use in your essay?	____	____
3. Examine the wording of your thesis statement. Does it clearly state the stance you will assume in your essay?	____	____
4. Check the opening section of your essay. Does it:		
• introduce the topic of your paper?	____	____
• capture reader interest?	____	____
• include your thesis statement?	____	____
5. Examine each section in the body of your essay. Do you:		
• focus on just one issue at a time?	____	____
• make clear assertions?	____	____
• support your assertions with evidence?	____	____
• explain the link between each assertion and its supporting evidence?	____	____
6. Check the organization of your essay. Do you:		
• follow the organizational plan indicated by your thesis?	____	____
• provide transitions to help guide your reader through your essay?	____	____
7. Have you supported your assertions with some combination of quoted, summarized, and paraphrased source material?	____	____
8. Have you documented all the material that needs to be documented?	____	____

	Yes	No
9. Have you checked the content of your essay to be sure it accurately communicates your position and intention?	_____	_____
10. Have you reviewed your sentences for accuracy and variety?	_____	_____
11. Have you reviewed your word choice for clarity and accuracy?	_____	_____
12. Is your works cited or reference list correct?	_____	_____

Chapter 11

....

PLAGIARISM

DEFINITION

Plagiarism occurs when writers take credit for work that is not really theirs. Because it encompasses a wide range of errors in academic writing, from improper citation to calculated fraud, plagiarism is an especially common problem for writers unfamiliar with the conventions of source-based writing. These writers often do not realize that any material they quote or paraphrase from a reading must be documented to avoid plagiarism.

Penalties for plagiarism vary from school to school, department to department, even instructor to instructor. They can range from a warning, to a failing grade on a paper, to a failing grade for a course, to expulsion from school. The academic community takes plagiarism seriously, but with care and honesty you can avoid problems and give the authors of the readings you use the credit they deserve for their work.

FORMS OF PLAGIARISM

Plagiarism is a difficult problem to address because it can assume so many different forms and involves so many different types of errors, some more serious than others. Understanding the various forms that plagiarism can assume will help you avoid problems.

PURCHASING A PAPER

Sometimes students will decide to purchase a paper rather than write one themselves. Whether you buy one from a fellow student or from a commercial vendor, purchasing a paper and turning it in as if it were your own is clearly a form of plagiarism. You are purposely taking credit for work that is not truly yours. Your teachers expect you to do your own work. Sometimes they may ask you to work with other students to write an essay, but even then you will be expected to do your own work in the group. Purchasing a paper—or even part of a paper—from someone and turning it in as if were your own is never acceptable.

TURNING IN A PAPER SOMEONE ELSE HAS WRITTEN FOR YOU

This form of plagiarism, related to the first, occurs when two students decide to let one take credit for work the other has actually completed—a student may ask his roommate to write a paper for him then turn it in for a grade. If caught, both students may face some sort of penalty for plagiarism. In other cases, roommates taking different sections of the same class may hand in the same paper to their instructors without permission. In this case, both students have committed plagiarism. Finally there are instances where a student retrieves a paper from the "fraternity" or "sorority" file, collections of papers written for various courses kept for students to copy and turn in (high tech versions of this file are the collections of student papers kept on university computer systems). These papers may have been written by people the student has never known; however, if the student represents it as her own work, that student is guilty of plagiarism.

TURNING IN ANOTHER STUDENT'S WORK WITHOUT THAT STUDENT'S KNOWLEDGE

This form of plagiarism has increased over the past few years as more and more students write their papers on computers. Here a student searches another student's computer files for a paper, copies the paper, then turns it in as if it were his own work. This is clearly a form of plagiarism.

IMPROPER COLLABORATION

More and more teachers are asking students to work together on class projects. If a teacher asks you to collaborate with others on a project, be sure to clarify exactly what she expects you to do individually when preparing the final essay. Sometimes a teacher will want a group of students to produce a single paper. The members of the group decide among themselves how they will divide the labor, and all group members get equal credit for the final essay. Though the group members should help each other complete the essay, if you are asked to complete a certain task as part of the larger project, make sure you give credit to others, when appropriate, for any material that was not originally your own. Other times a teacher will want the members of the group to work individually on their own papers; the other group members serve as each other's consultants and peer editors rather than as coauthors. In this case, you should acknowledge at the beginning of your essay or through documentation in the body of your paper any ideas or material you did not develop yourself.

COPYING A PAPER FROM A SOURCE TEXT WITHOUT PROPER ACKNOWLEDGMENT

This form of plagiarism occurs when a student consults a website, an encyclopedia, book, or journal article, copies the information directly from the reading into his paper, puts his name on the essay, and turns it in for a grade. Sometimes a student will compose an entire essay this way; sometimes he will copy only part of his paper directly from a source. In either case, copying from a reading without proper quotation and documentation is a form of plagiarism. So is copying material directly from a computerized encyclopedia. Even though your computer may come with an encyclopedia on CD, you cannot copy material from it and turn it in as your own work without proper documentation and acknowledgment.

CUTTING AND PASTING MATERIAL FROM SOURCES

Instead of copying all of the material for a paper from a single source text and passing the work off as their own, students increasingly lift material from several source texts and weave it together to construct a paper. This form of plagiarism is especially common when students gather information from the Web. Copying chunks of text from several Web sites into an essay and passing it off as your own work is unacceptable. All of the material drawn from Web sites must be properly documented.

LIFTING IMAGES FROM THE WEB OR OTHER SOURCES

If you copy photographs, pictures, charts, artwork, cartoons, or any other type of visual image from the Web or any other source, you need to document its source and give proper credit to its creator. Normally you would cite its source in a caption below the image or include the information as a way of introducing the image in your essay. Include a works cited or reference list entry for it at the end of your essay.

COPYING STATISTICS

Properly cite and document any statistics you use in your paper. If they come from a source text, including a Web site, they need to be documented. The same holds true if you include statistics from your own research in an essay you write. Indicate in your essay the source of these statistics and include a proper works cited or reference entry for them.

COPYING MATERIAL FROM A SOURCE TEXT, SUPPLYING PROPER DOCUMENTATION, BUT LEAVING OUT QUOTATION MARKS

Many students have a hard time understanding this form of plagiarism. The student has copied material directly from a source and has supplied proper documentation. However, if the student does not properly quote the passage, the student is guilty of plagiarism. The documentation a student provides acknowledges the writer's debt to another for the ideas she has used in the paper, but by failing to supply quotation marks, the writer is claiming credit for the language of the passage, language originally employed by the author of the source text. To properly credit the author for both the ideas and the language of the source text, the student needs to supply both proper quotation marks and proper documentation.

PARAPHRASING MATERIAL FROM A READING WITHOUT PROPER DOCUMENTATION

Suppose a student takes material from a source, paraphrases it, and includes it in his paper. Has this student committed an act of plagiarism? The student has if he fails to document the passage properly. The language is the student's own, but the original ideas were not. Adding proper documentation ensures that the author of the source text will receive proper credit for his ideas.

SELF-PLAGIARISM

The concept of self-plagiarism is difficult for many students to grasp: How is it possible to plagiarize or "copy" my own work? Self-plagiarism is considered an act of academic dishonesty for one primary reason: When teachers give students a writing assignment, they expect the student will turn in original work. If a student simply "recycles" an earlier paper—turns in a paper she or he had written in the past or for another class—the teacher is not receiving original work. Plagiarism also occurs if a student uses parts of an earlier paper in a current assignment without acknowledging their source. Keep in mind that unless otherwise indicated, teachers expect original work in the papers they assign—properly acknowledge and document material that comes from any outside source, including your own prior writing.

HOW TO AVOID PLAGIARISM

DO YOUR OWN WORK

Obviously, the first way to avoid plagiarism is to do your own work when composing papers—do your own research and write your own essay. This suggestion does not mean, however, that collaborating with others when you write or getting needed help from your teacher, tutor, or classmates is wrong. Many instructors will suggest or even require you to work with others on some writing projects—classmates, writing center tutors, friends. Just be sure the paper you turn in fairly and accurately represents, acknowledges, and documents the efforts you and others have put into the essay. If you get help on a paper you are writing, make sure that you can honestly take credit for the unacknowledged ideas and language it contains. If important or substantial ideas or words in the paper came from someone else, be sure to document those contributions properly. When you turn in a paper with your name on the title page, you are taking credit for the material in the essay. You are also, though, taking responsibility for that material—you are, in effect, telling your reader that you compiled this information, developed these arguments, or produced these findings and will stand behind what you have written. Taking that responsibility seriously, doing the hard work of writing yourself and composing papers that represent your best efforts, can help you avoid problems with plagiarism.

TAKE GOOD NOTES

One common source of unintentional plagiarism is poor note taking. Here is what can happen: a student goes to the library and looks up an article she thinks will help her write her paper. She reads the piece and, taking notes, copies down information and passages she thinks she might use in her essay. However, if she is not careful to put quotation marks around passages she takes word-for-word from the source, she can be in trouble when she writes her essay. If she later consults her notes when drafting her paper, she may not remember that the passage in her notes should be quoted in her paper—she may believe she paraphrased the material when taking notes. If she copies the passage exactly as she has it written in her notes and fails to place it in quotation marks in her paper, she has plagiarized the material, even if she documents it. Remember, to avoid plagiarism, passages taken word-for-word from a source must be quoted *and* documented. Therefore, be very careful when taking notes to place quotation marks around material you are copying directly from a reading. If you later incorporate that material in your essay, you will know to place the passage in quotation marks and document it.

To avoid problems, consider developing a consistent system for taking notes. In many high schools, students are required to write their notes on index cards with the source text's full bibliographic information on each card. If you find this system of note taking helpful, you can continue it in college. If you found this method too repetitive and time-consuming, you can make a few alterations. For example, you can take notes on lined paper, citing the bibliographic information at the top and the source text's page numbers along the left margin. Consider writing on only one side of the paper, though, so you're not flipping sheets around when you write your essay. You might consider using a research journal as a place to keep all of your notes for an assignment. One common practice among academics is to keep content notes from source texts on the left hand side of the journal and their own responses, insights, and questions on the right hand side so as not to confuse the two (these are frequently referred to as "dual entry" journals). Whatever system you use, employ it consistently and be sure to indicate in your notes what material is copied verbatim from a source and which is paraphrased.

PARAPHRASE PROPERLY

Another source of unintentional plagiarism is improper paraphrasing. When you paraphrase material, you have to be sure to change substantially the language of the source passage (see Chapter 3 for guidelines on paraphrasing material). If you do not do a good job paraphrasing a passage, you can be guilty of plagiarism even if you document the material. If in your paraphrase there are phrases or clauses that should be quoted (because they appear in your paper exactly as they appear in the source), you will be guilty of plagiarism if you do not place quotation marks around them, even if the whole passage is properly documented.

SUPPLY PROPER DOCUMENTATION

When you proofread a source-based essay, set aside time to look for problems involving documentation before you turn it in. Problems like these can be hard to detect; you need to pay close attention to finding them as you review your work. Make sure everything that should be documented is properly cited. If you ever have any questions about whether to document a particular passage or word, see your instructor. Because instructors know the documentation conventions of their particular fields of study, they can often give you the best advice. If you have a question about whether to document a passage and you cannot reach your teacher for advice, you should probably err on the side of documentation. When responding to your work, your teacher can indicate whether the documentation was absolutely necessary.

Remember, whenever you quote *or* paraphrase material, you need to supply proper documentation, indicating the source of those words or ideas. Most students remember to document quotations. Remembering to document paraphrased material can be more problematic, especially if you have been told *not* to document "common knowledge." Though this may appear to be a fairly simple guideline, in practice it can be confusing and vague. What is **common knowledge**? What qualifies as common knowledge varies from discipline to discipline in college and from audience to audience. Information that does not need to be documented in a history research paper may need to be documented in a philosophy research paper—the information is common knowledge for readers in history but not for readers in philosophy. Among one group of readers, certain facts, references, statistics, claims, or interpretations may be well known and generally accepted; among other readers, the same material may be new or controversial. For the first group of readers, documentation may not be necessary; for the second, it probably is. Again, if you ever have a question concerning whether something should or should not be documented, ask your instructor, who has expert knowledge about the discipline.

Many students express dismay over this guideline because it means that if they are writing a paper on a topic relatively new to them, they will have to document almost everything. When you are writing certain kinds of papers in certain classes, there may be no way to avoid having documented material in almost every paragraph. However, this situation is not "bad"; in fact, it is to be expected when you are writing on a subject new to you. There are ways to consolidate your documentation so the citations do not take up too much space in your essay (see the two "Consolidating References" sections in Chapter 12).

ONLINE PLAGIARISM CHECK

Many professors employ online plagiarism detection services like TurnItIn. com. These services search electronic versions of your paper to detect strings of words that match strings in the vast collection of source texts and prior student papers the company maintains on its server. At many schools, professors ask students to turn in the final drafts of their papers electronically so they can use a service like this. Other professors ask students to run rough drafts of their papers through the service in order to detect and fix passages that might be plagiarized. Check with your instructor or school librarian to see if you can take advantage of a service like this as you draft your essay.

CLARIFY COLLABORATION GUIDELINES

If you are asked to collaborate with others on a project, be sure to clarify the guidelines your teacher wants you to follow. You want to be sure you know what your teacher expects of each student in the group. Are the individual members of the group supposed to work together to produce a single essay? Are the group members supposed to help each individual member of the group write his or her own paper? How much help is acceptable? Can another student supply you with the material or arguments you will use in your essay? Can others help you with the organization, perhaps suggesting how you should structure your work? Can other students write part of your paper for you? Can others revise your paper for you, changing the language when needed? Be sure you know what your teacher expects before you begin work on a collaborative project, and be sure to ask your teacher to clarify how she expects you to acknowledge and document the help you receive from others.

Summary Chart

PLAGIARISM

1. **Forms of Plagiarism**

   Purchasing a paper

   Turning in a paper someone else has written for you

   Turning in another student's work without that student's knowledge

   Improper collaboration

   Copying a paper from a source text without proper acknowledgment

   Cutting and pasting material from multiple sources

   Lifting images from the Web or other sources

   Copying statistics

   Copying material from a source text and supplying proper documentation, but leaving out quotation marks

   Paraphrasing material from a reading without proper documentation

   Self-plagiarism

2. **How to Avoid Plagiarism**

   Do your own work.

   Take good notes.

   Paraphrase properly.

   Supply proper documentation.

   Use an online plagiarism check.

   Clarify collaboration guidelines.

PLAGIARISM CHECKLIST

	Yes	No
1. Are all of your quotations properly documented?	_____	_____
2. Is all paraphrased material properly documented?	_____	_____
3. Have you acknowledged or documented the help you have received in writing your paper?	_____	_____
4. If this is a group project, have you checked the original assignment to be sure your work conforms to the teacher's guidelines?	_____	_____
5. Does the paper truly represent your own original work and effort?	_____	_____

Chapter 12

....

DOCUMENTATION

DEFINITION AND PURPOSE

Proper documentation for your papers serves several functions. First, it allows your readers to know exactly where to find specific information if they want to check the accuracy of what you have written or if they want to learn more about the subject. When combined with a reference list or bibliography, proper documentation enables readers to locate information easily and efficiently. Second, documentation gives credit to others for their ideas, arguments, findings, or language. When you write from readings, you are joining an ongoing conversation—people have likely written on the topic before you began your research and will likely write on it after you have finished your essay. With documentation, you acknowledge the work of those previous authors and locate your work clearly in that conversation. Finally, as a practical matter, proper documentation helps you avoid plagiarism. Many instances of unintentional plagiarism result from improper documentation. You can avoid these problems if you take a few minutes to check the accuracy of your documentation before you turn your papers in for a grade.

TYPES OF DOCUMENTATION

In college, you will encounter two primary methods of documentation: (1) in-text parenthetical documentation and (2) footnotes or endnotes. When you use in-text parenthetical documentation, you indicate where that information can be found in the original source by placing a citation in parentheses right after the quoted or paraphrased material. With footnotes or endnotes, you place a raised (superscript) number after the quoted or paraphrased material, and then indicate where in the source text that information can be found. Your citation will be placed either at the bottom of your page (in a footnote) or at the end of your paper (in an endnote). Over the past few years, parenthetical methods of documentation have largely replaced footnotes and endnotes. You may still find professors, though, who prefer those older forms of documentation. Always check with your teacher if you have any questions about the type of documentation you should be using in a class.

PRIMARY ACADEMIC STYLE MANUALS

The biggest problem you will face when documenting papers in college is lack of uniform practice, as styles of documentation will vary from class to class. When you write papers in college, your teacher will expect you to follow the guidelines set out in the style manual commonly used in that field of study, a set of directions writers in that discipline follow when composing and documenting papers.

Teachers in humanities classes (English, history, philosophy, art) often follow the guidelines established by the Modern Language Association (MLA), as published in the *MLA Handbook for Writers of Research Papers* (7th ed., New York: Modern Language Association, 2009). Teachers in the social sciences (sociology, anthropology, psychology, criminal justice) tend to follow the rules set by the American Psychological Association (APA), which appear in *Publication Manual of the American Psychological Association* (6th ed., Washington, DC: American Psychological Association, 2010). However, you may have a class with a sociology teacher who prefers that you follow MLA rules or a philosophy teacher who wants you to use APA style. Also, teachers within a given field may want their students to follow different style manuals. During the same term, for example, you may be taking two communication courses, with one teacher asking you to use MLA documentation and the other wanting you to follow APA guidelines. If teachers do not specify the format they want you to follow, always ask them which style manual they want you to use when writing your paper. If a teacher voices no preference, then choose one format and follow it consistently.

The APA and MLA style manuals agree that writers should employ in-text parenthetical documentation and explanatory footnotes; however, they disagree over the exact form this documentation should assume. Though differences between the formats dictated by these style manuals may seem minor, knowing how to properly document your work helps mark you as a member of a particular academic or research community. Not knowing how may mark you as a novice or outsider.

The following are guidelines for using APA and MLA styles of documentation. The examples offered are not comprehensive. They may be sufficient for some of the papers you write, but you may have to use types of source texts not covered below. If you do, you can find each of the major style manuals in your college library; consult them if the following examples do not answer your questions.

APA GUIDELINES

IN-TEXT DOCUMENTATION

The APA recommends an author-date-page method of in-text documentation. When you quote material, note parenthetically the last name of the author whose work you are using, the year that work was published, and the page number in the reading where that material can be found. When you paraphrase material, you need to note the last name of the author whose work you are using and the year that work was published, but you do not need to include a specific page number in the documentation. What you include in a parenthetical citation can change, though, depending on the information you have already included in the body of your paper. For example, if the author's name has already been used to introduce the material, you do not repeat the name in the parenthetical citation.

Source with One Author

When you quote a passage from a source that has only one author, place the author's last name in parentheses, followed by the year the work was published and the page number where the passage can be found in the source text, all separated by commas. Precede the page reference with "p." if the passage is located on one page in the source text ("p. 12") and with "pp." if the passage runs on more than one page ("pp. 12–13"):

Example 1

> "Drug-using women may be in a position to capitalize most on the advantages of women-inspired prevention methods, and be hindered the least by the disadvantages, as compared with other groups of at-risk women" (Gollub, 2008, p. 108).

If you were to paraphrase that passage, following APA guidelines, you would not include in the documentation a specific page number, only the author and year of publication:

Example 2: Paraphrase

> Prevention methods designed and inspired by women may offer more help to drug-using women than to other similar at-risk groups (Gollub, 2008).

Note the space between the end of the paraphrased passage and the parenthetical citation. Also, the period for the sentence follows the documentation (which is not the case with block quotations). Remember not to repeat information in your parenthetical citation that is included in the body of your essay. For example, if you mention the author's name to introduce a quotation or paraphrase, that information does not need to be repeated in the parenthetical citation. The year of publication should be in parentheses (preferably right after the author's name), and the page number, also in parentheses, should be after any quoted source material:

Example 3

> According to Erica L. Gollub (2008), "Drug-using women may be in a position to capitalize most on the advantages of women-inspired prevention methods, and be hindered the least by the disadvantages, as compared with other groups of at-risk women" (p. 108).

Source with Two Authors

If a work has two authors, cite the last names of both authors when you refer to their work. Separate the names with an ampersand (&) if you are citing them parenthetically, but use "and" if they appear in the body of your text:

Example 4

> "At the beginning of the AIDS epidemic, the large size of high-risk groups, and their lack of organization around public health issues virtually guaranteed that high levels of collective action to combat AIDS would be extremely low" (Broadhead & Heckathorn, 1994, p. 475).

Example 5: Paraphrase

> According to Broadhead and Heckathorn (1994), because the group of people most likely to be affected by AIDS was so large and tended not to focus on health issues, a poor response to the epidemic was almost certain.

Source with Three to Five Authors

The first time you refer to work from a source with three to five authors, list the last names of all the authors in the order in which they appear in the source. Again, use an ampersand before the last name when citing the authors parenthetically. In subsequent references to the work, cite the last name of the first author followed by "et al." (which means "and others"):

Example 6

> A recent study has shown that people who are infected with the HIV virus live longer and healthier lives when they receive various combinations of antiretroviral treatments (Kalichman, Eaton, Cain, Cherry, & Pope, 2006).

Example 7

> A recent study by Kalichman, Eaton, Cain, Cherry, Pope, and Kalichman (2006) has shown that people who are infected with the HIV virus live longer and health-ier lives when they receive various combinations of antiretroviral treatments.

Example 8

> Kalichman et al. (2006) found that . . .

If shortening a citation through the use of "et al." will cause any confusion (that is, if two or more citations become identical when shortened), include as many names as necessary to distinguish the works.

Source with Six or More Authors

If a work has six or more authors, cite only the last name of the first author followed by "et al." and the year of publication:

Example 9

> A recent study in Africa confirms that among sexually active people, regular con-dom use helps prevent the spread of HIV and AIDS (Laga et al., 1994).

Example 10

> A recent study in Africa by Laga et al. (1994) confirms that among sexually active people, regular condom use helps prevent the spread of HIV and AIDS.

As in the previous examples, if shortening a citation through the use of "et al." will cause any confusion, list as many authors' last names as needed to differen-tiate the works, and then replace the remaining names with "et al."

Source with No Author

When a work has no author, cite the first word or two of the title and the year of publication. If the source text is a journal article or book chapter, the short-ened title will appear in quotation marks; if the work is a pamphlet or a book, the shortened title should be italicized:

Example 11

> "The world has recognized that an adult with AIDS in Zambia has as much right to treatment as one in Norway. Children should not be left to die simply because they cannot pay" ("Children," 2005, p. 16).

Example 12

> In "Children and AIDS" (2005), the editors of the *New York Times* argue, "The world has recognized that an adult with AIDS in Zambia has as much right to treatment as one in Norway. Children should not be left to die simply because they cannot pay" (p. 16).

Because the title of the article is used to introduce the quotation in Example 12, it is not repeated in the parenthetical citation.

Sources Whose Authors Have the Same Last Name

If two authors have the same last name, differentiate them by their first initials:

Example 13

> Surveys have found that many people avoid discussing AIDS because they feel they know too little about the topic (J. Brown, 1991); consequently, a number of companies are beginning to develop programs to educate their workers (L. Brown, 1991).

Two or More Sources by the Same Author

If you are referring to two or more works by the same author, differentiate them by date of publication separated by commas. If both are included in the same parenthetical citation, order them by year of publication:

Example 14

> Because AZT has proved to be ineffective in controlling the effects of AIDS (Brown, 1993), scientists have been working hard to develop a vaccine against the virus, especially in Third World countries where the epidemic is spreading quickly (Brown, 1994).

Example 15

> A series of articles in *New Scientist* by Phillida Brown (1993, 1994) traces efforts to develop adequate treatments to combat AIDS.

Two or More Sources by the Same Author Published the Same Year

If you are referring to two or more works by the same author published in the same year, differentiate them by adding lowercase letters after the dates:

Example 16

> Two recent articles (Brown, 1994a, 1994b) trace the efforts to improve AIDS treatment in Third World countries.

The "a" article is the reference that appears first in the reference list, the "b" second, and so on.

Electronic Sources of Information

If you refer to the work as a whole, include the author's last name and the year of publication. If, instead, you are citing specific information in the source text, include the author's last name, the year of publication, and the page number.

If the pages are not numbered, include the paragraph or section number in the source text where the material can be found preceded by "para.":

Example 17

According to one expert, AIDS has killed 14 million people over the past 20 years (Underwood, 1999, para. 1).

As always, do not repeat information in the citation that is already present in your essay.

Consolidating APA-Style References

If you want to include references to two or more sources in one parenthetical citation, arrange them alphabetically by the last name of the authors and separate them with semicolons:

Example 18

Many recent studies have examined the best treatment options for women who suffer from HIV infection (Gollub, 2008; Kalichman et al., 2006; Wanjama, Kimani, & Lodiaga, 2007).

FOOTNOTES AND ENDNOTES

Some style manuals still advocate using footnotes or endnotes as the primary means of documenting source-based essays, but the APA suggests they be used sparingly, only to supply commentary or information you do not want to include in the body of your paper. These notes are numbered consecutively in the text with superscript numerals.

Example 19

A survey of recent articles published on AIDS shows a growing interest in developing reliable research methods to test high-risk groups, such as drug abusers and prostitutes.[1]

The notes may be placed at the bottom of the page on which they appear or on a separate page at the end of the paper with the word "Footnotes" centered at the top. The footnotes are double spaced in numerical order, preceded by superscript numerals. The first line of every note is indented five to seven spaces.

MLA GUIDELINES

IN-TEXT DOCUMENTATION

MLA style uses an author-page system of in-text documentation. When you quote or paraphrase material, you tell your reader parenthetically the name of the author whose work you are using and where in that reading the passage or information can be found. If your reader wants more information on this source text (for instance, whether it is a book or an article, when it was published, or what journal it appeared in), she will refer to the works cited list at the end of your paper, where you provide this information.

The exact form of the parenthetical documentation—what information goes into the parentheses and in what order—varies depending on the type of source you are referring to and what you have already mentioned about the source in the body of your essay.

Source with One Author

When you quote or paraphrase information from a reading that has just one author, place the author's last name in parentheses, leave a space, and then indicate the page number or numbers in the source where the passage or information can be found. Whether you are quoting or paraphrasing material, the period follows the parentheses. In the following examples, pay particular attention to spacing and the proper placement of quotation marks:

Example 20

> "Drug-using women may be in a position to capitalize most on the advantages of women-inspired prevention methods, and be hindered the least by the disadvantages, as compared with other groups of at-risk women" (Gollub 108).

Example 21: Paraphrase

> Prevention methods designed and inspired by women may offer more help to drug-using women than to other similar at-risk groups (Gollub 108).

When using the MLA format, do *not* include "p." or "pp." before the page number or numbers. Again, notice that the final period is placed *after* the documentation. The only exception to this punctuation rule occurs when you block quote information, in which case the period comes before the parenthetical documentation.

Do not repeat in the parentheses information that is already included in the text itself. For example, if you mention the author's name leading up to the quotation or believe your reader will know who the author is from the context of the quotation, you do not need to repeat the author's name in parentheses:

Example 22

> According to Erica L. Gollub, "Drug-using women may be in a position to capitalize most on the advantages of women-inspired prevention methods, and be hindered the least by the disadvantages, as compared with other groups of at-risk women" (108).

MLA style requires you to record specific page references for material directly quoted or paraphrased. If you are quoting or paraphrasing a passage that runs longer than one page in a reading, indicate all the page numbers where that information can be found:

Example 23

> According to Gollub, many recent studies have investigated the sexual practices of drug users who are infected with the HIV virus (107–8).

Source with Two Authors

If a work has two authors, list the last names of the authors in the order they appear in the source, joined by "and." If you mention the authors in the body of your essay, include only the page number or numbers in parentheses:

Example 24

> "At the beginning of the AIDS epidemic, the large size of high-risk groups, and their lack of organization around public health issues virtually guaranteed that high levels of collective action to combat AIDS would be extremely low" (Broadhead and Heckathorn 475).

Example 25: Paraphrase

> According to Broadhead and Heckathorn, because the group of people most likely to be affected by AIDS was so large and tended not to focus on health issues, a poor response to the epidemic was almost certain (475).

Source with Three Authors

If a work has three authors, list the last names of the authors in the order they appear in the source, separated by commas, with "and" before the last name:

Example 26

> Recently, researchers have begun to examine the AIDS epidemic by combining a wide range of scientific and social perspectives and methodologies (Fan, Conner, and Villarreal).

Since this citation refers to the entire work, no specific page reference is provided.

Source with More Than Three Authors

If a source has more than three authors, include the last name of the first author followed by "et al.":

Example 27

> A recent study has shown that people who are infected with the HIV virus live longer and healthier lives when they receive various combinations of antiretroviral treatments (Kalichman et al. 401).

Source with No Author

If a work has no author, parenthetically cite the first word or two of the title. If the work is a journal article or book chapter, the shortened title will appear in quotation marks. If the work is longer, the shortened title should be italicized. If you mention the title of the work in the body of your essay, you will need to include only the page number or numbers in parentheses:

Example 28

> "The world has recognized that an adult with AIDS in Zambia has as much right to treatment as one in Norway. Children should not be left to die simply because they cannot pay" ("Children" 16).

Example 29

> In "Children and AIDS," the editors of the *New York Times* argue, "The world has recognized that an adult with AIDS in Zambia has as much right to treatment as one in Norway. Children should not be left to die simply because they cannot pay" (16).

Sources Whose Authors Have the Same Last Name

If two different authors have the same last name, differentiate them in your documentation by including their first initials:

Example 30

> Surveys have found that many people avoid discussing AIDS because they feel they know too little about the topic (J. Brown 675); consequently, a number of companies are beginning to develop programs to educate their workers (L. Brown 64).

Two or More Sources by the Same Author

If you are referring to two or more works by the same author, differentiate them in your documentation by putting a comma after the last name of the author and adding a shortened version of the title before citing the specific page reference:

Example 31

> Because AZT has proved to be ineffective in controlling the effects of AIDS (Brown, "Drug" 4), scientists have been working hard to develop a vaccine

against the virus, especially in Third World countries where the epidemic is spreading quickly (Brown, "AIDS" 10).

Again, the shortened title of an article or chapter is placed in quotation marks; the shortened title of a longer work would be italicized.

Electronic Sources of Information

If the pages in the electronic source text are numbered, include the author's last name and the page number. If, instead, the paragraphs or sections in the source text are numbered, include the author's last name and the paragraph or section number or numbers (use "par." for one paragraph, "pars." for more than one paragraph). *Separate the author's last name and the paragraph numbers with a comma.* If the source text does not number pages, paragraphs, or sections, include only the author's last name.

Consolidating MLA-Style References

Many times in papers, you will include in one paragraph information you gathered from several different sources. When you document this passage, arrange the references alphabetically by the last names of the authors and separate them with semicolons:

Example 32

> Many recent studies have examined the best treatment options for women who suffer from HIV infection (Gollub; Kalichman et al.; Wanjama, Kimani, and Lodiaga).

No page numbers are included here because the passage refers to the general topic of the articles, not to specific information in them.

FOOTNOTES AND ENDNOTES

The MLA suggests that footnotes or endnotes be used only to supply commentary or information you do not want to include in the body of your paper. Whether you are adding content notes (explanations of or elaborations on ideas you have discussed in the body of your paper) or bibliographic notes (a list of sources your readers might want to consult if they are interested in learning more about the topic you are discussing), try to keep them to a minimum because they can be distracting.

Number footnotes and endnotes consecutively in the body of your essay with superscript numerals:

Example 33

> A survey of recent articles published on AIDS shows a growing interest in developing reliable research methods to test high-risk groups, such as drug abusers and prostitutes.[1]

If you are using footnotes, the citation appears at the bottom of the page on which the corresponding number appears. If you are using endnotes, all the citations appear in numerical order at the end of your paper on a separate page with the heading "Notes" centered one inch from the top margin. Double-space after typing this heading; then begin the citations. All the citations are double-spaced and begin with the corresponding superscript number followed by a space. Indent the first line of each note five spaces or one-half inch from the left margin.

Chapter 13

REFERENCE LISTS AND WORKS CITED ENTRIES

DEFINITION AND PURPOSE

A reference or works cited list comes at the end of your paper. In it you provide all of the bibliographic information for the sources you used when writing your essay. You have one entry for every source you refer to in the body of your paper, an entry that lists for your readers the information they would need to locate the source and read it themselves.

With in-text documentation you indicate where you found the specific information or language you used in your paper, usually including only the last name of the author and the page number on which the material is located. In your reference list you will give your reader much more information concerning this reading: the author's full name, the full title of the piece, and the place and year of publication. Also, while in-text documentation indicates a specific page where the material can be found, a reference list citation indicates all the page numbers of the source.

A works cited or reference list is sometimes also called a *bibliography*, but the two may not be the same, depending on the style you are following. While the entry format for each is the same, in a bibliography you might include an entry for every source you *consulted* when researching your paper; in a works cited list you include an entry only for the sources you actually *included* in your paper. Suppose you consulted ten books or articles when researching a topic for a paper but used only seven of them in your final draft. If your teacher asked you to put together an APA bibliography for your essay, you would have ten entries. If she asked you for a works cited or reference list, you would have only seven entries. If you are unsure what to include in your list of references, consult with your teacher.

Putting together a works cited or reference list can be tedious and time-consuming because there are specific forms you have to follow. These forms are dictated by the type of source you are using and the style manual you are following. Your job is to follow these forms exactly. There is an important reason for this uniformity. When you put together a works cited list in the proper form, you are providing a valuable service for your readers: when writers in a discipline agree to follow the same format for reference lists, readers can easily determine where to locate the sources that interest them because they know how to read the entries.

Complicating your efforts to put together a proper reference list is the fact that each field of study has its preferred ways of structuring entries. While the information in the entries generally stays the same across the disciplines, the order in which you present that information varies widely. As described in the previous chapter, teachers in the humanities tend to follow the guidelines established by the Modern Language Association (MLA) and those in the social sciences typically employ the guidelines established by the American Psychological Association (APA). When putting together a works cited or reference list, your best approach is to follow the guidelines and sample entries as closely as you can, placing the information from your source exactly where it appears in the model. Pay very close attention to capitalization, spacing, and punctuation.

The samples provided in this chapter follow the guidelines of the major style manuals, but they are not comprehensive. As you write a paper, you may use types of readings not covered in these examples. If this occurs, you can obtain a copy of each style manual at your library and follow the sample entry it contains for the type of text you are employing.

APA FORMAT

SAMPLE REFERENCE LIST ENTRIES

In an APA reference list, you include the name of the author, the title, and the publishing information for all of the readings you use in the body of your essay. You include the authors' last names, followed by a comma and the initials of their first and middle names. If a source has more than one author, list their last names first followed by their initials and a comma, then use an ampersand (&) to introduce the final name. Book and journal titles are italicized; article titles are not (neither are they placed in quotation marks). In the titles of books and articles, you capitalize only the first word of the title and subtitle (if any) and any proper nouns and proper adjectives. The format for listing the publishing information varies by the type of source, so pay close attention to the accompanying sample entries and follow them precisely. The first line of every entry is flush with the left margin; all other lines are indented, and all entries end with a period.

Journal Article, One Author

Gollub, E. L. (2008). A neglected population: Drug-using women and women's methods of HIV/STI prevention. *AIDS Education & Prevention, 20*(2), 107–120.

- Note how the author's first and middle initials are used.
- Note where the year of publication is listed.
- Note how the title of the article is not placed in quotation marks.
- Note which words are capitalized and which are not in the title of the article.
- Note how the journal title and volume numbers are italicized.

Journal Article, Two Authors

Broadhead, R. S., & Heckathorn, D. D. (1994). AIDS prevention outreach among injection drug users: Agency problems and new approaches. *Social Problems, 41*(3), 473–495.

- Note the order of the names: last name first followed by initials. The names are separated by a comma and the second name is introduced by an ampersand.
- The year of publication comes next, noted parenthetically.
- Note that the "A" in "Agency" is capitalized because it is the first word in the subtitle.
- Note that the volume number follows the title of the journal; it is also italicized.

Journal Article, Three to Seven Authors

Kalichman, S., Eaton, L., Cain, D., Cherry, C., Pope, H., & Kalichman, M. (2006). HIV treatment beliefs and sexual transmission risk behaviors among HIV positive men and women. *Journal of Behavioral Medicine, 29*(5), 401–410.

- When there are three to seven authors, list all of their names.

Journal Article, More Than Seven Authors

Laga, M., Alary, M., Nzila, N., Manoka, A. T., Tuliza, M., Behets, F., . . . Pilot, P. (1994). Condom promotion, sexually transmitted diseases treatment, and declining incidence of HIV-1 infection in female Zairian sex workers. *The Lancet, 344,* 246–248.

- When there are eight or more authors, list the first six, then include an ellipsis and the last author's name.
- When you cite an article like this in the body of your essay, you will use the first author's surname followed by "et al." (Laga et al., 1994).

Article from a Monthly Periodical

Minkel, J. R. (2006, July). Dangling a carrot for vaccines. *Scientific American*, *295*, 39–40.

- For a monthly periodical, indicate the month of publication after the year, separating the two with a comma.
- Be sure to include the volume number as well, after the journal title.

Article from a Weekly Periodical

Clinton, B. (2006, May 15). My quest to improve care. *Newsweek*, *147*, 50–52.

- Indicate the month and day of publication after the year, separating the year and month with a comma.
- Include the volume number after the journal title.

Newspaper Article

Dugger, C. W. (2008, March 9). Rift over AIDS treatment lingers in South Africa. *New York Times*, p. 8.

Chase, M. (2005, April 20). Panel suggests a 'Peace Corps' to fight AIDS. *Wall Street Journal*, pp. B1, B5.

- Note the placement of the date: year followed by month and day, with a comma separating the year and month.
- The title of the newspaper is capitalized and italicized.
- Precede the page number with "p." if the article is on one page and with "pp." if it runs longer than one page.
- If the newspaper is divided into sections, indicate the section along with the page number.

Newspaper Article, No Author

Children and AIDS. (2005, February 16). *New York Times*, p. 16.

- When there is no author, begin the citation with the title.

Book with One Author

Hinds, M. J. (2008). *Fighting the AIDS and HIV epidemic: A global battle*. Berkeley Heights, NJ: Enslow.

- Note that the order of information for citing a book parallels the order of information for citing an article.
- Book titles are italicized. The first word in the title is capitalized and so are all proper nouns and proper adjectives and the first word in the subtitle.
- Following the title, indicate the city of publication and the publisher.

Books with Multiple Authors

Douglas, P. H., & Pinsky, L. (1991). *The essential AIDS fact book*. New York: Pocket Books.

Wanjama, L. N., Kimani, E. N., & Lodiaga, M. L. (2007). *HIV and AIDS: The pandemic*. Nairobi: Jomo Kenyatta Foundation.

- List multiple authors by their last names and initials, separating them with commas, and using an ampersand to introduce the final author.
- If a book has up to seven authors, list all of their names in your reference citation. For more than seven authors, see the previous guideline for periodicals. In the body of your paper, when you parenthetically cite a source with six or more authors, use only the first author's name followed by "et al." and the year of publication.

Two or More Works by the Same Person

Squire, C. (1997). *AIDS panic*. New York: Routledge.

Squire, C. (2007). *HIV in South Africa: Talking about the big thing*. London: Routledge.

- Arrange the citations in chronological order, the earliest first.

Book, Corporate Author

National Gay and Lesbian Task Force. (1987). *Anti-gay violence: Victimization and defamation in 1986*. New York: Author.

- If the publisher is the same as the corporate author, simply write "Author" after the city where the work was published.

Book, Later Edition

Fan, H. Y., Conner, R. F., & Villarreal, L. (2007). *AIDS: Science and society* (5th ed.). Sudbury, MA: Jones and Bartlett.

- If you are using a later edition of a book, list the edition number parenthetically after the title.

Edited Book

Cohen, A., & Gorman, J. M. (Eds.). (2008). *Comprehensive textbook of AIDS psychiatry*. New York: Oxford University Press.

- If one person edited the book, place "(Ed.)" after his name. If more than one person edited the work, place "(Eds.)" after their names.
- Pay particular attention to the periods in this citation. It is easy to leave some of them out.

Book, No Author or Editor

Corporate responses to HIV/AIDS: Case studies from India. (2007). Washington, DC: World Bank.

- When the title page of a book lists no author, begin your citation with the title.
- Note that in this type of entry, the edition number will precede the year of publication.

Multivolume Book

Daintith, J., Mitchell, S., & Tootill, E. (Eds.). (1981). *A biographical encyclopedia of scientists* (Vols. 1–2). New York: Facts on File.

- Indicate for your reader how many volumes comprise the work. This information follows the title.

One Volume of a Multivolume Book

Daintith, J., Mitchell, S., & Tootill, E. (Eds.). (1981). *A biographical encyclopedia of scientists* (Vol. 1). New York: Facts on File.

- When you use just one volume of a multivolume work, indicate the volume number parenthetically after the title.

English Translation of a Book

Jager, H. (Ed.). (1988). *AIDS phobia: Disease pattern and possibilities of treatment* (J. Welch, Trans.). New York: Halsted Press.

- Open the citation with the name of the author or editor.
- Following the title, give the translator's name followed by a comma and "Trans."
- Note that in giving the translator's name, you begin with her initials, followed by the last name.
- Again, pay attention to all the periods included in this citation.

Article or Chapter from an Anthology

Many times in writing a source-based paper you will use a work contained in an anthology of readings. When this is the case, follow this format in your reference list:

Bethell, T. (2006). The African AIDS epidemic is exaggerated. In D. A. Leone. (Ed.), *Responding to the AIDS epidemic* (pp. 18–22). Detroit: Greenhaven Press.

Patton, C. (1993). "With champagne and roses": Women at risk from/in AIDS discourse. In C. Squire (Ed.), *Women and AIDS* (pp. 165–187). London: Sage.

- Open your citation with the name of the author whose ideas or language you included in your paper.
- Next, give the title of the specific reading you referred to in the body of your essay.
- Next, give the name of the author or editor of the anthology and the larger work's title (the title of the book is italicized). Precede this information with the word "In" (note capitalization).
- Follow the title with the specific page numbers on which the article can be found. In this case, Patton's article can be found on pages 165–187 of Squire's book; Bethell's article can be found on pages 18–22 of Leone's book.
- Close the entry with the publishing information.

Article in a Reference Work

Acquired immune deficiency syndrome. (1990). In *The new encyclopaedia Britannica* (Vol. 1, p. 67). Chicago: Encyclopaedia Britannica.

Haseltine, W. A. (1992). AIDS. In *Encyclopedia Americana* (Vol. 1, pp. 365–366). Danbury, CT: Grolier.

- When the entry in the reference work is signed, begin the citation with the author's name; when it is not signed, begin the citation with the title of the entry.
- Include the year the reference work was published, the title of the work (italicized), the volume number and inclusive page numbers of the entry (noted parenthetically), followed by the publishing information.

Personal Interview

Under APA guidelines, all personal communications are to be cited in the text only. Include the name of the person you interviewed (first and middle initials, full last name), the words "personal communication," and the date of the interview (month, day, year), all separated by commas:

(F. Smith, personal communication, June 24, 1995)

Electronic Sources of Information

The standards for citing electronic sources of information are still in flux. You can find the most current version of the APA's standards online at www.apa. style.org/elecref.html.

In 2007, APA updated its guidelines for including electronic sources of information in reference lists. The major changes include these:

- When possible, include the Digital Object Indicator (DOI) number rather than the URL for online articles.
- Still include the URL for online reference sources, such as dictionaries and encyclopedias.
- Including the name of the database used to locate online articles is no longer required.
- Include the retrieval date only if the material is likely to be changed or updated.

Information on CD-ROM

AIDS. (1995). *The 1995 Grolier multimedia encyclopedia.* [CD]. Danbury, CT: Grolier.

- List the name of the author or authors (if known), last name first followed by first and middle initials. Because this source text has no author, the entry begins with the title.
- List the date of publication in parentheses.
- Give the title of the chapter or entry you consulted for your paper.
- Give the title of the publication that contained the chapter or entry.
- Indicate the electronic medium (i.e., CD) in square brackets.
- List the publication information.

Online Information Database

AIDS. (2008). In *Encyclopaedia Brittannica online.* Retrieved July 1, 2008, from http://www.britannica.com

- Give the author's name. If the entry is unsigned, begin with the entry's title.
- Give the date of publication.
- Give the title of the database (preceded by "In").
- Give the retrieval date.
- Give the database's URL.
- DO NOT end the entry with a period (someone might think the period is part of the URL).

Article from an Online Publication

This is the format to use if your source text exists only electronically. If the article does not also appear in print somewhere, use this form for your reference list entry:

Ambinder, M. (2007, December 8). Huck and AIDS. Retrieved from http://theatlantic.com

- Give the name of the author followed by the date of publication.
- Give the title of the article.
- Give the URL where the article can be retrieved.
- You do not need to give the date of retrieval.

Previously Published Article Found Online

Underwood, A. (1999, February 8). How the plague began. *Newsweek, 133,* 59. Retrieved from http://www.newsweek.com

Kalichman, S. C., Eaton, L., Cain, D., Cherry, C., Pope, H., & Kalichman, M. (2006). HIV treatment beliefs and sexual transmission risk behaviors among HIV positive men and women. *Journal of Behavioral Medicine, 29*(5), 401–410. doi: 10.1007/s10865-006-9066-3

- Give the name of the author(s).
- Give the date of publication.
- Give the title of the article.
- Give the journal's title and volume number (along with the issue number when relevant).
- Give the inclusive page numbers of the article.
- If the article has a DOI indicator, give it.
- If the article does not have a DOI indicator, give the retrieval URL.
- If the entry ends with an URL or DOI number, do not place a period at the end.

E-Mail

The sixth edition of APA's *Publication Manual* considers e-mail messages to be "personal communication," which should be cited in text only. In parentheses, include the name of the person who sent you the e-mail message (first and middle initials followed by the full last name), the words "personal communication," and the date of the communication (month, day, year):

(F. Smith, personal communication, December 1, 1998)

SAMPLE APA-STYLE REFERENCE LIST

List all of your references at the end of your paper, beginning the list on a new page. At the top of the page, center the word "References." After the heading, double-space and list your citations in alphabetical order according to the last name of the author or first key word in the title if there is no author. The first line of every citation should be set flush left. Indent subsequent lines.

References

AIDS. (2008). In *Encyclopaedia Brittannica online*. Retrieved July 1, 2008, from http://www.brittannica.com

Ambinder, M. (2007, December 8). Huck and AIDS. Retrieved from http://www.theatlantic.com

Bethell, T. (2006). The African AIDS epidemic is exaggerated. In D. A. Leone (Ed.), *Responding to the AIDS epidemic* (pp. 18–22). Detroit: Greenhaven Press.

Chase, M. (2005, April 20). Panel suggests a 'Peace Corps' to fight AIDS. *Wall Street Journal*, pp. B1, B5.

Children and AIDS. (2005, February 16). *New York Times*, p. 16.

Clinton, B. (2006, May 15). My quest to improve care. *Newsweek, 147*, 50–52.

Cohen, A., & Gorman, J. M. (Eds.). (2008). *Comprehensive textbook of AIDS psychiatry*. New York: Oxford University Press.

Corporate responses to HIV/AIDS: Case studies from India. (2007). Washington, DC: World Bank.

Douglas, P. H., & Pinsky, L. (1991). *The essential AIDS fact book*. New York: Pocket Books.

Dugger, C. W. (2008, March 9). Rift over AIDS treatment lingers in South Africa. *New York Times*, p. 8.

Fan, H. Y., Conner, R. F., & Villarreal, L. (2007). *AIDS: Science and society* (5th ed.). Sudbury, MA: Jones and Bartlett.

Gollub, E. L. (2008). A neglected population: Drug-using women and women's methods of HIV/STI prevention. *AIDS Education & Prevention, 20*(2), 107–120.

Hinds, M. J. (2008). *Fighting the AIDS and HIV epidemic: A global battle*. Berkeley Heights, NJ: Enslow.

Kalichman, S. C., Eaton, L., Cain, D., Cherry, C., Pope, H., & Kalichman, M. (2006). HIV treatment beliefs and sexual transmission risk behaviors among HIV positive men and women. *Journal of Behavioral Medicine, 29*(5), 401–410. doi: 10.1007/s10865-006-9066-3

Laga, M., Alary, M., Nzila, N., Manoka, A. T., Tuliza, M., Behets, F., . . . Pilot P. (1994). Condom promotion, sexually transmitted diseases treatment, and declining incidence of HIV-1 infection in female Zairian sex workers. *The Lancet, 344*, 246–248.

Minkel, J. R. (2006, July). Dangling a carrot for vaccines. *Scientific American, 295*, 39–40.

Squire, C. (1997). *AIDS panic*. New York: Routledge.

Squire, C. (2007). *HIV in South Africa: Talking about the big thing*. London: Routledge.

Underwood, A. (1999, February 8). How the plague began. *Newsweek, 133*, 59. Retrieved from http://www.newsweek.com

Wanjama, L. N., Kimani, E. N., & Lodiaga, M. L. (2007). *HIV and AIDS: The pandemic*. Nairobi: Jomo Kenyatta Foundation.

MLA FORMAT

SAMPLE WORKS CITED ENTRIES

In a works cited list following MLA style, include the name of the author and full title of the works you cited in the body of your essay, along with relevant publication information. When listing the authors, include their full names, last name first. Titles of articles are placed in quotation marks; titles of books are italicized. In titles, the first and last words are capitalized along with any key words, proper nouns, and proper adjectives in between. Journal titles are italicized, and you should list all the pages you read in the source text. Do not precede page numbers with "p." or "pg."; simply list inclusive page numbers. Finally, MLA style employs hanging indentation: begin the first line of each entry at the left margin and indent all subsequent lines one-half inch.

Note: 2008 saw the publication of the third edition of the *MLA Style Manual and Guide to Scholarly Publishing*. In this edition of its style manual, MLA substantially revised its guidelines for works cited entries. Over the next few years, as teachers and scholars become more familiar with these new guidelines, expect to see articles in print that use both old and new versions. The sample works cited entries below follow the new, third edition guidelines.

Major changes made in the third edition of the *MLA Style Manual and Guide to Scholarly Publishing* include the following:

- Add the medium of publication to each entry (e.g., "Print," "Web," or "CD").
- Place book, journal, or Web titles in italics; do not underline them.
- Include the volume and issue number for every journal citation.
- When working with online sources, only include the URL when your reader would not otherwise be able to find your source.

Journal Article, One Author

Gollub, Erica L. "A Neglected Population: Drug-Using Women and Women's Methods of HIV/STI Prevention." *AIDS Education & Prevention* 20.2 (2008): 107–20. Print.

- Give the full name of the author as it is printed with the article, last name first. Place a period after the name.
- The title of the article is placed in quotation marks. Note how the first and last word of the title are capitalized as are all key words in between. Also note that the period at the end of the article title goes inside the closing quotation mark.
- The title of the journal is italicized.
- Indicate the inclusive page numbers of the article.
- Indicate the medium of publication.

Journal Article, Two or Three Authors

Broadhead, Robert S., and Douglas D. Heckathorn. "AIDS Prevention Outreach among Injection Drug Users: Agency Problems and New Approaches." *Social Problems* 41.3 (1994): 473–95. Print.

Mitchell, Roger E., Paul Florin, and John F. Stevenson. "Supporting Community-based Prevention and Health Promotion Initiatives: Developing Effective Technical Assistance Systems." *Health Education & Behavior* 29.5 (2002): 620–39. Print.

- When there are two or three authors, list all of them in the order they appear in the article. Give the first author's last name, then his first name. Give the other authors' names first name first. Separate the names with commas and introduce the last name with "and."

Journal Article, More Than Three Authors

Kalichman, Seth, et al. "HIV Treatment Beliefs and Sexual Transmission Risk Behaviors among HIV Positive Men and Women." *Journal of Behavioral Medicine* 29.5 (2006): 401–410. Print.

- When there are more than three authors, list only the first author, last name first. Follow that name with the expression "et al." (which means "and others").

Article from a Monthly Periodical

Minkel, J. R. "Dangling a Carrot for Vaccines." *Scientific American* July 2006: 39–40. Print.

- Note the month of publication after the title. Months can be abbreviated, except for May, June, and July.
- Note that there is *no* comma between the month and year.
- Note that you do *not* include the volume number of the work, only the month and year.

Article from a Weekly Periodical

Clinton, Bill. "My Quest to Improve Care." *Newsweek* 15 May 2006: 50–52. Print.

- After giving the title of the piece, list the day, month, and year of its publication in that order, without any punctuation between them.

Newspaper Article

Chase, Marilyn. "Panel Suggests a 'Peace Corps' to Fight AIDS." *Wall Street Journal* 20 Apr. 2005: B1+. Print.

Dugger, Celia W. "Rift over AIDS Treatment Lingers in South Africa." *New York Times* 9 Mar. 2008: 8. Print.

- If the newspaper article is signed, give the writer's name, last name first.
- After the title of the piece, give the name of the newspaper, italicized.
- Next, give the date of publication: day, month, then year without any intervening punctuation.
- Give the page number, indicating the section number or letter when applicable.
- Use a plus sign (+) to indicate interrupted pagination.

Newspaper Article, No Author

"Children and AIDS." *New York Times* 22 Feb. 2005: 16. Print.

- If the article is unsigned, begin the entry with the title.

Book with One Author

Hinds, Maurene J. *Fighting the AIDS and HIV Epidemic: A Global Battle.* Berkeley Heights: Enslow, 2008. Print.

- Again, note how the entry begins with the author's last name.
- Note how the title is italicized and how the first, last, and key words are capitalized.

Book with Multiple Authors

Douglas, Paul Harding, and Laura Pinsky. *The Essential AIDS Fact Book.* New York: Pocket Books, 1991. Print.

Wanjama, Leah Niambi, et al. *HIV and AIDS: The Pandemic.* Nairobi: Jomo Kenyatta Foundation, 2007. Print.

- When a book has two or three authors, list all their names. Begin with the last name of the first author; the names of the other authors are listed first name first. Separate the names with commas and use "and" before the last name.
- If there are more than three authors, list only the first author and follow it with "et al."

Two or More Books by the Same Person

Squire, Corinne. *AIDS Panic.* New York: Routledge, 1997. Print.

—. *HIV in South Africa: Talking about the Big Thing.* London: Routledge, 2007. Print.

- When you have two or more books by the same author or authors, list them on your works cited list in alphabetical order by the first key word in the title.
- For the first work by the author, give his or her full name, last name first. For subsequent entries by the author, instead of repeating the name, type three hyphens followed by a period. Then list the title of the work and the relevant publishing information.

Book, Corporate Author

National Gay and Lesbian Task Force. *Anti-gay Violence: Victimization and Defamation in 1986.* New York: National Gay and Lesbian Task Force, 1987. Print.

- Treat a corporate author just as you would an individual author.

Book, Later Edition

Fan, Hung Y., Ross F. Conner, and Luis Villarreal. *AIDS: Science and Society.* 5th ed. Sudbury: Jones and Bartlett, 2007. Print.

- Indicate the edition number after the title.

Edited Book

Squire, Corinne, ed. *Women and AIDS: Psychological Perspectives.* London: Sage, 1993. Print.

Cohen, Ann, and Jack M. Gorman, eds. *Comprehensive Textbook of AIDS Psychiatry.* New York: Oxford UP, 2008. Print.

- If one person edited the work, place "ed." after his name. If there is more than one editor, use "eds."

Book, No Author or Editor

Corporate Responses to HIV/AIDS: Case Studies from India. Washington, DC: World Bank, 2007. Print.

- When there is no author, begin the entry with the title.

Multivolume Book

Daintith, John, Sarah Mitchell, and Elizabeth Tootill, eds. *A Biographical Encyclopedia of Scientists.* 2 vols. New York: Facts on File, 1981. Print.

- Indicate the number of volumes in a multivolume work after the title.

One Volume of a Multivolume Book

Daintith, John, Sarah Mitchell, and Elizabeth Tootill, eds. *A Biographical Encyclopedia of Scientists.* Vol. 1. New York: Facts on File, 1981. Print.

- If you use only one volume of a multivolume work, indicate the volume number after the title.

English Translation of a Book

Jager, Hans, ed. *AIDS Phobia: Disease Pattern and Possibilities of Treatment.* Trans. Jacquie Welch. New York: Halsted, 1988. Print.

- Begin the entry with the name of the author or editor whose work has been translated, followed by the title of the work.
- Next, write "Trans." followed by the name of the translator, first name first.

Article or Chapter from an Anthology

Bethell, Tom. "The African AIDS Epidemic Is Exaggerated." *Responding to the AIDS Epidemic.* Ed. Daniel A. Leone. Detroit: Greenhaven, 2006. 18–22. Print.

Patton, Cindy. "'With Champagne and Roses': Women at Risk from/in AIDS Discourse." *Women and AIDS.* Ed. Corinne Squire. London: Sage, 1993. 165–87. Print.

- First, list the name of the author whose article or chapter you are using.
- Next, give the title, in quotation marks. If the title of an entry already contains quotation marks, the original quotation marks are shifted to single quotation marks in the citation.
- Next, give the title of the work that contained the article and the name of the editor or editors, preceded by either "Ed." if one person edited the work or "Eds." if more than one editor was involved.
- Finally, list the publication information and the page numbers in the larger work where the article or chapter can be found.

Article in a Reference Work

"Acquired Immune Deficiency Syndrome." *Encyclopaedia Britannica: Micropaedia.* 1990 ed. Print.

- If the author of the entry in the reference work is listed, begin with that. If it is not, begin with the heading of the entry, in quotation marks.
- After indicating the heading of the entry, list the name of the reference work and the edition.

Personal Interview

Alexander, Jane. Telephone interview. 16 June 2008.

Smith, John. Personal interview. 16 June 2008.

- List the name of the person interviewed, the nature of the interview (whether done in person, over the telephone, etc.), and the date of the interview: day, month, and year.

Electronic Sources of Information

The most up-to-date information on MLA formats for citing electronic sources of information is available at www.mla.org.

Information on CD-ROM or Diskette

"AIDS." *The 1995 Grolier Multimedia Encyclopedia*. Danbury: Grolier, 1995.
   CD-ROM.

- Give the name of the author (if known), last name first.
- Give the title of the chapter or entry from which you drew the informa-
   tion (in quotation marks).
- Give the title of the CD.
- Indicate the place of publication, the publisher, and the date of publication.
- Indicate the medium of publication (in this case, CD-ROM).

Online Information Databank

"AIDS." *Encyclopaedia Brittannica Online*. Encyclopaedia Britannica, 2008.
   Web. 1 July 2008.

- Give the author's name (if known), last name first.
- Give the title of the article or entry. This particular source text is unsigned,
   so the entry begins with the title.
- Give the title of the online database, in italics.
- Give the name of the databank's sponsoring institution or organization
   and the date of publication.
- Indicate the medium of publication (in this case, "Web").
- List the date of access. Note how it is listed and punctuated.

Article from an Online Publication

This is the format to use if your source text exists only electronically. If the
article does not also appear in print somewhere, use this form for your works
cited entry:

Ambinder, Marc. "Huck and AIDS." *TheAtlantic.com*. Atlantic Monthly, 8
   Dec. 2007. Web. 2 July 2008.

Underwood, Anne. "How the Plague Began." *Newsweek.com*. Newsweek, 8
   Feb. 1999. Web. 3 July 2008.

- Give the author's name, last name first.
- Indicate the title of the work, in quotation marks.
- Give the title of the online database, in italics.
- Give the name of the databank's sponsoring institution or organization.
- Give the date of publication or posting.
- Indicate the medium of publication.
- Indicate the date of access.

Work from an Online Service

"AIDS: Education Cuts the Toll." *Business Week* 5 Dec. 2005: 112. *Academic
   Search Premier*. Web. 1 July 2008.

Parkhurst, Justin O. "'What Worked?': The Evidence Challenges in Determining the Causes of HIV Prevalence Decline." *AIDS Education & Prevention* June 2008: 275–83. *Academic Search Premier.* Web. 1 July 2008.

Shadlen, Kenneth C. "The Political Economy of AIDS Treatment: Intellec-
tual Property and the Transformation of Generic Supply." *International
Studies Quarterly* 51.3 (2007): 559–81. *Academic Search Complete.*
Web. 5 July 2008.

- Give the name of the author, last name first.
- Give the title of the article in quotation marks.
- Give the title of the publication (in italics) and the relevant dates of publi-
  cation and volume/issue numbers (the first sample is from a weekly pub-
  lication, the second from a monthly publication, and the third from a
  quarterly publication).
- Give the inclusive page numbers of the article.
- Give the name of the database, in italics.
- Give the medium of publication.
- Give the date of access.

E-Mail

Give the name of the writer (last name first), the title of the message (taken
from the "subject" line), an indication of who received the message, and the
date of the message.

Edwards, John. "Re: AIDS Sources." Message to author. 31 July 2008. E-mail.

Francis, Heather. Message to Karen Wilhoit. 24 June 2007. E-mail.

- If the subject line of the message is blank, leave out that part of the entry.
- Note how the date of the message is listed: day, month, year.
- Note the medium of publication (in this case, "E-mail").

SAMPLE MLA-STYLE WORKS CITED LIST

Begin the works cited list on a separate sheet of paper at the end of your essay.
Centered at the top, write "Works Cited" and then double-space before you
begin listing your entries. Entries are alphabetized by the author's last name or
by the first key word in the title if there is no author. The first line of each entry
begins on the left margin, and all subsequent lines of each entry are indented
one-half inch. The entire list is double-spaced.

Works Cited

"AIDS." *Encyclopaedia Brittannica Online*. Encyclopaedia Britannica,

    2008. Web. 1 July 2008.

"AIDS: Education Cuts the Toll." *Business Week* 5 Dec. 2005: 112.

    Academic Search Premier. Web. 1 July 2008.

Alexander, Jane. Telephone interview. 16 June 2008.

Ambinder, Marc. "Huck and AIDS." *TheAtlantic.com*. Atlantic Monthly,

    8 Dec. 2007. Web. 2 July 2008.

Bethell, Tom. "The African AIDS Epidemic Is Exaggerated." *Responding*

    to the AIDS Epidemic. Ed. Daniel A. Leone. Detroit: Greenhaven P.,

    2006. 18–22. Print.

Broadhead, Robert S., and Douglas D. Heckathorn. "AIDS Prevention

    Outreach among Injection Drug Users: Agency Problems and New

    Approaches." *Social Problems* 41.3 (1994): 473–95. Print.

Chase, Marilyn. "Panel Suggests a 'Peace Corps' to Fight AIDS." *Wall*

    Street Journal 20 Apr. 2005: B1+. Print.

"Children and AIDS." *New York Times* 22 Feb. 2005: 16. Print.

Clinton, Bill. "My Quest to Improve Care." *Newsweek* 15 May 2006:

    50–2. Print.

Cohen, Ann, and Jack M. Gorman, eds. *Comprehensive Textbook of*

    AIDS Psychiatry. New York: Oxford UP, 2008. Print.

Corporate Responses to HIV/AIDS: Case Studies from India.

    Washington, DC: World Bank, 2007. Print.

Douglas, Paul Harding, and Laura Pinsky. *The Essential AIDS Fact Book*. New York: Pocket Books, 1991. Print.

Dugger, Celia W. "Rift over AIDS Treatment Lingers in South Africa." *New York Times* 9 Mar. 2008: 8. Print.

Edwards, John. "Re: AIDS Sources." Message to author. 31 July 2008. E-mail.

Fan, Hung Y., Ross F. Conner, and Luis Villarreal. *AIDS: Science and Society*. 5th ed. Sudbury, MA: Jones and Bartlett, 2007. Print.

Francis, Heather. Message to Karen Wilhoit. 24 June 2007. E-mail.

Gollub, Erica L. "A Neglected Population: Drug-Using Women and Women's Methods of HIV/STI Prevention." *AIDS Education & Prevention* 20.2 (2008): 107–20. Print.

Hinds, Maurene J. *Fighting the AIDS and HIV Epidemic: A Global Battle*. Berkeley Heights: Enslow, 2008. Print.

Kalichman, Seth, et al. "HIV Treatment Beliefs and Sexual Transmission Risk Behaviors among HIV Positive Men and Women." *Journal of Behavioral Medicine* 29.5 (2006): 401–10. Print.

Minkel, J. R. "Dangling a Carrot for Vaccines." *Scientific American* July 2006: 39–40. Print.

Mitchell, Roger E., Paul Florin, and John F. Stevenson. "Supporting Community-based Prevention and Health Promotion Initiatives: Developing Effective Technical Assistance Systems." *Health Education & Behavior* 29.5 (2002): 620–39. Print.

National Gay and Lesbian Task Force. *Anti-gay Violence: Victimization and Defamation in 1986*. New York: National Gay and Lesbian Task Force, 1987. Print.

Parkhurst, Justin O. "'What Worked?': The Evidence Challenges in Determining the Causes of HIV Prevalence Decline." *AIDS Education & Prevention* June 2008: 275–83. *Academic Search Premier*. Web. 1 July 2008.

Patton, Cindy. "'With Champagne and Roses': Women at Risk from/in AIDS Discourse." *Women and AIDS*. Ed. Corinne Squire. London: Sage, 1993. 165–87. Print.

Shadlen, Kenneth C. "The Political Economy of AIDS Treatment: Intellectual Property and the Transformation of Generic Supply." *International Studies Quarterly* 51.3 (2007): 559–81. *Academic Search Complete*. Web. 5 July 2008.

Smith, John. Personal interview. 16 June 2008.

Squire, Corinne. *AIDS Panic*. New York: Routledge, 1997. Print.

—. *HIV in South Africa: Talking about the Big Thing*. London: Routledge, 2007. Print.

Underwood, Anne. "How the Plague Began." *Newsweek.com*. Newsweek, 8 Feb. 1999. Web. 3 July 2008.

Wanjama, Leah Niambi, et al. *HIV and AIDS: The Pandemic*. Nairobi: Jomo Kenyatta Foundation, 2007. Print.

Appendix

PEER REVIEW GUIDELINES

In most cases, your instructor will provide you with a set of guidelines to follow when you review a peer's writing. If your teacher does not give you a set of guidelines to follow, you may want to employ the peer review procedures outlined below. To apply any set of guidelines effectively, though, you need to understand the purpose of peer review and commit yourself to improving your peer's writing. When peers review your work, remember that they are merely suggesting ways you might improve your writing. As the author of the piece, you are responsible for all final editing decisions.

PURPOSE

When you review a peer's writing, you can play three related roles, each serving a unique purpose: average reader, adviser, and editor. As an **average reader**, you offer your genuine response to the manuscript. You should let your peers know which aspects of their writing you find interesting, which parts you find boring, what is clear, what is confusing, what you would like to know more about, and what questions you have. As an **adviser**, along with offering your response to the manuscript, you also make specific suggestions to improve the piece. You can suggest changes in content, organization, format, or style. Finally, as an **editor**, you make specific suggestions for improving the piece and correct any problems you find in the writing.

Whatever role you play, your goal remains the same: to help your peer produce the most effective piece of writing possible. Peer review works best when it is truly reciprocal in nature: you do your best to improve your peer's writing because you know your peer is doing his or her best to improve your writing.

PROCEDURES TO FOLLOW

If you are asked to review a peer's writing, follow the guidelines your instructor distributes. If your teacher does not provide you specific guidelines to follow, employ the following procedures.

Step 1:   **Read through the entire paper** carefully without marking anything.

Step 2:   Consider whether the paper (or any part of it you are reviewing) **meets the needs of the assignment**. If it does not, tell your peer why you think it does not answer the assignment.

Step 3:   Examine the paper's **content**. Point out which sections of the essay are clear, which need further development, which specifically address the assignment, and which seem to stray from it. Offer any suggestions you have for improving the paper's content.

Step 4:   Examine the paper's **structure**. Note any problems with the paper's thesis statement or topic sentences. Comment on whether the writer provides clear and effective transitions between paragraphs or among sentences within the paragraphs. Note any passage where you lose track of the writer's train of thought. Finally, comment on the effectiveness of the opening and closing sections of the essay.

Step 5:   Examine the paper's **style**. Note any awkward or confusing sentences (if you have a suggestion about how to improve the sentence, offer it). Look for consistency in voice, diction, and point of view, commenting on any problems you find. If you think that any passage is stylistically inappropriate given the assigned audience, let the writer know.

Step 6:   **Proofread** for errors in spelling, punctuation, or typing. You can either circle errors you find and leave them for the author to correct or offer corrections of your own.

Step 7:   Examine the paper's **documentation**. First, check to see that the author has documented every passage that needs to be documented, noting any questions you have. Second, note any errors you find in the documentation the author provides, such as problems with the documentation's placement, formatting, or punctuation. Finally, proofread the paper's works cited or reference list if there is one.

ACTING ON PEER REVIEWS

As an author, you have the final say concerning the changes you make to your essay. You can accept or reject your peer's suggestions, but whatever decision you make, base it on a careful consideration of your peer's comments.

Accepting every suggestion a peer reviewer offers is usually a bad idea, as is summarily rejecting every suggestion a reviewer makes. Consider each comment individually. Decide whether the peer reviewer's suggestion will improve your manuscript. If it will, make the change. If you think it will not, do not act on the suggestion. If you are unsure about making any change, talk it over with your instructor before you decide.

CREDITS

Bauerlein, Mark. "Generation Text," from *America,* November 2009, Edition 12, pp. 20–22. Copyright © 2009 by America Press Inc. Reprinted with permission. All rights reserved. For subscription information call 1.800.627.9533 or visit www.americamagazine.org.

Blumberg, Fran C., Kristen P. Bierwirth, and Allison J. Schwartz. "Does Cartoon Violence Beget Aggressive Behavior in Real Life? An Opposing View," from *Early Childhood Education Journal,* 36, 2008. Copyright © 2008 by Fran C. Blumberg, Kristen P. Bierwirth, Allison J. Schwartz. Reprinted with permission of Springer.

Cantor, Joanne. "Media Violence and Children's Emotions: Beyond the 'Smoking Gun'," from a paper presented at the Annual Conference of the American Psychological Association, Washington, DC, August 2000. Copyright © 2000 by Joanne Cantor. Reprinted with permission of the author.

Crain, Michael. "Animal Suffering: Learning to Care and Not to Know," from *Encounter,* 22.2, 2009. Copyright © 2009 by Michael Crain. Reprinted with permission of the publisher. All rights reserved.

Essex, Nathan L. "Zero Tolerance and Student Dress Codes," from *Principal,* September/October 2004. Copyright © 2004 by National Association of Elementary School Principals. Reprinted with permission. All rights reserved.

"From *Animal House* to *Big Brother:* Student Privacy and Campus Safety in an Age of Accountability," from *Student Affairs Leader,* Edition 36(7), pp. 1–5. Copyright © 2008 by Magna Publications. Reprinted with permission.

Konheim-Kalkstein, Yasmine L. "A Uniform Look," from *American School Board Journal,* 2006. Copyright © 2006 by National School Boards Association. Reprinted with permission. All rights reserved.

Medina, Leticia V. "Building a Culture of Animal Welfare: Past, Present, and Future," from *Annual Review of Biomedical Sciences,* Edition 10, pp.104–111. Copyright © 2008 by Annual Review of Biomedical Sciences. Reprinted with permission.

INDEX

Abstracts, 66, 75
  how to write an abstract, 66
  sample abstract, 75
"Animal Suffering: Learning Not to Care
  and Not to Know," 253–259
APA Documentation Guidelines, 277–281
  consolidating references, 281
  electronic sources of information,
    280–281
  footnotes and endnotes, 281
  source with no author, 279–280
  source with one author, 277
  source with six or more authors, 279
  source with three to five authors, 278–279
  source with two authors, 278
  sources whose authors have the same last
    name, 280
  two or more sources by the same author,
    280
  two or more sources by the same author
    published in the same year, 280
APA Reference Lists, 288–296
  book, corporate author, 291
  book, edited, 292
  book, later edition, 291
  book, multiple authors, 291
  book, multivolume, 292
  book, multivolume, one volume of, 292
  book, no author or editor, 292
  book, one author, 291
  book, translation, 292
  chapter from an anthology, 293
  electronic sources of information,
    294–295
  journal article, monthly periodical, 290
  journal article, more than seven authors,
    290
  journal article, one author, 289
  journal article, three to seven authors, 289
  journal article, two authors, 289
  journal article, weekly periodical, 290
  newspaper article, 290
  newspaper article, no author, 290
  personal interview, 293
  reference work, 293
  sample reference list, 295–296
  two or more works by the same author,
    291

Argumentative Synthesis, 213–263
  definition, 213–214
  elements of argument, 214–219
  how to write an argumentative synthesis,
    223–230
  persuasion, 219–223
  revision checklist, 262–263
  sample argumentative synthesis, 230–234
  summary chart, 260–261

Bauerlein, Mark, 34
Bierwirth, Kristen P., 189
Blumberg, Fran C., 189
"Building a Culture of Animal Welfare: Past,
  Present and Future," 243–253

Cantor, Joanne, 173
Chesbrough, Ron, 69
Claims, 214–215
Crain, William, 253
Critical Reading, 1–27
  definition and purpose, 1–3
  marking texts, 11–17
  questioning texts, 3–11
  note taking, 18–19
  summary chart, 24–25
Critiquing a Text, 95–125
  definition and purpose, 95–96
  film review as a critique, 96–98
  how to write a critique, 99–111
  revision chart, 125
  sample critique essay, 119–122
  summary chart, 123–124

Documentation, 275–286
  APA documentation guidelines,
    277–281
  definition and purpose, 275
  MLA documentation guidelines,
    281–286
  primary academic style manuals,
    276–277
  types of documentation, 275–276
"Does Cartoon Violence Beget Aggressive
  Behavior in Real Life? An Opposing
  View," 189–195

Essex, Nathan L., 112

"Four Legs Good, Two Legs Bad: The Anti-human Values of 'Animal Rights'," 235–243
"From *Animal House* to *Big Brother:* Student Privacy and Campus Safety in an Age of Accountability," 69–75

"Generation Text," 34–36
"Getting Serious about Eradicating Binge Drinking," 20–23
Grounds, 215–218

"Hard Choices," 15–17

Informative Synthesis, 171–211
  definition and purpose, 171–172, 195–196
  how to write an informative synthesis, 197–203
  revision check list, 210–211
  sample informative synthesis, 204–207
  summary chart, 208–209
  types of synthesis essays, 172
Integrated Quotations, 33, 38–41

Konheim-Kalkstein, Yasmine L., 115

Lincoln, Abraham, 135
Lincoln's Second Inaugural Address, 135–136
  rhetorical analysis of, 136–137, 143–144

Marking Texts, 11–17
  annotating texts, 12–14
  highlighting texts, 11–12
  sample annotated text, 15–17
  summary chart, 26
"Media Violence and Children's Emotions: Beyond the 'Smoking Gun'," 173–180
Medina, Leticia V., 243
MLA Documentation Guidelines, 281–286
  consolidating references, 285
  electronic sources of information, 285
  footnotes and endnotes, 285–286
  source with more than three authors, 283–284
  source with no author, 284
  source with one author, 282–283
  source with three authors, 283
  source with two authors, 283
  sources whose authors have the same last name, 284
  two or more sources by the same author, 284–285
MLA Works Cited Lists, 297–306
  book, corporate author, 300
  book, edited, 300
  book, later edition, 300

book, multiple authors, 299
book, multivolume, 300
book, multivolume, one volume of, 300
book, no author, 300
book, one author, 299
book, translation, 300–301
chapter from an anthology, 301
electronic sources of information, 301–303
journal article, monthly periodical, 298
journal article, more than three authors, 298
journal article, one author, 297
journal article, two or three authors, 298
journal article, weekly periodical, 298
newspaper article, 298–299
newspaper article, no author, 299
personal interview, 301
reference work, 301
sample works cited list, 303–306
two or more works by the same author, 299
Moore, Patrick, 15

National Center for Family Literacy, 155
Note Taking, 18–19
  summary chart, 27

Paraphrasing Texts, 47–59
  definition and purpose, 47–48
  documentation of, 57
  how to paraphrase material, 50–57
  qualities of a good paraphrase, 48–50
  revision checklist, 59
  summary chart, 58
Peer Review Guidelines, 307–309
Persuasive Appeals, 220–223
  ethos, 222
  logos, 220
  pathos, 220–221
Plagiarism, 265–273
  checklist, 273
  definition, 265
  forms of plagiarism, 265–268
  how to avoid plagiarism, 269–271
  summary chart, 272

Questioning Texts, 3–11
  questions to ask as and after reading a text, 7–11
  questions to ask of visual texts, 150–155
  questions to ask prior to reading a text, 4–5
Quoting Texts, 29–45
  altering quoted material, 41–42
  block quotations, APA, 36–37
  block quotations, MLS, 37–38
  definition and purpose, 29–30

integrating quoted material into texts, 33–34
revision checklist, 45
summary charts, 43–44
when not to quote material, 32–33
when to quote material, 30–32

Reference Lists and Works Cited Entries, 287–306
APA guidelines, 288–296
definition and purpose, 287–288
MLA guidelines, 297–306
Response Essays
definition and purpose, 81–82
how to write a response essay, 84–89
qualities of a good response essay, 82–84
revision checklist, 93
sample response essay, 89
summary chart, 91–92
Rhetorical Analysis of Visual Texts, 149–169
definition and purpose, 149–150
example of rhetorical analysis of visual text, 155–158
how to write a rhetorical analysis of a visual text, 158–163
reading visual texts critically, 150–155
revision checklist, 169
sample rhetorical analysis of a visual text, 163–166
summary chart, 167–168
Rhetorical Analysis of Written Texts, 127–147
definition and purpose, 127–128
example of rhetorical analysis of a written text, 136–137
how to write a rhetorical analysis of a written text, 137–142
revision checklist, 147

rhetorical analysis of texts, 128–130
rhetorical strategies, 130–134
sample rhetorical analysis of a written text, 143–144
summary chart, 145–146
Rhetorical Situation of Texts, 128–130
Rhetorical Strategies, 130–134

Schwartz, Allison J., 189
Simmons, Betty Jo, 181
Smith, Wesley J., 235
Stalsworth, Kelly, 181
Summarizing Texts, 61–79
abstracts, 66
definition and purpose, 61–62
documentation of, 69
explanatory summary, 68–69
how to summarize a text, 66–67
how to write an abstract, 66
informative summary, 67–68
qualities of a good summary, 63–65
revision checklist, 80
sample abstract, 75
sample explanatory summary, 76–77
sample informative summary, 76
summary chart, 78–79
types of summaries, 62–63

"Television Violence and Its Effects on Young Children," 181–188

"A Uniform Look," 115–119

Warrants, 218–219
Wechsler, Henry, 20
Wentzell, Heather, 181

"Zero Tolerance and Student Dress Codes," 112–115